THE MAN WITH
MARADONA'S SHIRT

Steve Hodge was a fixture of Brian Clough's Nottingham Forest teams in the eighties and early nineties. He also won the league with Leeds, and played for Spurs, Aston Villa and QPR. He played at the Mexico World Cup in 1986 and was in the England squad at Italia 90.

Rob Jovanovic has written books on Beck, Pavement, Richey Edwards and R.E.M. He's also the author of several books about Nottingham Forest.

STEVE HODGE

THE MAN WITH MARADONA'S SHIRT

An Orion paperback

First published in Great Britain in 2010
by Orion
This paperback edition published in 2011
by Orion Books Ltd,
Orion House, 5 Upper St Martin's Lane,
London WC2H 9EA

An Hachette UK company

1 3 5 7 9 10 8 6 4 2

A CIP catalogue record for this book is available
from the British Library.

ISBN 978-1-4091-1735-3

Printed and bound in Great Britain by
CPI Mackays, Chatham, Kent

The Orion Publishing Group's policy is to use papers that
are natural, renewable and recyclable products and
made from wood grown in sustainable forests. The logging
and manufacturing processes are expected to conform to
the environmental regulations of the country of origin.

www.orionbooks.co.uk

This book is dedicated to Ali, Josh, Elliot and Amber, Mum and Dad, my family and everybody who helped me fulfil my ambitions. Thank you all.

Foreword

It is both an honour and privilege to write a foreword for Steve Hodge's autobiography. The book details the career of one of the finest members of our profession and an illustrious career that the majority of our members would aspire to, playing with top quality teams for a remarkable seventeen years.

He has played under legendary managers such as Brian Clough, Sir Bobby Robson and Terry Venables and continues to be involved in the game as a qualified A licence coach at the Nottingham Forest Academy and as an FA ambassador as part of our World Cup bid.

Whilst the book is a fascinating inside view of success, it also has its high drama and tragedy. Steve participated in the tragic semi-final at Hillsborough in 1989 and whilst Maradona vanquished his World Cup hopes in 1986 with his Hand of God goal, at least Steve has some compensation as he has Maradona's shirt from that game!

I hope all readers will enjoy the book as much as I did watching Steve perform and progress throughout his football career.

Gordon Taylor OBE
Chief Executive – PFA

Introduction

It gives me very great pleasure to pen a few words as a tribute to an excellent professional footballer who scaled all the barriers to reach the very top.

What makes Steve Hodge special is that despite a wonderfully successful career of over 500 games and an outstanding scoring rate at the highest level, he was one of the most unassuming, humble guys you could ever wish to meet. You could never guess by his straightforward, unflashy manner and lifestyle that he was one of the most gifted left-sided players that England produced in his era. He was an honest, totally dedicated and selfless player.

My memories of Steve are many: discussing his early career with Brian Clough; watching him provide Gary Lineker with England's second goal in Monterrey during Mexico '86; making an outstanding contribution to Tottenham Hotspur's left side of our super five man midfield which had purists praising but left hearts broken when failing in the May 1987 classic cup final. He did get medals, though, and collected a proud reward!

Steve was a player who played with his heart on his sleeve, 100 per cent dedicated, a workaholic with an eye for goal.

His recollections of his time on the grass recalling his great moments and disappointments with a host of fascinating stories will certainly be an honest account. Steve Hodge knows no other way!

David Pleat

Prologue

Saturday 21st June 1986.
Holiday Inn, Mexico City.

Had a team meeting today, only one change. Terry Fenwick is back in for Alvin Martin. No special instructions for Maradona, just that whenever he gets the ball our nearest player has to close him down as quickly as possible. Sometimes we might have to double-up on him. So glad that we moved hotels. The last one, next to the motorway, was a nightmare, but everyone can sleep now. The Italian squad have been staying here as well; it's a bit strange walking through the lobby and saying hello to the likes of Cabrini and Zoff. But they're out now and we've got the hotel to ourselves. Got an early start in the morning – we kick-off at midday. Still can't quite believe that I'll be playing in a World Cup quarter-final tomorrow.

Sunday 22nd June 1986, Mexico City. A World Cup quarter-final against Argentina, the first time that the countries had faced each other since the 1982 war. Without doubt this was going to be the biggest game of my career so far. Of course I wanted to go two games further but I couldn't look beyond today's encounter. We'd been relieved just to get out of the group after a pretty horrendous start. Bobby Robson was under a lot of pressure and we all knew that, but we'd breezed past Paraguay in the round of 16 with a good performance and confidence was high. Now we'd be facing the best player in the tournament, a worldwide phenomenon. I'd played against him previously in Barcelona and so I knew what he was all about. On that day Brian Clough had showed me not to stand on ceremony where reputations are concerned. Back then I was in the Nottingham Forest side that played Barcelona at the Camp Nou in 1983 and on that occasion, as we lined up in the tunnel, Clough walked down the line of players before stopping right in front of a bewildered Maradona. "You might be able to play a bit," said the manager, "but I can still grab you by the balls!" He then did just that before striding off towards the pitch.

In Mexico we had Gary Lineker, the tournament's in-form goal scorer and we'd come across a good formation with him and Peter Beardsley up front. They really linked well together and we were strong at the back, and very experienced, so why wouldn't confidence be high? When you reach the quarter-finals you know you've got a chance. We'd had meetings leading up to the game but Bobby was never one for too much tactical analysis. He was more of a motivator and he'd pull out the telegrams he'd received from people back home. They could be from an old friend in Newcastle or from an old lady in Bristol wishing us all the best. He was keen to portray the excitement back home and keep up the patriotic fervour that he always liked to instil into the squad. He always tried to drill into us that the people back home were pinned to their televisions, willing us to win, because we were somewhat cocooned from what was going on in England. No WAGs, no mobile phones, no satellite TV. We knew the press were always close by and we'd felt their wrath early on. Bobby had said that if anyone were to ask us about the Falklands we were to say it's none of our business. We didn't want to get anywhere near revving them up or giving them any more reason to really want to win the game, but I think they did use that to motivate their players anyway.

The game was being played just seven days before the final, which would be taking place at the same venue. We were up at 8 a.m., breakfast thirty minutes later and then leaving the hotel at 9 a.m. Footballers don't like early kick-offs because it messes up their routines and we were kicking-off at noon in the midday sunshine to keep European TV companies happy. We filed on to the coach and pulled away from the hotel, driving through pretty empty streets. We'd played at the Azteca Stadium a few days before against Paraguay and when we returned to the massive stadium I think I knew that, short of winning the World Cup, this was going to be the pinnacle of my career. We hoped we could get two games further but I was in dreamland, thinking back to where I'd been in a relegation fight just two months earlier. The bus arrived at the Azteca and then slowly drove down, under the actual stadium where it was dark. I knew this was something special, something historic. I'd been waiting all my life for today. Then we descended into a sodium-lit underworld, hidden away from the harsh Mexico morning sunshine.

○ ○ ○

In the changing rooms the usual suspects were being loud. Terry Butcher was loud, that helped him get aggressive. Kenny Sansom was chirpy and would share a joke to relax himself and the other players. Gary Lineker was always quiet. Some of the people you might have thought would be loud weren't, I think the enormity of the occasion had sunk into some of the players. I was my usual quiet self, gathering my thoughts until I went on my own to a warm-up area where there was some AstroTurf under the stands along a corridor from the dressing room. I just loosened up a bit by knocking a few balls against the wall. I could hear a loud hum outside; it wasn't a thumping noise but obviously a lot of people were arriving and the occasion was building. My old Forest teammate Viv Anderson came over and said a few words. "Can you believe it?" he asked. "You're playing in a World Cup quarter-final. I've been to two World Cups and haven't kicked a ball yet." He made me realise how lucky I was; I could only smile in return.

Back in the room Don Howe would usually have something to say; he was more tactical than Bobby but he hadn't singled out Maradona specifically. At the team meeting the day before we'd briefly addressed the Maradona situation and what we'd do to combat him when he had the ball. Bobby didn't want us to lose our own self-belief so we didn't talk about him too much, it was more about how we were going to play. He reiterated that sometimes we'd have to double up on him, but we were just to play our own game.

As we readied to go out for the anthems Bobby said a few last words, "We're England. We play our way!" People around me were shouting out, "No regrets!" and "Don't let it pass you by!" For the older pros this would be their one-and-only chance to get to a World Cup semi-final. The Argentinians were waiting for us in the tunnel as we walked out. I had a little look to see where Maradona was, but I was at the back of the line and didn't see him until we got onto the pitch. We were hit with a blast of noise and blinding sunshine as we emerged from the tunnel. I was also hit by the vastness of the stadium. I saw his mop of black hair and people, if not in awe of him, were certainly aware of his presence. Whatever happened in the game, history was about to be created.

In the Beginning

Tony Hateley was a football legend in Nottingham. He'd played for Notts County before moving to high-profile clubs like Liverpool, Chelsea, Aston Villa, Coventry and Birmingham City then returned to County at the end of his career. I was about ten years old when I saw him standing on the top bank at Stanhope Junior School. Every now and then he'd bellow out, "Come on, son!" I didn't keep a diary as a child, but many images easily stuck in my mind during my formative years and this is one of those moments. I was playing for Stanhope and our opposition that day included Tony Hateley's son, Mark. Later we'd end up in some of the same England World Cup squads. I also faced Brian Kilcline, who was at Christ the King, the local Catholic school. He became known as this six-foot-tall thirteen year old who had a beard and he would scare everybody to death. Later he beat me in an FA Cup final. Looking back it seems strange that three successful players made it from such a small area.

I grew up in Gedling, a mining village in Nottinghamshire. During the 1970s most of my schoolfriends' dads were miners, but my dad, Brian, was a local government officer while mum, Violet, worked at a lace factory in Nottingham. Dad was a good local non-league winger and our family was always quite sporty. We'd have holidays in Blackpool and Bournemouth, and I have great memories of being in Stanley Park playing football or cricket with parents, grandparents and cousins or out at Mablethorpe on the East coast in a caravan. Like many children in the 60s and 70s I spent much of my free time outside kicking a ball about. In the school holidays I'd play with my cousin at the local Westdale Lane school where my grandfather was the caretaker and we'd have the whole school to ourselves. It would be one versus one across the whole playground or, on another day, it would be just bowler versus batsman at cricket. Whatever the game it was always competitive. In term time we'd sneak through a neighbour's garden as a short cut on to another local school where we'd play until dark. It sounds very old-fashioned now, but that's how it was. Sport was a huge part of my life and it really was jumpers for goalposts all the time. Sundays were spent at my Granddad Hodge's house with all the family. He had a long driveway and we'd play cricket with six or seven fielders.

My dad started taking me down to see Forest from about the age of eight. I was lucky enough to see Ian Storey-Moore in his last year at the City Ground. He was exciting and scored some memorable goals. I was there when he netted a famous one against Arsenal as he beat about eight Arsenal players from the halfway line, but he couldn't save Forest and they went down to the Second Division. Then Duncan McKenzie became the Forest star. I was at the FA Cup game when Forest beat First Division Manchester City 4–1 in the first Sunday game. I was almost in tears because I also supported Manchester City as a kid and Francis Lee was my hero. City had a great team in the late 1960s and early 1970s. They won the League Championship in 1968, the FA Cup in 1969 and both the League Cup and European Cup Winners' Cup in 1970. I especially loved the way Lee played, the goals he scored, and the fact that he was a big character. I was able to see England games on television; Mexico '70 was my first memory of a big tournament, and the FA Cup final was shown but there wasn't much other football on TV for a youngster to watch. I managed to go to the 1974 League Cup final but Wolves beat Man City that day and I was devastated.

My dad and granddad would take a little stool for me to stand on at the City Ground where we'd go on to the old East Stand terracing. We'd park near Colwick and walk over Lady Bay Bridge which was a little way along the river from Trent Bridge. When you got on to the bridge in winter time you'd see the lights of the stadium in the middle distance across the misty river and the atmosphere was so exciting. The away fans were placed in the old wooden stand behind the Forest fans, where we stood. There was little sign of any police planning or crowd control back then. I don't remember ever seeing any stewards. The sway of the crowd could be scary and sometimes the crush could carry you across the steps, even with your dad looking out for you. For a youngster it could be a daunting experience and it was always likely that something nasty would happen.

In 1974, after beating Manchester City, Forest got to the FA Cup quarter-finals for the first time in several years. They drew Newcastle away and my dad drove us up to St James to see the game. We stood behind the goal with the rest of the Forest fans and I got a place right at the front so I could just about see over the wall at the front of the terracing. Forest controlled the game and went 3-1 up against ten men, but then things took a turn for the worse. I could see some trouble at their end behind the goal and we knew that in that era there might be a pitch invasion by the home fans so they could get the game abandoned and replayed. I saw one chubby Geordie get out on to the pitch and then hoards of them spilled on to the pitch. The Newcastle fans came running the length of the pitch towards us. It was like the Zulus coming towards us! There was no security to speak of and the police were pitiful and just couldn't cope with what was happening. I couldn't move or go anywhere and for an eleven year old it was very frightening. My Dad just said, "Get your head down!" which I did. Then I can just remember people climbing over us and past us and people roaring. After a few minutes it died down and the police managed to wrestle some semblance of order. The police came in and cordoned off the Forest fans and I was still right at the front. The players had been taken off but when they returned I just saw Forest collapse in the last half hour and they lost 4–3. The Newcastle fans got away with it but the FA decided to replay the game and after a second replay that Newcastle won 1–0, they eventually reached the final where they lost to Liverpool. The whole episode really gave me an insight into what could happen on the terraces and showed me that sometimes you have no control over what might happen to you and it was a day that I'd never forget.

It was a complete contrast when I went to watch cricket in the sedate environment of Trent Bridge. I would go and watch Test matches with my cousin Paul where we'd be allowed to spend the day by ourselves. I saw Viv Richards score 200 and lots of the great players passed before me each summer. To a kid from Gedling seeing someone from Australia in the early 1970s was like seeing someone from Mars. We got to watch them in the nets and it was like seeing a different species. I lapped it all up and just wanted to absorb everything that I could.

○ ○ ○

Back in the beginning I played as a striker for Stanhope Junior School and would get loads of goals; knowing how to finish would be very important for me later in my career. I was first spotted by the local area scout, Graham Cordell, who scouted for Forest and had been a goalkeeper for Aston Villa. He came to speak to me after a game and asked if my dad was there so that he could arrange a trial for me. He later said to my dad that the thing that made his mind up about me was that I'd received a ball and I'd let the ball run through my legs because I knew a teammate was behind me. It was that bit of awareness that had impressed him.

Back then, before the days of football academies, you went for trials in the school holidays. A chap called Jack Nesbitt saw me playing at the Clifton All-Whites ground. He asked for my dad and set me up for a trial at Derby County. So by the age of eleven I had both Forest and Derby knocking on my door. It was like being in dreamland. Even if you think you're not bad you don't know how good the other kids are going to be. At the trials you'd meet kids from all over Nottingham but no one would know what to say to each other because everyone there was there with the same aim. It was actually a good grounding in how to break the ice when meeting new people, just as I'd have to throughout my career. The trialists would meet at the City Ground and eleven of us would be thrown together to play against a side from, say, Corby. There'd be some lads from Ireland and Scotland thrown in too. The early trials weren't a make-or-break situation and most players would go on to sign schoolboy forms at the age of fourteen so you knew you'd got two years. You just wanted to impress and you'd get a boost if you knew you'd played well. A couple of ex-Forest players, Alan Hill and Liam O'Kane, were in charge of the trials, which seemed to come around during every school holiday.

By secondary school I was playing for South Notts which encompassed a large area and we'd go to places like Coventry, Doncaster and Sheffield. I was still quite small and was constantly up against physically bigger players. We'd play on

Saturday mornings and we'd meet at 8 a.m. in the city centre for the team bus. We'd play the game and be back in Nottingham for about 2 p.m. when my Dad would pick me up and take me to play for Parkhead, my local club side, on the Saturday afternoon. Another future professional from this team was Nigel Pearson, who played for Shrewsbury, Sheffield Wednesday and Middlesbrough and later managed South-ampton and Leicester City. I'd be back home for about 6 p.m., shattered but having loved every minute of it. For most players, two games in a day would be enough for the weekend but on a Sunday I'd often play for the league representative team as well, so on some weekends I'd play three full matches. We trained just once a week; it was the games which were really the training. I'd also play for my school once a week as well so you could improve pretty quickly playing that many games against the best players in the area for about four years. It's very different to the regime imposed on young players today who do more training but don't learn and develop in the same way because they don't get enough games to play.

I was fortunate that my upbringing revolved around sport and luckily I had the talent and physical attributes to be able to pursue that dream. I can well remember the days when my dad would take me to the school football ground and watch as I did laps of the pitch and got me to hop from the halfway line to the goal-line in order to build up my calves. I used to go for runs as a thirteen or fourteen year old and it became clear that fitness was one of my main strengths and the jogging routine is something which I've kept up to this day. I won the 1975 South Notts Cross Country Championship, which proved I had excellent stamina.

My trials took me all over the place. Before you signed schoolboy terms at fourteen, you could play trial games for as many different clubs as you liked. When I was twelve I was put on a train to Derby which was quite daunting for me. Jack Nesbitt was supposed to be waiting for me at the other end but when I arrived he wasn't there. I panicked a little bit: I didn't have a mobile phone to use, but after about half an hour wandering around Derby train station someone turned up to collect me. The brother of legendary Arsenal manager Bertie Mee lived in Nottingham and he got me a trial down at Arsenal, but I didn't want to play so far from home, although I often played games at West Brom and at Notts County, and I had a week at Manchester United arranged by a chap called Bill Barrowcliff. He invited myself and another Nottingham lad to stay at Salford University, and at the age of fourteen we had a fantastic time. At United there were lots of players from Wales, Scotland and Ireland. I think Ronnie Whelan might have been there. I thought I might look out of place but I did OK against all these Under-14 internationals. We got a tour of Old Trafford and thirteen lads and two scouts managed to get stuck in a lift for over an hour. One of the adults was Bob Bishop, a United legend for finding George Best. It was all a really good experience.

I was never at home during the holidays but my parents were very supportive. They were also cautious and very realistic. If I got a "well done" I knew I'd done really well because the compliments weren't free flowing. When I got one I knew I'd earned it.

Another time at Derby I was up against Dave Mackay in the training dome playing one versus one like I had against my cousin just a few years earlier. I remember telling my dad about it. He knew all about Dave from his days at Spurs. At the Derby training ground I was walking around with the likes of Roy McFarland and Colin Todd, players who had recently won the League Championship. It was a slightly surreal time for me.

After three years playing at South Notts I was dropped for

a year for being too small, even though I'd been the captain during the previous season. For a year I was out of the trips around the Midlands and I missed the England Under-15 trials. For a while it could have been the end of my world as I lost confidence and doubted myself, but luckily the trial games still kept coming. West Brom were still keen and they had me over to watch their reserves. I saw an unknown forward called Cyrille Regis score and soon afterwards he got into their first team where his career just took off. It gave me an insight into how you can quickly make a name for yourself if things go your way.

Even though I was dropped from South Notts I eventually signed schoolboy terms at Forest in October 1977. My original scout, Graham Cordell was pally with Peter Taylor and after one game he told Graham that, "I want to see young Hodgey and his parents at the ground tomorrow to meet me and the gaffer." Brian Clough was probably the most famous manager in the country; he'd performed miracles at two provincial clubs and now I was going in to meet him. As we walked in Chris Woods had just signed as an apprentice. He was this big, blond-haired lad from Lincolnshire with a potato-growing father. Then we were called into the manager's office. It was my parents that Clough wanted to chat with. For me it was very much a case of speak when you're spoken to. "Come in, pet, will you have a drink?" he asked my mum. Both my parents declined a drink but he was persistent. "Well, you will have one because you're in my office now. We rate your son not bad for his age." He went on to ask about my dad's work, just normal banter. Forest had just been promoted to the First Division and had had a great start to life in the top flight. It was a straight choice for me between Forest and Derby, but Brian Clough was the draw and that made up my mind for me. I knew he'd give kids the chance if they were good enough and so I signed for him. I had two years left at school before my exams but would be playing for the Forest Colts side in the Notts Youth League under the guidance of Trevor Patterson.

Patterson was like a sergeant major, a real nasty piece of work. Once we lost a cup final and he was really annoyed with us. He stormed in and said, "You lot are a shower of shit! None of you will ever make it as footballers! You're useless!" Those words have always stuck with me. I thought, "Does he really mean it? Are we really not very good? Is this reality checking in?" Today it would be classed as real verbal abuse and it was scary to fourteen and fifteen-year-old kids. My dad later said he saw a real change in me mentally during that year with Trevor Patterson. I survived it though and we occasionally saw the first-team management taking an interest. That was the light at the end of the tunnel but nothing was guaranteed.

The Apprentice

July 1979 seems a really long time ago now. Margaret Thatcher was the new prime minister, punk was still in fashion and English football was far from the multi-million pound industry that it is today. I was just a sixteen-year-old kid and the chance to jump on board the professional football merry-go-round was incredibly exciting and even the one-in-a-million odds of making it weren't going to stop me having a go. Forest had just had an unbelievable two years and I had been lucky enough to witness it all from fairly close quarters without actually being a part of the squad. They'd won the championship at the first time of asking and then went and beat holders Liverpool in the European Cup before becoming champions of Europe themselves. I'd had a front row seat as they knocked holders Liverpool out of Europe in September 1978 and I met Bill Shankley that night and got his autograph. I also saw first hand the respect that Brian Clough had for Shankley and also Jock Stein, who visited later.

I got a treat when Trevor Francis found out that I was a big ELO fan. He knew the lead singer, Jeff Lynne, and invited me along with some of the first-team players to go and see them in concert. We all went backstage and I felt like an imposter but loved being close to a band I loved.

I was offered a two-year contract as an apprentice with the reigning champions of Europe – not many people got that chance. Five of the youth side were taken on and seven dumped, with a few new ones being brought in, including a tricky winger called Calvin Plummer. We were suddenly thrust into the world of professional players at the absolute pinnacle of their careers – who could want for a better education?

I'd taken my O-Levels in June and had just five weeks before I reported for preseason training in July. Alan Hill had always told me to make sure I worked hard for my exams because they were my back-up for a life outside of football. There were no guarantees that I'd make it in the game. Liam O'Kane was in charge of giving us our duties at Forest and we started a week before the first team came back from their summer break. It was probably the sweetest break they'd ever had, because the last match of the season had seen them beat Malmo 1–0 to win the European Cup. We were given our own towels, own kit, and four other sets to look after for the senior players. Each first teamer had four lots of kit and four sets of boots, so we had to look after around twenty or so kits and sets of boots. We'd arrive before the senior players in the morning and set out their training kit; we also had to clean out the big bath, showers and toilets after training. We'd have to clean all the boots and sometimes Larry Lloyd would throw them back at me and I'd be told to do them again in no uncertain terms.

During our first day's lunch break we all went up to the Trent Bridge chip shop for pie and peas, which soon became our regular haunt, not something which would be tolerated today. Then we were soon involved in preseason training with the first-team squad. It started with lots of runs around Wollaton Park in Nottingham. I was now training with what would today be the likes of Barcelona or AC Milan.

Jimmy Gordon took most of the training. He was an old-school coach having been with Clough and Taylor for years and previously represented Scotland while playing for Newcastle and Middlesbrough. He'd lead us through run after run around the Wollaton Park lake. I didn't really enjoy it, but it wasn't a problem for me, but some players would come back a stone overweight and literally needed to be run back into shape. I didn't say much but listened to the stories and it was great to be around a team which you knew would go down in the annals of history. The banter would be flying around and I sponged it all in even if it wasn't nice sometimes. The young players had to sink or swim in a very tough mental school with the manager, with the senior players and with your younger peers.

When the footballs came out after about two weeks, the apprentices and first team went separate ways, but occasionally we'd have a first teamer train or play alongside us. Once we were joined by Kenny Burns, a hard player who Clough and Taylor had transformed from a centre-forward to a centre-half. They'd done such a good job that he'd been voted PFA Player of the Year in 1978. On this day Burns joined us for a preseason session and he was caught on the leg by a six-foot youth player called Simon Worthington. Burns didn't take kindly to it and without any ceremony he turned around and head-butted him. As Simon hit the deck, Kenny just turned and walked straight off the pitch, up the embankment and back to the dressing rooms. I was shocked and couldn't believe what I'd just seen. I'd never seen anything so violent on a football pitch, especially between players of the same club. It was an extreme example of the way things were done at Nottingham Forest. The first team were encouraged by the manager not to let the young lads in, but then he'd come to us and say, "Go and sort out so-and-so!" He'd have everyone fighting each other to prove their place and everyone thought they'd have a chance of getting into the first team. Clough would often tell me in training to go and kick John Robertson, who he felt was the best player at the club. "Well done, son," he'd intone. "Now go and kick him again!" Robbo would be grumbling in the background but Clough loved it that I'd go and kick an old pro, that I wasn't intimidated even though I respected them.

My daily routine would involve getting a bus into Nottingham at 7.15 a.m., where I'd arrive for about 8 a.m. Then I had to wait around for thirty minutes for a connecting bus to take me to the ground where I'd arrive at about nine to start in the boot room and set out two sets of kit. The first team would start arriving for their ten-thirty start. This instilling of discipline, while being surrounded by people who had reached the very pinnacle and succeeded in their careers, made you more than willing to go through the humbling stuff. You could see what could be achieved right in front of you every day, it was a positive environment to learn in and I was surrounded by winners.

The youth side was called the "A" team and we played in the Midlands youth league, a league that we were expected to win every year, so we were under pressure right from the start. I knew that I'd have to push myself to the limit to get anywhere near the first team when they could go out and break transfer records to bring in new players. I also had competition within the A team. A lad called Jim McKechnie came down from Scotland and we all called him "four-grand Jim" because his dad had allegedly been paid £4,000 for him to sign for Forest. Like me, he played in midfield which was obviously a problem for me as they'd already invested hard cash in him.

I think when many players retire they look back at those two years as some of the most enjoyable of their career in terms of camaraderie. We'd all head to the local snooker hall after training and on Saturday nights after a game we'd all go around town having a few drinks. We also had the occasional celebrity visitor. One time I played with Trevor Francis in a game between youth team players and *The Sun* came down for a photo. We all went out and bought a copy the next day! It was just another fantastic experience for a first year apprentice playing with the first million pound player. As an apprentice I'd been allowed to join the Professional Footballers' Association. I had to pay the princely sum of 25p as an 'entrance fee' with my annual subscription costing £3.

Friday afternoons were the worst. You'd be there late, getting all of your own kit ready for Saturday morning, and if the first team were at home you had to get all of their kit ready or pack it up for an away trip. Sometimes I'd be called upon to clean Brian Clough's shoes, or sometimes his car. Then we had to sweep the stands and clean up litter. Ron Fenton took charge of the apprentices and every Friday he'd put us through an extreme physical test. We'd be lined up against a wall because he wanted to check that we'd been doing our stomach exercises that week. I wasn't the best, to be honest, and I didn't really like doing them. It was up to each player to go and do them in their own time during the week. Fenton would walk along the line and each week he'd pick someone and say, "Tense them!" The unfortunate apprentice would then get punched ten times in the stomach. He rained them in quickly, one after another, and Ronnie was a strong man. Some lads would crumple up after two punches and we'd all be in the background laughing but if it was your turn you just had to take it, and it did hurt. It was another toughening experience, I can't imagine that being in the Arsene Wenger book of training techniques.

Amongst ourselves the apprentices also had routines and sometimes forfeits had to be taken. Whenever one of us had a birthday the unlucky lad would get stripped and put in the showers where he'd be covered all over in black boot polish. When it wasn't your turn it was great, but everyone got it at some point; it was a really good laugh. We were quite a close-knit bunch but we all knew we'd lose a few players along the way. I remember Peter Taylor coming to me at half-time during a friendly game and he said, "Young Hodge, if you don't pick up your performance I'll send you to Hartlepool for a month!" I knew Hartlepool was up north somewhere and it didn't sound very appealing! I didn't really get to know Peter that well, but he gave me one of those stares and he had a real snarl on his face when he said it.

Forest had a couple of mavericks around briefly in 1980 and I was given Charlie George's boots to clean. I didn't mind though, especially when he gave me an extravagant £50 Christmas tip! George didn't stay long but he did score as Forest defeated Barcelona to win the European Super Cup. Before the first league game after they returned from Spain the gaffer came to me outside the dressing room and handed me the Super Cup trophy. "Young Hodge, go and show our fans this trophy," he ordered. And so I had to go out and do a solo lap of honour around the pitch with the trophy, which I'd had nothing to do with. Stan Bowles was also signed. He would turn up for training in a taxi and leave it in the City Ground car park with the meter running while he trained. Not only that, but his girlfriend would be sitting in the back waiting as well!

In the January of the second year most players knew where they stood against the others and had a good idea of whether or not they'd be retained. Calvin Plummer was already in the reserve team, so obviously he'd been picked out. Colin Walsh, Stuart Gray and John Robertson were all ahead of me in the left-sided areas I wanted to get into. Gray was a left-back and left-sided midfielder and Walsh was seen as Robertson's eventual replacement, so I saw a lot of barriers ahead of me. By January I wasn't sure what would happen to me. I was then thrown into the reserve team to see what would happen; once again it was a case of sink or swim. On the Friday Brian

Clough pinned up his handwritten team sheets for the first and reserves team games for the following day. The first-team line-up was one of legend. Shilton, Anderson, Gray, McGovern, Lloyd, Burns, O'Neill, Bowyer, Birtles, Woodcock, Robertson. The reserve team XI was slightly less known with Kent, Thrower, Lilley, Haire and MacLeod starting the game. My eyes scrolled down the list and there I was at the bottom: '12. Hodge'. I hung around until everyone had gone home then went over to the noticeboard, took down the sheet of paper and stuffed it into my bag. When I got on that day at Preston for a few minutes I knew that I'd made a start; I was making progress and moving from youth football to the men's game where I'd be given no favours.

My full reserve-team debut came later. Frank Clark was the second string's manager and I played at Blackpool with Larry Lloyd in the team on a beautiful afternoon. I got off to a great start and scored in a 3–1 win. I recall going into the toilets at half-time and John O'Hare was sat smoking in one of the cubicles with smoke billowing out over the top. I remember thinking: footballers don't smoke! Getting a regular game in the reserves was a fantastic education off and on the field. One week I played against a Liverpool side with Phil Thompson, who'd won the European Cup, and the next time they included Ian Rush, Jimmy Case, Avi Cohen, Steve Heighway and Ronnie Whelan – an unbelievable side. At Everton I was faced by Howard Kendall, who was playing in the reserves while he was the first-team manager! Graeme Sharpe was forever saying, "Yes boss, yes boss." These days you wouldn't get that chance to play in the reserves against the top pros, the European Cup winners. At Aston Villa it was the same, as they fielded Noel Blake, Gary Williams and Nigel Spink.

Brian Clough took a great interest in the reserves – he had to, because the club was broke and he couldn't afford to buy anybody. During games we'd know if he was there because his voice would be booming out from the mostly empty stands. Trialists would come and go until one day a lad called Peter Davenport came in and scored on his reserve team debut. He was a real natural finisher, two footed, quick. He was signed and in the first team very quickly. It proved to me that there *was* a route to the first team through the reserves: Forest weren't able to just go and buy a player when they needed one any more.

During that second year of my apprenticeship I went on Forest's annual trip to the Blau Witt tournament in Holland and another one in Dusseldorf. I can remember seeing a young David Moyes with a mop of red hair walking along the street with Paul McStay of the Celtic youth side. Leicester City had a speed merchant by the name of Gary Lineker in their team and we faced the likes of Bayern Munich and Ajax. You had to grow up very quickly because these were some of the best youth teams in Europe. Brian Clough went with us to the Blau Witt and during one game he was in a foul mood. Nigel Thrower took a throw-in but delivered it to the recipient's neck area while shouting, "Hold it!" Clough was enraged. "Hold it!" he screamed. "He's not a fucking seal!" At half-time he asked David Campbell where he thought he was playing. "Er, right midfield, breaking out wide ... " the young Irishman began. Clough cut him short. "You couldn't break a fucking egg!" Then he asked Steve Sutton how old he was. "Eighteen," came the reply. "Well, if you play like that you'll be out of the game by twenty-one!" Clough spat back. In the second half it was my turn. "How many O-Levels have you got?" he shouted when I came near the bench. I held up my hand to indicate five. "You'll get none in fucking football!" he replied.

Brian Clough was watching me by the end of the 1980–81 season. I saw an article in the *Nottingham Evening Post* by

Duncan Hamilton in which the manager picked out myself and Chris Fairclough as names for the future. If I saw something in the local paper written by Hamilton, or by John Lawson, then I knew it was from the horse's mouth. Because I was a good athlete and had had a decent season on the left wing, Clough called me in and said I'd be offered a one-year professional contract with a wage of £70 a week. It was take it or leave it. I took it gladly.

The Professionals

The 1981–82 season was the worst at Forest since they'd won promotion in 1977. Since then they'd been to three League Cup finals and won the championship and two European Cups. The fans had quickly come to expect success but a series of high-profile transfers hadn't quite worked out and the glory team was being broken up. I saw them lose at home to lowly Wrexham in the FA Cup, Justin Fashanu couldn't buy a goal and the team were struggling. The current methods weren't working so it was a good time to be a young player at Nottingham Forest.

In October I got a call on a Sunday afternoon and was called into the ground where the first team were at home to Vancouver Whitecaps in a friendly game. The Canadians were touring with Peter Lorimer and Ray Hankin in their side. I only got to the ground at about ten past two for a three o'clock kick-off as I'd played for the reserves on Saturday, and when I arrived I was told that I was playing! Things couldn't have started better for me as I scored at the Trent End in the first twenty minutes and we drew 2–2. That game gave me such a buzz, but then, of course, I was out of the team again. A few weeks later we were at Grantham for a friendly and I was picked again and bagged a hat-trick in a 5–2 win, so I must have been putting myself in the frame.

Defender Chris Fairclough was a year younger than me and was getting a few first-team chances before me, but towards the end of the season Clough asked me to come and watch a home game against Spurs and be on the bench with him. "Come and learn your trade" was how he put it. Clough was always aware that Spurs liked to play a passing game and when they were inspired by Glenn Hoddle, he'd say, "If you let this lot play today they'll take the piss out of you!" During the game we had a chance and it looked like we might be about to score, though it was scrambled away. Graham Lyas, our physio, half jumped up and shouted "Yes!" but he sat down quickly, realising he'd made an error. Cloughie angrily turned to him and said, "Physio, when the ball's being placed back on the halfway line, then I'll tell you it's a goal! Until then, sit down and shut up!" So I sat very quietly through the whole game, just watching and learning, not daring to say a word. Davenport scored and we won 2–0, I knew that I must be in his thoughts. When someone took a long shot, Clough said, "Who does he think he is, shooting from forty yards!" And when someone missed from close range he exclaimed, "He's entitled to hit the target from there!" All the sayings that I'd be hearing for the next ten years were coming out. When a Forest player misplaced a pass he'd bellow, "Pass the ball to a red shirt!" He once told me, "You'd be amazed how many players can't pass a ball five yards from A to B when they're under pressure."

"A footballer needs to practise his job every day," he'd intone and another favourite of his was, "If you're not sure what to do, do nowt, sleep on it."

The last game of the season was away at Ipswich and I was included in the squad that travelled. I had to make all the teas and coffees on the bus for the whole three-hour trip on the Friday. I was made to feel welcome but knew my place as everyone would be gently taking the mickey out of me. "One more sugar, please." "Can you stir it gently for me?" But I was just happy to be in the fourteen-man squad.

Saturday was a lovely sunny day and Willie Young came into my room and said, "You're playing today. Justin's pulled out." I thought, "Well, he's a striker. I don't play as a striker. I'm not sure about that. I'll wait and see." My parents had travelled down as well just on the off-chance that I might be the sub or be involved in some way. We got to the ground and we were all waiting to hear the team – no one from the management had given me any hint as to whether I'd be involved or not. Clough read the team out and said, "Young Hodge, you're playing centre-forward." I thought, "Wow, I don't care where I play. I'm actually starting a game!" Justin Fashanu had pulled out for some unknown reason and the manager was clearly angry with him about it, so now, right at the end of my contract, I was being thrown in at the deep end.

It was a massive game for Ipswich Town, because if they won and Liverpool lost they'd be the league champions. Liverpool were a point ahead and playing at home, so it meant a lot for them. Both games were being covered on *Match of the Day*, which was a big deal back then, and the main chance for fans to see football on TV. I went out and saw some Forest fans in the corner, which we appreciated, because three hours each way for a meaningless game, for us, was a big undertaking. I've since seen on a video Bobby Robson asking his assistant manager, Bobby Ferguson, "Have you seen that little centre-forward?" before the game, and he told Terry Butcher and Russell Osman to look out for me. Obviously his brain was ticking over about me and it was ironic that our paths would meet so much later in my career. As we walked out the noise hit me; I wasn't used to that kind of reception playing for the youth team or in reserve games. Clough just told me to go out and enjoy myself and to run around, which I did for eighty-five minutes. As it turned out, the two managers that day would become the two most important men in my career.

At half-time I'd been running around like an idiot in the heat and it was 0–0. I'd been able to get the ball down and lay it off, I didn't feel out of place. It had been drummed into me to receive the ball, get turned and run at the defender, so I tried to do that whenever I could. We scored within five minutes of the restart. Peter Davenport got one, then another, before Alan Brazil pulled one back. After seventy minutes we counter-attacked and I had a run at Mick Mills; a change of pace got me a half-yard in the box, I drilled the ball low and hard and Davenport got his hat-trick from close in. By then I was shattered. Nervous energy had got me through it; I'd made a goal and I was happy to have had an input in a great win. I was substituted with five minutes to go and as I walked off Cloughie came off the bench and hugged me and picked me up in the air. I was just eager to get in the shade, but then he started untying my boot laces! I was thinking, "Brian Clough is taking my boots off! I must have had a really good game today! He's really pleased with me!" I was slightly embarrassed but inwardly I was buzzing.

"Well done, son," he said. "You'll be doing this forty-odd times again next season if you're lucky!" which was music to my ears. It was a huge game for me. If we'd lost 4–0 that might have been the end of my professional career, you just never knew. Before we left Portman Road I saw what could happen if you got on the wrong side of Cloughie. Justin Fashanu, who had pulled out and given me my chance, was denied access to the team coach by the manager. Cloughie was livid and shut the door behind him and said, "Let him walk!" I was shocked to see a million-pound player being shut out of the team bus. I went away from that game absolutely shattered, sitting at the back of the bus just gazing at the East Anglian countryside as we made our way back home, happy and contented with my debut.

Justin Fashanu –
The Sad Story of a Million
Pound Flop

I always found Justin Fashanu to be an articulate and friendly character but his ways were very different to your average First Division footballer in the 1980s. All the first-team players at Forest had a blue towel with a number stitched on but Justin preferred to bring in his own towels for use after training; it was little things like that that made him stand out from the crowd, never a good thing in a football dressing room. He also went through a period of bringing his own personal masseur into the changing room to give him a massage before training. This was questioned by some of the players because in the macho world of professional football it was a bit precious! Justin's little eccentricities might have been overlooked if he had been successful on the pitch, but at Forest he really struggled. While I was still an apprentice he asked me and two or three others to stay behind after training for some extra shooting practice. He was still new to the club then and I hadn't really seen what he could do, but on this occasion no words were needed. These simple shooting drills turned into a nightmare for him, and us apprentices displayed far better technique than the one-million-pound player. His shots continually flew high and wide or were miscued and in a strange way it gave me a confidence boost because I saw that my technique was better than a one-million-pound player's.

It seemed to go from bad to worse for Justin; his scoring was minimal and the first team struggled. Brian Clough obviously felt let down that the money he'd spent wasn't being repaid and things between him and Fashanu disintegrated. It came to a head later while we were training at the Holme Road training ground one day, when a police car arrived and two policemen strolled on to the pitch. Justin had been suspended by the manager but had turned up to train anyway. I watched with the other apprentices from another pitch and saw the officers walk towards Justin and inform him that the manager wanted him to be removed from the grounds. It was a measure of the power that Brian Clough had in Nottingham that he could get uniformed policemen to come to training and remove a player. Justin initially refused and stood his ground, but after some gentle persuasion he strode off and into the police car which took him back to the City Ground to get changed. It was another surreal day at Nottingham Forest and it was sad to see Justin humiliated in such a way, walking off with his head bowed and clearly upset by what was happening to him.

To Europe

After the Ipswich game I was out of contract, but soon afterwards I was called in by Cloughie, which I took to be a good sign. "I thought you did all right at Ipswich, young man," he said. "I'm going to offer you a one-year contract with a rise to £90." Relieved to still have a future in the game, I took it. I was pleased because I'd never been one of the blue-eyed boys but had managed to take my chance when it came. The last game of my contract could easily have gone the other way and I might not have been kept on at all. So I had a full season to look forward to. Our preseason preparations continued to Gibraltar, Nuremberg and then a tournament in Huelva. We reached the final against Recreativo de Huelva and it was a real kicking match, something else that I'd never been involved with or seen before. We won 1–0 and the trophy was a massive Spanish galleon. Myself, Bryn Gunn and Colin Walsh were put in charge of getting it back to the hotel and then back to England. It was a nightmare getting it through customs and on to the plane, where it had three seats to itself. It's still in the Forest trophy room to this day.

The league season opened at West Ham; I was in the starting XI and we won 2–1. The league had ordered a referee's clampdown, the sort of thing that comes along every few years and then fades away as the season progresses. Colin Todd got sent off for us after he handled the ball on the halfway line and we lost at home to Manchester United, 3–0, with my idol Bryan Robson scoring one of the goals. As I'd grown up I'd always wanted to be like Robson, captain of both his club and country with an all-action, swashbuckling style that I tried to emulate. I always thought he had an aura about him, and perhaps I put him on a pedestal because all through my later England career I'd be watching to see how he acted and carried the responsibility of being the captain. Soon afterwards I was in the team that travelled to face Liverpool at Anfield. When we ran out I saw Graeme Souness and thought he looked menacing, but despite the youngsters in the team we still had our share of experience. Ian Bowyer was great to have around; he was full of old-pro nous and said, "Don't worry about them. We're Nottingham Forest!" He'd frequently beaten Liverpool in the European Cup and in finals and semifinals. He knew how the game worked, he was tough, rugged and knowledgeable, the perfect mentor. We also had Hans van Breukelen in goal, who'd been brought in from Utrecht. He was a fantastic character who everyone loved, a great influence. Garry Birtles had come back to Forest for a second chance after struggling at Manchester United. So I had lots of experience around me and I was full of confidence after scoring in front of the Kop to give us the lead. They came back to score twice but I got another one just before half-time and we went in at the break all-square. It was such an adrenaline rush going in at half-time, having played less than half a dozen first-team games and getting two at Anfield. In the second half we traded goals again before Ian Rush won it in the last seconds. There are certain games in your career that you lose but you can look back and know you really enjoyed it, and this was one of those games. I was making people aware of my name and my confidence was sky-high.

Then we hammered West Brom 6–1 in the League Cup. I was up against the experienced Martin Jol. While I would buzz around the midfield, he was more of a big lanky stroller.

I must have been annoying him that day because whenever he got close to me he'd reach out and pinch my skin. He was obviously trying to put me off my game, but it didn't work and when I was taken off near the end of the game I was given a standing ovation. By now Bobby Robson had been installed as the England manager and he watched the game that night. Afterwards he said I was a very interesting young player and that he'd be watching me closely. After less than ten games it was amazing to get that kind of attention. Now I was in the centre of midfield and had a bit of a free role alongside Ian Bowyer. I was hard to mark because I didn't really know where I "should" run, I'd just look for space and get into it.

Without getting complacent, I felt like I'd arrived. The team had a good mix of youth and experience. The latter was provided by Colin Todd, Viv Anderson, Ian Bowyer, Garry Birtles, Kenny Swain, Willie Young and Hans van Breukelen. The tradition amongst the first-team squad was that every Friday lunch we'd all go to McKay's Café for butties and a cup of tea and talk about football. It wasn't anything like the strict diets that top level players adhere to today, but to be accepted into that group was a big deal for me. We'd have the usual chit-chat about the gaffer's team selection, who we'd be playing next and where we'd all be going out to together after the game on Saturday. One day we sat there going through the bonus sheet, which paid us a set amount for the place we occupied in the league table at the end of each week, over a bacon and egg butty.

I was still just trying to take it all in, but some of the things that happened at Forest wouldn't have happened anywhere else. There was never a dull moment when you played in a Brian Clough team. A couple of games from the autumn of 1982 stick in my mind, both against Graham Taylor's Watford. Taylor had them flying – they eventually finished as runners-up that season, but we comfortably beat them 2–0 at the City Ground in the league. The most memorable part of the game occurred when someone dressed as a clown ran on to the pitch. I saw Cloughie sprinting on behind him, looking red in the face. He was really angry and he grabbed hold of the clown and forced him off the pitch, but that was not enough. He then forced him across the path around the pitch and then over a small wall and into the stand. The pitch was sacrosanct to Clough, he called it "My pitch" and no one was allowed on to it.

The second game at home to Watford was in the League Cup. They liked to launch the long ball but that night we passed rings around them and were 7–2 ahead in the closing minutes before Luther Blissett scored for them right at the end to make it 7–3. He sprinted in to the back of the net to get the ball back quickly and I was thinking, "What's he doing that for, the game's over?" It was just that he'd been taught to always do the right thing and keep going to the final whistle. I'd served my apprenticeship but was still very much learning my trade. I missed a 3–0 win over Arsenal and sat on the bench. In the last minute Brian Talbot chased a ball to the corner flag. Brian Clough turned to me and said, "Did you see that, son? A professional at work." He really admired the effort. He was keen that we were ready to play for ninety minutes, never to harass the referee and to play the ball on the floor. At Norwich I scored after twenty-two seconds on an icy pitch. Cloughie used to say, "Lads, you can win or lose a game in the first minute. Be switched on from the start." That night we won 1–0 and I was praised by Cloughie: "You want to get forward naturally, son. There's not many who want to do that. Keep doing it."

In December we went to play an indoor five-a-side tournament in Milan, something else that would never happen with a Premiership side today. Ajax were also there and just before we played them Cloughie called over to me, "Young

Hodge, you mark young Cruijff !" Here I was, one year into my first-team career and being asked to mark one of the world's greatest-ever players. I didn't get near him, but what an education. A couple of youngsters called Marco van Basten and Frank Rijkard were in the Ajax side and I think our 6–4 loss was a creditable result. We also played Internazionale in the tournament and they boasted recent World Cup winners such as Bergomi, Conti and Altobelli. We got thrashed again!

In the third round of the FA Cup we were drawn away to Derby County. Forest–Derby games were always special, but this one generated more interest than ever. When Peter Taylor had left Forest at the end of the previous season he'd announced that he was going to retire, but not long afterwards he was unveiled as Derby's new manager, returning to the club that he and Clough had left in such controversial circumstances almost a decade earlier. The two had fallen out over Taylor's appointment and the buildup to the game was intense. I'd never really got to know Peter Taylor so I always wondered if he rated me as a player, because it was strange that I got my debut at Ipswich just a week after he resigned at Forest. Some players remember him as a joker and Cloughie always used to say that Taylor made him laugh, but he had a ruthless side too. Forest had had a coach by the name of Brian Bates and one day, out of the blue, Peter Taylor called him in to say, "Brian, one of us is leaving the football club and it isn't me."

The Baseball Ground was a muddy bog of a pitch that day, which had been watered on purpose – an old Brian Clough trick – and we lost 2–0 to our Second Division opponents. Brian Clough was year by year gaining a stigma for never having won the FA Cup and after this loss he was gutted. "Well, that's another year gone for us to get to the twin towers," said Ian Bowyer. He would always say, before any cup game, no matter what the round, "Boys, the twin towers are beckoning" and it's something I took up throughout my career whenever I played in a cup match.

Despite his failure to win the FA Cup, Clough always, always preached the importance of the league. "This is our bread and butter," he'd say. "This is what we do week in week out. Anyone can win a cup, but not anyone can win the league." After a home game someone would come in with a sheet of the afternoon's scores and he'd say, "Read it out then, son." When the scores had been announced, Cloughie would add, "Hang on, there's only one result today, lads. Nottingham Forest won!" It's the only thing that bothered him.

We finished the season in fine style. Peter Davenport came back from injury and we surged to seven wins and two draws in our last nine games. During half-time at home to Liverpool the manager shouted, "Will somebody go and sort Souness out. He's sitting in my centre circle like he owns the joint!" Ian Bowyer went and got stuck into him and we won 1–0. Our good run saw us climb to fifth in the table, just two points behind Watford, the runners-up, and we qualified for the UEFA Cup. I finished with ten goals, not bad for a first-year midfielder. I was also named as the fans' player of the year, which meant an awful lot to me.

If I were a player today I'd have been looking forward to a summer's rest, but back then we still had a trip to Canada before our season was over. We faced Manic de Montreal, who had the ex-French international Jean François Larios playing for them. He was the only player in my whole career who spat in my face. I was defending a corner and had no idea what was coming as he rolled his lips and spat in the middle of my forehead. As it ran down on to my nose, I was in shock. It was an end-of-season friendly – there was just no need. I scored twice that day, including the winner with a rare long-range effort, but Larios is my abiding memory of that game – it was disgusting. We also played in Toronto against a side featuring the legendary Roberto Bettega. We had the customary trip to Niagara Falls, met the prime minister Pierre Trudeau, and had a night out to a lap-dancing bar, something that back then I'd never even heard of!

The Overseas Midweek Break

Though it doesn't seem that long ago, many things that I experienced as a professional player would never be allowed or tolerated today. One thing that has gone for ever is the midweek overseas trip to play a friendly. Today players get rested because they have "too many games" but we regularly had over seventy matches in a season, and included in that were long trips to play friendly matches with the only reason being a chance to get a hefty appearance fee for the club. A typical jaunt was a trip to Kuwait. We'd played Luton on the Saturday and then flew out the next day. The manager would order that wives and girlfriends would get flowers or chocolates delivered to their house on a Wednesday or Thursday and they'd know what was coming next. We could be away on a Saturday, be missing all week then play away again before getting home eight days later. This time we were greeted by an all-male crowd, dressed in traditional head-to-toe floor-length white robes and head-gear for a game in Kuwait City, then flew by private jet to Riyadh. We were treated like rock stars before another game. We'd meet the local British embassy staff and the ambassador; we were like royalty. Then we flew back Thursday night and stayed overnight in another hotel. We'd played four games in seven days, travelled who knows how many miles and all for the PFA daily allowance of about £10 a day. I was seeing the world for the first time, really, and took it all in my stride, but if you had a family it wouldn't have been great to keep jetting around leaving the wife and kids at home. Another trip took us to play an Oman Select XI. They kicked the shit out of us and it was nasty. I saw Ian Wallace flatten one of their players with a punch. They were decent players but had no discipline. Again, the club was paid a lot of money to get us out there. Slightly shorter trips included one to Malta, where the manager got us on to a Royal Navy boat. He'd walk into a restaurant anywhere and everyone would turn and stare. And so it went on.

One trip was to Iraq and two games in Baghdad. Cloughie ducked out of that one, but before we left, he advised us to pack our "tin helmets". A week after we left, the hotel where we'd stayed was blown up in a bomb attack. At the end of the 1981–82 season we flew out to Casablanca to play Kuwait as part of their build-up for the 1982 World Cup finals. I got a shock to see abject poverty first hand and recall seeing a little pot-bellied kid of about five or six wandering the streets alone during the night. A couple of months later during our preseason preparations we flew out to Malaysia. The name of Nottingham Forest, recent European champions, opened a lot of doors. When we arrived in Kuala Lumpa Justin Fashanu went out on his own while the rest of us went to a bar. When he met up with us later he'd come back from visiting some Sultan or other. He was never really part of the group and always went off on his own somewhere. One night at a hotel in Spain I woke up to the sounds of screaming and went out in to the corridor where I found Viv Anderson standing in shock and a gaping hole in the door which Justin Fashanu had smashed through in a fit of rage. Justin wasn't in a good place mentally, and he'd just exploded. Wherever we went and whatever we did there was never a dull moment!

One preseason Cloughie took the whole squad to a brothel in Amsterdam. I don't know if the manager knew it was a brothel or just thought it was a bar. All the Forest hierarchy was there and I thought it wasn't a typical bar when I noticed all the women in there had numbers on their wrists! When we finished our drinks we had a walk through the red-light area, past rows of windows behind which sat women showing their wares, all with an Alsatian dog sat beside them. We strolled on to another bar, all the while with our legendary manager leading the way, not something I could imagine being done by any of today's top-flight managers.

If the manager was on a flight home with us I knew he'd be coming down the aisle at some point to give me a tap on the shoulder. "Are you carrying anything through?" he'd ask, and because I rarely was he'd give me a bottle of whisky or 200 cigarettes to take through customs to ensure he got the maximum out of his "allowance".

We'd usually go to Majorca at the end of the season and the manager would make the bus detour on the way home from an away game to go past East Midlands Airport. "We'll be here for our holidays soon," he'd say. "Now everybody wave at the airport." And there we'd be. A team full of professional sports-men. On a bus. Waving at an airport.

Robbed

We had two whole months break before we started our next preseason in Holland and we had a total of eight preseason games including a tournament in Barcelona. Our first game against the hosts gave me a first look at Diego Maradona. Barcelona were managed by Cesar Menotti the chain-smoking, World Cup-winning Argentinian legend. During the game Cloughie marched over to him and said right in his face, "Hey, put that cigarette out, don't you know they're bad for you!" He'd just grabbed Maradona's balls and now he was giving the manager a bollocking. He just didn't care. We lost that game 2–0 and played Anderlecht in the third/fourth place play-off. It was the usual preseason routine of playing lots of games to get match fit. During the game I made a harmless gesture to the referee, just asking if he was sure about a decision, and he booked me! I couldn't believe it. Afterwards the manager asked me, "What am I going to fine you?" I didn't want to get fined. I thought I'd done nothing wrong. "I don't deserve to get fined," I argued. He said "Son, I'm going to let you decide." Early in my career my enthusiasm would sometimes get me booked because I was keen to do well. He wanted to make a point that this should be a deterrent and eventually he fined me £100. I was on £90 a week at the time, but his view was that no matter what happened you leave referees alone. Sometimes before games when the referee and linesmen would come into the dressing room Cloughie would say to them, "Any trouble with this lot [meaning his own players], you let me know. We have no trouble with referees here!" Then after the pleasantries had been exchanged and the officials had left, the gaffer would call them a bunch of shithouses!

In our second game of the season we won 2–1 at Old Trafford, something we did quite regularly in those days. At five-to-three I saw United full-back John Gidman watching the horse racing on TV with his boots on and his socks down round his ankles in a room on his own. I couldn't believe what I was seeing!

I was still living at home and travelling to training on the bus, even though I was an established first-team player and playing in the UEFA Cup. Can you imagine a current Premiership player getting on a bus to go anywhere? I still hadn't learned to drive at this point, so for an evening UEFA Cup game I'd be with the commuters in my tracksuit. It sounds like something out of Stanley Matthews' era now, and it wasn't glamorous at all.

Forest's first European game for a few years was against the unknown quantity of Vorwearts from East Germany. I scored a header and we won the first-leg 2–0 at home.

Then we flew behind the Iron Curtain to East Germany, close to the Polish border. Once we'd checked into our hotel the manager said, "Come on, we're going for a walk. See how the other half lives." We all set off together, peering in at little drinking establishments full of men. It was an area of dimmed street lights, an eerie place from another era. You did wonder if you were being watched, but it was exciting; it was another, albeit sad, strange world.

Back home we had a trip to Wimbledon in the League Cup. They were just starting to get noticed around the football world. I used to lie down at the back of the bus and get a kip for a couple of hours. The bus always had bowls of sweets and Crunchies and chocolates, a load of unhealthy stuff from the

Clough family newsagents in West Bridgford. We'd get coffee in a flask, and a packet of crisps. Plough Lane was a nasty place to go and they were a nasty team to play against: lots of verbals, lots of elbows. They out-muscled us, but, then again, we never practised set-plays and they always battered us. There'd be salt in the sugar pot, cold showers and they always went route one. We lost 2–0.

Notts County were back in the First Division. Cloughie always had a lot of respect for Jimmy Sirrel and what he had achieved on a meagre budget across the river. We played at the City Ground quite early in the season and were comfortably ahead 3–1 late in the game. I got the ball and took it to the corner flag where County's David Hunt came up and whacked me. He got a red card and we saw the game out. Job done. Or so I thought. In the papers the next day Brian Clough had his say. Splashed across *The Sun* in inch-high letters he said, "I'd have kicked him myself!" I didn't understand that and the FA pulled him up on the comment. I thought it was the right thing to do; if I'd lost the ball and they'd scored I'd have been in real trouble. He was full of contradictions, and of course he made the national press. In typical Clough fashion he also said in the same article that I could expect to play for my country one day. A bonus comment in an otherwise confusing read.

Forest have been involved in a lot of firsts over the years; the first shin-pads, first referee's whistle, the first million-pound player and so on. This season we were also in the first-ever live league game on TV when we visited Tottenham Hotspur. Our team bus got stuck in some bad traffic on the way down so Cloughie told Albert, our bus driver, to drive down the hard shoulder. When the police arrived, the manager simply said, "Sorry, but I've got a game to play!"

We were having a good season in the league and our UEFA

Cup games were a nice bonus rather than a distraction. We were used to flying off for all kinds of midweek friendlies anyway. In the second round we were drawn against PSV Eindhoven. The first away leg was another great education. They had the likes of van der Kerkoff and Arie Haan. They were a top team playing at the highest level. Peter Davenport scored a memorable solo goal, I was up and down the left wing and we won 2–1. The players would usually go out to Madison's nightclub in Nottingham after a midweek game; as we often flew back right after a UEFA game we still made it to our regular haunt well before closing time, even though we'd just been playing in Holland. The beauty of charter flights!

Peter Davenport was one of the rare players that Brian Clough would let get away with things. After a game Cloughie would say to him, "What time suits you next week for training?" and Peter would often reply "Friday". "OK, we'll see you Friday," Clough would reply in front of us all. Basically he was allowed to have a week off while we had to train every day. Clough knew that Davenport was a home bird and struggled a little bit with homesickness. Clough would say that a professional player needed to practise his trade every day. But he was a master and treated players in the way he thought would bring out the best in them. Rather than get a week off I was more likely to be told "Harry, get forward or fuck off!" during a game or afterwards it might be, "Well played, son. Not bad for a player who can't play."

The third round of the UEFA Cup drew a lot of press and media interest. Back then, British teams rarely played each other in Europe but we drew Celtic and all of the usual "Battle of Britain" stuff was wheeled out. The first leg at home was a special European night by the Trent. Celtic had brought 10,000 fans with them and it was a really icy night. Shortly before we went out Clough pulled the back four to one side and said, "All I want from you tonight is a clean sheet. I don't care what the other six do. I don't want to concede a goal tonight!" He'd heap praise on people who would defend his goal at any cost. Even in a five-a-side if you dived back and cleared a shot off the line he'd go berserk and shout, he'd love it.

His usual take on big European ties was that, "I've got one hundred and eighty minutes to win this match; whatever happens tonight it's only half-time. I'll wait until the last minute of the second leg if I have to. Just go out and play your normal game. Don't go trying to win it in the first leg."

The conditions made sure that little football was played. The Scottish fans were happy with the 0–0 draw and a couple of times they spilled out of their enclosure and on to the pitch. We weren't exactly disappointed and afterwards we all headed off to Madison's. There we found some of the Celtic lads and I ended up chatting with Roy Aitken about football well into the early hours.

The lead up to the away leg was pure Clough at his best. He dropped me for the preceding game against Leicester, simply to wind me up. Then we flew to Glasgow on a Sunday and he took the whole squad on a bus into the city. We pulled up at a tough-looking pub and he took the twenty or so of us inside. He ordered that all of us have a lunchtime beer and we were there for no longer than twenty minutes then he ordered us right back to the bus. Then we realised that the bar belonged to Celtic manager David Hay. As we exited Clough called out to the lad serving behind the bar, "Tell David, thanks for his hospitality and add it to his bill!"

We travelled down to Troon that Sunday night but our kit and everything else stayed in Glasgow. On Monday he took us to the Troon harbour for five hours in the bars. It was December and there wasn't anyone there apart from us playing pool and kicking our heels. We must have had six or seven pints each, and didn't train. On Tuesday it was the same again. On Wednesday we went for a walk, had an afternoon kip, then travelled to the game. We'd done no training. Without our kit we couldn't, even if we'd wanted to. Almost 70,000 were inside Celtic Park that night. And when we walked out for an early look around the stadium, the "jungle" was already quite full and started giving us some abuse. Ian Bowyer went right over and gave them a big wave then turned back with a big smile on his face while they went ballistic behind him, screaming at him and gesturing but he sent us the message, "Don't worry, we can handle that lot." Any fear of the crowd just melted away; it was really reassuring. We kept it to 0–0 into the second half and then I scored the vital first goal with a late run into the box. Colin Walsh scored to make it 2–0 and it was all over. All I could hear was the 2 or 3,000 Forest fans. Brian Clough would always say enjoy the moment, but let's get away quickly, so we flew right home and were in the club to top off the night. The coach from East Midlands airport got us in to town by 12.30. We had a great team spirit. The manager let us have a long leash but he trusted us and encouraged us to do that. On the pitch it was great fun too. We had lots of goal scorers with Birtles and Davenport up front while myself, Bowyer and Walsh could score our share from midfield. Using two wide players meant we could play an open game, but as we proved in Europe, we could keep clean sheets and put Ian Bowyer into a more defensive role.

After we were drawn against Sturm Graz in the UEFA Cup quarter-finals we realised that we hadn't had any bonus payments agreed in our contracts for the European games. Financially we'd got to the quarter-finals for nothing. Without agents or advisers we'd just hadn't thought to ask about it. The senior players went to see the manager as we'd won three rounds of the UEFA Cup and thought we deserved something. They agreed a deal by which we'd get a payment for the first three rounds but only if we got a win or draw in our next league game at Wolverhampton Wanderers. Avoiding a loss at Molineux would pay us £3,000 cash each, not bad considering I was on £90 per week. We'd already beaten them 5–0 at home and they were rock bottom of the table – they'd eventually be relegated and finished twenty-one points from safety. Less than 11,000 turned out to witness a dire game on a poor, muddy pitch. Little football could be played in the conditions and late on it was dragging out to a 0–0 draw. Then Wolves got a corner with about three minutes to go and Paul Hart scored an own goal. A lot of unhappy players trudged off that day but the manager, while always preaching that the bread and butter of the league was always his priority, could take some solace from the fact that Hart had saved the club somewhere in the region of £40,000.

Chris Fairclough and I had had a couple of pints in a local pub after training one day and thought that the manager was way out of line regarding the European bonuses. So, half-drunk, we somewhat courageously went to see him in his office. We said we thought he just wasn't being fair and that a fair day's work deserved a fair day's pay. He just said he had agreed it with the senior pros and that was that. I think we both felt good that we had got it off our chests, even if we hadn't managed to change his mind. And whoever did that anyway? Willie Young was one player that I saw really have a go back at Cloughie. He didn't care about the gaffer's reputation and that was probably why he was sold and replaced by Paul Hart from Leeds.

By now I had passed my driving test and would leave my car at the Ground during away trips. I got back late from one midweek away game and pulled out of the car park.

Immediately another car parked at the side of the road pulled out and began following me; it was a police car. Having not been driving for long I was worried when it followed me over Trent Bridge and then a good three miles towards home. Eventually it flashed me and I pulled over, trying to think what I might have done wrong. The police officer got out and walked to my window. "Oh, it is you, Steve," he said. "Can I have your autograph?"

We had to prepare for the first leg at home to Graz knowing that we again had no bonus agreements for the rest of the competition. As usual we went up to a hotel at junction 28 of the M1 and treated the home European game like an away trip, and as was also usual, that season we got another European clean sheet at home. Paul Hart scored in a 1–0 win and we had one foot in the last four. We had two days in Austria before the second leg and again we cut back on the training and spent our time going on walks. On one of these wanders through the Austrian countryside the manager stopped us by a tree. "This," he announced, "is a punch tree." We all looked at the tree, then at the manager, then back at the tree. "Everyone has to punch it." Such was the absolute power that he held over his players, no one was going to say 'no' to Brian Clough. So one by one we stepped forward and punched the tree trunk. When the last player had cracked his knuckles on the bark we carried on with the walk.

The next day I went for a walk with Steve Wigley and Chris Fairclough. It was a beautiful day, "It's a good to be alive day!" Clough had announced at breakfast, and we saw this picturesque little village. We called in to the church, said a couple of prayers for the game the next day, then stopped off at a little bar. We ended up chilling out and enjoying the scenery for about three hours and had one too many. We staggered back to the hotel where all the squad was having dinner. We snuck in and I got my head down but the others knew we were half-cut. Ian Bowyer was taking the mickey saying, "You've got a big European game tomorrow. Who do you think you are?" Chris felt so guilty that he decided to go out for a run, still a little bit inebriated. The game itself was very tight. They scored and we went to extra time. I was pushed in the back for a penalty and we went 2-1 ahead on aggregate and had an away goal. The gaffer never moved from the touchline for the whole of extra time and at half-time in extra time he just kept shouting, "Come on lads! Come on lads! Come on lads!" constantly for about two minutes. That's all I could hear, Brian Clough shouting. It was as if he had nothing else to say, as though he couldn't do anything else to help us. He would verbally support us but we were on our own and he looked a little bit helpless.

Forest were still a big name in Europe and we were expected to get to big finals and win them. We faced Anderlecht in the last four and some quality players like Enzo Scifo, future Denmark manager Morten Olsen, van den Berg and Franky Vercauteraen. Clough played them a massive compliment by putting five across midfield in the home leg. It was very unusual to change from our standard 4-4-2. The match was goalless late on and we got a corner. I managed to sneak in at the back post to give us the lead with a header and then four minutes later I scored one of the favourite goals of my whole career. My diving header at the Trent End made it 2-0 and should have clinched our place in the final. Everyone went berserk and we walked off on a real high. Deep down we all thought we'd get a goal in Belgium and that would be it. We stayed in Ostend and the day before the second leg Clough had some comments in the paper about the referee. He knew what could go on in Europe, having been robbed at Juventus in 1973. His fears would prove to be well-founded.

We played in front of 38,000 but it was a strange atmosphere. We were almost there but not quite. Then Scifo scored and it was game on, but we survived until half-time at 1–0. We were still OK, we just needed a goal. The referee, Carlos Guruceta of Spain, wouldn't talk to anyone. He was like a schoolmaster: if you tried to approach him he'd just shush you and wave you away. Then they got into the box and a really dramatic dive got them a penalty though Kenny Swain hadn't fouled Kenneth Brylle. It was a travesty, but suddenly we were pegged back to 2–2 on aggregate and the crowd was giving them some momentum. We didn't really think anything was amiss with the referee until time began to get on in the second half. We never got the very important decisions from the officials when we played away in Europe anyway. I was booked after about an hour and Clough took me off for the last twenty minutes or so. Garry Birtles went on to try and get a goal. They scored a good third goal and we were going out. We got a corner in the last minute and, as the ball came in, I heard a whistle before it even reached the penalty box. Paul Hart headed it in but it had been disallowed. I didn't even jump up. No one had seen anything wrong at all.

Moments later it was all over. I remember Hans van Breukelen kicking the ball at the ref from fifty yards. Cloughie realised that he'd been done again in a European semi and he was pretty quiet. In the changing room immediately after the game a UEFA official approached him.

"Mr Clough. I believe you have grounds for a complaint?"

His reply: "Young man, I've never complained about referees in twenty years and I'm not about to start now."

In my eyes we lost 2–1 and should have been in the final. The UEFA official said he'd investigate but we didn't expect anything. At the airport Clough came and sat next to me. He said, "Son, tonight I took you off before you got sent off." A lady Forest fan came towards us with a big smile on her face. She said, "Brian, don't worry about it, there's always next season." He was really accommodating and said, "Yes, OK, thanks, pet." As she wandered off he turned to me and said, "Harry, they haven't got a fucking clue, have they? They'll never know how much it hurts." On the plane that night I'd never seen him so flat after a defeat; I think he really wanted to make his mark on Europe on his own. As Brian Clough, not Brian Clough and Peter Taylor.

The truth came out eventually. Years later it transpired that people had been paid to keep things quiet and that the referee had been paid £20,000 by Anderlecht, although by then Guruceta had been killed in a car crash. So at least we had a reason for losing, but we'd still been robbed of a possible European medal. A few players got together to try and go down the compensation route. Some of them had been out of work for a while and were keen to get some money for their families, but it didn't get anywhere. It wasn't pushed as far as it should have been and, just as UEFA hoped, it was all brushed under the carpet. It remains, and will always be, one of the biggest regrets of my career. We had been cheated but no one in authority seemed to care. I would later be cheated again, and that would be on an even bigger stage.

The bribery overshadowed a good end to the season when we finished third in the First Division, the club's best position since 1979. We had been beaten by the champions Liverpool home and away that year and those defeats ensured that we finished six points behind them. We also won the prize for being the top-scoring team and had plenty to look forward to.

England's Last Champions

If I could draw any consolation from the season it was representing my country in the Under-21 European Championships. Ever since I'd read in an article that Brian Clough had said I could play for England one day I'd had a great boost in confidence. I thought, "Wow, does he really mean that?" As ever though, you couldn't predict what Clough might do next. I was picked for my first England Under-21 squad in October 1983, having only played ten first-team games. Howard Wilkinson picked me for a trip to Thessaloniki and he drove me and Brian Kilcline down to the West Lodge Park hotel to meet the other players. I saw Manchester City's Tommy Caton at reception, he was well known having played in an FA Cup final already, so I went over to say hello. "Hi, I'm Steve Hodge, Nottingham Forest" and we shook hands but I thought, "He probably doesn't know who I am."

The game was a qualifier for the Euro 84 finals and though we lost 1–0 I came on for the last five minutes and earned my first England cap. When the cap later arrived through the post it was a proud moment for me. My first full game followed against Denmark at Carrow Road alongside Paul Walsh and Brian Stein. The Under-21 games were a bit strange because we didn't really know each other and weren't a team in the real sense of the word. It was more a gathering of players who wanted to stand out and so were a little bit greedy. That wasn't my style because I was a real team player and in this scenario it was to my detriment because some of the flashier players got promoted ahead of me to the full England squad.

England qualified from their group but despite Brian Clough previously talking me up on the international stage he then knocked me back down. He pulled me out of a friendly game because I needed a single solitary stitch in my leg. He came into the treatment room and said, "That looks a bit bad. I'll call up and pull you out." He wasn't keen on anyone going to international friendlies. "What have the England coaches taught you this time?" he'd snipe when we reported back to Forest. "What has Don Howe taught you that I couldn't teach you? I know football better than they do!" He was clearly still very bitter not to have been given the England manager's job.

The Under-21s format was different back then, with the knockout stages being played throughout the season like a traditional cup competition. We faced France in the quarter-finals and played really well. Dave Sexton had succeeded Howard Wilkinson as manager by now. He was a thoughtful, quiet man and technically a good coach and we got on well. We beat the French 6–1 with Mark Hateley getting four of the goals. It took me back to my junior school days. Mark would go on to have a successful career with Rangers and AC Milan amongst others.

The semi-finals pitted us against Italy and the first million-pound teenager, Roberto Mancini. I missed the first leg at home which we won 3–1, but travelled to Florence for the return. In front of a big crowd we lost 1–0 but hung on to reach the final. You could see that Mancini was a class act, even at that age. He could do everything on the pitch, but it wasn't enough for them that night.

The European Championship final was not as big a thing then as it is now, but it was still a huge event for us and we were up against a quality side in Spain – they had some big names like Michel, Zubizaretta and Butragueno. The first leg took place in Seville, where it was pouring down with rain. Rumours spread through the camp that Bobby Robson was in town to watch the game and when we assembled for tea and toast at 5 p.m. he was sitting there waiting for us. He gathered us together and said, "There's a World Cup coming in two years and I see you lads as the future. Go out and impress me, because I will give kids a chance." This gave us all a massive incentive to do well on the muddy pitch. Mel Sterland scored and we won 1–0. Back at home for the decider there were just 12,000 at Bramall Lane. Though they were technically a better team, we out-battled them and won 2–0 to secure my first medal. We'd beaten France, Italy and Spain along the way and we are still the last England team to win a major trophy, and that's over a quarter of a century ago now! It's frightening that we haven't won anything since then with the players that we've had.

A week later Mark Hateley was called up to the senior side and scored against Brazil. That goal changed his life for ever. Bobby Robson had been true to his word and I could see that if I proved myself he'd give me a chance, but I didn't realise how long I'd wait for it. Before making my full debut I served some time as an over-age player for the Under-21s. We played Romania at Ipswich where I scored twice as captain, which was a massive honour. I first met Tony Adams during these games. He was in the England squad even though he hadn't yet played for Arsenal. He was big and confident and greeted me with a handshake and the words, "Hi, I'm Tony Adams." I was captain again against Turkey at Ashton Gate where I scored again. This was now late 1985 and I hoped I might get a chance with the seniors who had friendly games planned for early 1986. The World Cup was nowhere in my thoughts.

Asking for it

After beating Spain I enjoyed a fantastic trip to Australia with Forest and got the chance to play at the MCG against Manchester United, which being a big cricket fan I loved. I arrived late after my England duty and found that at some point on the long journey I'd taken the wrong case when I changed plane. When I got to the hotel and opened it I thought, "These aren't my clothes" and "Why are there vegetables in here?" Luckily there was nothing dodgy or I might have had a lot of explaining to do. Apparently my case had been diverted to Ireland and I had to buy new clothes while spending most of the three week trip in my tracksuit. During the trip we had a night out to watch Torvill and Dean on their Bolero World Tour and met them afterwards. Nottingham was making an impact down under!

○ ○ ○

The first game of the 1984–85 season was a 3–1 loss at Howard Wilkinson's Sheffield Wednesday. We got a lot of abuse from the Wednesday fans that day in the wake of the miners' strike and shouts of "scabs" rang out. It was also mercurial Dutch midfielder Johnny Metgod's first game in English football. "You tackle like a butterfly," Clough said to Metgod, "but you can pass a ball like a dream." As we walked off at Hillsborough I asked him how he thought he'd done. "I've got a stiff neck from watching the ball sail over my head for ninety minutes," he replied. To be fair, we hadn't exactly had the best preparation for the game as we'd only flown home from a game at Panathinaikos on the Friday night. Things soon picked up though and we reeled off a string of wins. Johnny had been signed from Real Madrid, a sign that Forest were still a big name on the European circuit, to play alongside Ian Bowyer in the centre of midfield. Consequently I often found myself shuffled out to the left wing where I felt restricted and not able to play to my full potential which was built around making well-timed runs into the box and getting a decent number of goals. I knew I could cause damage from the centre. Among the Forest squad the left wing was referred to as the 'graveyard'. It was the position where careers went to die because there was so much physical output required it could kill your career. You also had to rely more on your teammates to get the ball to you, unlike the centre of midfield where I had much more freedom. On the left wing I'd be forever told to stay out wide and I got fed up hearing the manager call out, "Harry, get your feet on that touchline!"

We won 5–0 at Aston Villa but afterwards the manager was singing the praises of Villa midfielder Gordon Cowans. "Did you see how he got stuck in for a small lad?" We beat Arsenal at home and the manager instructed me to kick their fullback Viv Anderson whenever I got the chance, something he liked to do to ex-Forest players when they returned to the City Ground. At home to Sunderland we won 3–1 but when our fullback Bryn Gunn gave away a goal he was hauled off after only twenty minutes, just to make a point.

We went out to Brugge in the first round of the UEFA Cup, which was a disaster, and more changes were made. Midway through the season Nigel Clough arrived. Though it was soon evident that he could pass the ball and was very brave I wasn't sure whether the pace of the First Division would be too much for him, but he showed what he could do when he got in the team. The manager usually referred to him as "the centre-forward". Another new signing was Gary Megson. During an early preseason game it became apparent that Megson's time at the City Ground would be limited. Cloughie turned to Ron Fenton and asked, "Who's that red-haired player in my midfield?"

"That's Gary Megson," came the reply.

"That's not the player I saw last season," said Cloughie.

"It is. You signed him from Sheffield Wednesday, boss."

"No, Ron. You signed him, not me, and I suggest you get rid of him!"

All the younger lads kept out of the way when the gaffer appeared. Even an established player like Megson was extremely intimidated by him. Gary never actually played a game for Forest. Like Asa Hartford before him and John Sheridan later on he came in but Cloughie didn't fancy him as a player.

I eventually got twelve goals from the wing but I wasn't happy and after Christmas there was press talk of a move, which was quite unsettling. Manchester United were mentioned and who, at the age of twenty-two, wouldn't relish a move to Old Trafford? I decided to do something that much more experienced players hadn't dared to do at Forest: I asked for a transfer. I got my mum to type out the request for me, but with her not being a typist it came out a bit amateurish. I went to see Brian Clough in the intimidating atmosphere of his office. He kept me waiting outside for about forty-five minutes. I saw Howard Wilkinson and Peter Eustace walk by – Sheffield Wednesday were playing Forest in a reserve game that night – and they had already tapped me up.

When Clough called me in I was pretty terrified at what might happen, and I knew he wouldn't like what I was going to do. With no agent or adviser I was on my own against one of the most feared men in the game. I had the letter tucked inside my jacket pocket. My heart was pounding when I went in and I told him that I wanted to leave the City Ground. "You can't just ask verbally!" he snapped, "You need to put it in writing!" At that point I pulled out the envelope and handed it over. I could tell he wasn't expecting me to be prepared, but he opened it and slowly read it to the end. "Who typed this?"

"My mum."

"Tell her not to give up the fucking day job!"

I thought that was as bad as it was going to get, but just as I was about to leave he added, "Now remember, young man, that anything that happens to you now is because of this letter!" I walked out shaking and almost in tears. I bumped into Paul Hart but just acknowledged him and headed straight to my car. I was in a right state.

In 1985 things were about as bad as they could get between Brian Clough and Peter Taylor. Word had seeped out about my transfer request and I got a call from a guy named Brian Newton. He said, "Taylor knows how he can get you away from Forest." He just wanted to upset the apple cart at Forest and get me away; not to Derby, just away from Forest, which perfectly illustrated the depths to which their once-great relationship had sunk. At the time there was some hatred there. I thought long and hard about meeting him and I don't know what he would have said but I bottled it and I think I was right to bottle it. If Clough had found out I'd have really suffered.

The last game of the season was at Tottenham. We sat down for tea and toast at about five-thirty and Neil Webb appeared at the next table with his girlfriend, father and the gaffer. It was obvious that he'd be signing for Forest and he did so a few days later. I took that as an indication that I was likely to be sold. I'd sulked for about a month after I'd hinted in the papers that I'd be interested in speaking to Manchester United – this was after Ron Atkinson had written that United were interested in me. Clough told me in no uncertain terms that he wouldn't sell to United because he saw them as a threat. I was getting regular phone calls from a "Mr Smith" at Aston Villa making it known that they were interested in me and Peter Eustace used to call me up from Sheffield Wednesday. But in 1985 I didn't have an agent; I was twenty-two years old and had to deal with it.

At the end of the season I'd also been named as a stand-by player for the England first team. Manchester United were facing Everton in the FA Cup final and if there had been a replay there were about twelve players going to be involved and unavailable for the full international in Finland. As the match was played I was walking through the streets of Nottingham, not wanting to know the score, not wanting to see a TV screen. Then I heard a roar from a bar and knew someone had scored and I missed my chance. I knew that might be the only chance I got. It must have been strange for people to see me in the middle of town, shopping for clothes while the biggest football match of the season was being played. I was gutted. It was going to be an uncertain summer.

Shoe String Finances –
The Boys on the Bus

Forest were skint. They'd wasted over £3 million on Ian Wallace, Justin Fashanu and Peter Ward, plus they were in debt from building the two-tiered Executive Stand. Cutbacks had to be made and of course the players felt it. Overnight stays before away games were cancelled; instead we'd take long coach journeys on the day of a game. Bargain-basement signings and non-league players were coming in and, luckily for me, the youngsters were given a chance to come through. One thing that Brian Clough stuck to was making sure that the committee members went on a different bus to away games than the players and coaching staff. One day the members' coach started to pull out of the car park at the City Ground and Clough shouted, "Come on lads, give the nice board members a big wave!" And to a man the players had to get up and go over to the side of the bus and wave. "Keep smiling lads! Keep smiling while they have their smoked salmon dinners. Keep smiling at the shithouses, every last one of them!" Meanwhile the players were down to having soup and a roll as the pre-match dinner. We didn't even get off the bus to eat it; someone would come along handing out rolls and thermos flasks of soup.

The players' bus had a curtained partition part way along. The manager, his coaches Liam O'Kane and Ron Fenton, club secretary Ken Smales and physio Graham Lyas would sit at the front, we'd be at the back. The curtains would whoosh back every now and then to reveal Clough standing there. "What are you lot up to?" he'd demand. "So-and-so. Go and get me a cup of tea." It was just to let us know that he was about, but generally he left us to get on with it. Sometimes on the way back, especially after a loss, he might get angry and the verbal abuse would be dished out. After one bad loss he pulled the curtains back and said, "Thanks for spoiling my weekend, you shithouses!" He then described me and Steve Wigley as a pair of traffic cones because we hadn't worked enough in the game, before he called me down the bus to talk to him. "We've had a bid from QPR. Would you like to go?" This was right out of the blue. "No, I'm fine thanks, I'll stay here."

"Well, I just wanted to mark your card," he replied, which was something he'd say a lot. That was the end of it. I wondered why he told me because he didn't need to. Was he marking my card as he was thinking of moving me on? Eventually the selling of me and Peter Davenport helped to reduce the club's debts, but for now it was back to the soup and a roll. Our next trip might have been to Highbury, or Old Trafford or Anfield. No one would have believed it. Trying to go and win at these places (which we often did) after a three-hour coach journey and a meal of soup and a roll.

Out of the Frying Pan

With Neil Webb now in the squad I reported back for preseason training but was hoping that a deal could be done to get me away before the start of the season. Clough had made five new signings during the summer. Alongside Webb he added defenders Stuart Pearce and Ian Butterworth, another midfielder in the shape of Brian Rice and he'd made his peace with John Robertson, who returned from Derby. I found it strange that I was still a Forest player when everything was pointing to me being gone. I was picked for the opening league game at Luton and played alongside Neil Webb in the centre of midfield, which is where I'd wanted to play all along. Neil scored and we drew 1–1 on the plastic pitch. I was picked again four days later when we hosted Sheffield Wednesday at the City Ground and was again picked in the middle. It was a really frustrating game to play in and just as much so for the Forest fans watching. Howard Wilkinson set his team out to play a high line of defenders and I, for one, kept getting caught offside as I made runs from midfield. They grabbed a goal and killed the game off with a dour defensive display. Wilkinson had got what he wanted, no matter that the game as a spectacle was dead. Brian Clough certainly had his own ideas about how the game should be played that were a million miles from Wilkinson's. As the managers returned to the dressing rooms after the game he turned and bellowed twenty yards along the corridor at Wilkinson, "Howard, you'll get the game done away with, playing football like that!" He really meant it.

A couple of days later I reported for Friday-morning training and was kitted up and walking out when the manager called me back. "Harry, darling, I've got Graham Turner in my office," he said. "I've given him permission to speak with you and I think you should go and make yourself a few bob." As far as he was concerned he'd solved his problem, i.e. me, by arranging a fee with Aston Villa. I'd known nothing about these developments beforehand; I was a commodity to be bought and sold. I didn't really have a choice as I'd asked for the move and could hardly back out now. I got changed out of my kit and went to see him for ten minutes. Villa had lots of young players like Mark Walters and Tony Dorigo and, from the outside, seemed to be a good young up-and-coming club. Plus they'd won the European Cup only three years earlier. They were a big club in every sense.

My major ambition at that point was to play for England, and I felt a move to Villa would give me the best chance of achieving that. I'd won six Under-21 caps and a B international one and I felt I was on the periphery of Bobby Robson's plans.

Graham Turner drove me to Doug Ellis's house in Sutton Coldfield that afternoon. Doug took me out in his Rolls Royce around Bodymore Heath, the training ground, and told me his plans for the club and all about his latest fishing trip to Scotland. Then I went to a local hospital for a medical and I signed that night at his house. From arriving for training at Forest to becoming a Villa player took only a few hours. It was all a bit of a whirlwind. I was offered a four-year contract on better money than I was getting at Forest, where the local boys always got less. There was no negotiation. I just said, "Thank you very much. I'll take that." Which, in hindsight, was absolutely crazy.

That night I had to go back to a darkened City Ground to get my boots. It was quite a sad moment after seven years, but

I'd made my bed ... I'd asked for it and so we all moved on. I'm not one for sentimentality in football. I may be sentimental as a person but football is a job. The next day I was back at Villa Park in a suit and led out on to the pitch to wave to fans before a game against Queen's Park Rangers. I found that really tough. A microphone was thrust into my hands in front of the massive Holt End and I wheeled out some niceties about being happy to sign, hoping to score lots of goals, blah, blah. Then it was up into the stands to watch the game.

In the director's box I bumped into the QPR manager, Jim Smith, who told me that if he'd had the money he would have bought me. It was nice of him to say it and as I watched his Rangers side win at Villa Park I wondered if that would have been the better move. I found out that this was Steve McMahon's last game for Villa. He was moving to Liverpool and I was his replacement, which suddenly made me the most experienced midfielder at the club. I hadn't realised just how young the Villa side was. Nigel Spink in goal, Allan Evans at the back and Andy Gray up front were the only experienced players. I was supposed to add to that experience having played a few seasons of top-flight football and played in Europe but I was only twenty-two myself. I didn't want the burden of being a leader in the middle of the park. I hoped that more players would be brought in with me as I soon realised that it wouldn't be as smooth as I thought it would be. I'd been naïve and hadn't really looked into things as closely as I might have before taking such a big step. It was too late now, but the doubts were there already. Maybe I'd made a big mistake, but there was nothing I could do. I just had to get on with it. I did think back to another of Brian Clough's stock phrases though: "The grass isn't always greener."

Monday was the day I first really got a chance to meet my new teammates. I knew Mark Walters from the England

Under-21 squad but no one else and was a little apprehensive when I arrived. I needn't have been, because as soon as I walked in to the canteen area at the training ground Andy Gray immediately came over to talk to me. He was very loud and brash and confident. "Come on, Hodgey boy! How ya doing?" He introduced me to everyone and it was just what I needed. On my first day at Villa an experienced player like Allan Evans asked me, "What's Cloughie like, then?"

I made my Villa debut at Southampton. Afterwards Graham Turner told everyone, "It's good to have Steve in the middle of the park. He's got bags of experience." But I didn't want to be Mr Experienced. We had seven of our eleven players under twenty that day.

I scored on my home debut against Luton and we went on a good run with lots of goals until we played Forest. I was naturally keen to impress that day and I got hardly any boos from the away fans which I appreciated. I think the Forest fans knew that the club needed to sell me for financial reasons. Forest won 2–1 but I was all over the place, trying to save the defeat. I was surprised that no one really kicked me or said anything. When I got kicked or riled I would try harder, so perhaps they'd been told not to wind me up.

Soon after I was back in the England Under-21 squad but I wasn't completely happy. Villa weren't what I wanted, too inconsistent. Turner tried to change things around and keep people's confidence up but there was never a chance that we'd beat any of the big boys. At Liverpool we were down 3–0 in thirty minutes. It was literally men against boys. When the third goal went in I shouted over to the back four, "No more!" It was the Forest doctrine coming out: even if we're getting beat, make sure we don't get embarrassed here.

We badly needed some new blood because we were physically lightweight. The kids had been given the chance but had not really taken it like they had at Forest. We needed a spark and badly missed Gary Shaw, who was out injured. Simon Stainrod came in from Sheffield Wednesday but he wasn't really what we needed. Simon had great ability but he liked to do his flicks and would drive me mad. I would be making my runs but he liked to have the ball to himself and the pass never arrived. After a while I stopped making the runs because I was just wasting my time. He was more interested in entertaining the crowd. I'm not sure he was the right player in a struggling team. If he lost it, I had to get it back because he wouldn't. He scored eight goals all season, not enough for a striker. Andy Gray got six or seven but I'd been getting 12 from midfield at Forest. Even at Villa I'd scored five by Christmas in a holding midfield role.

As our league form worsened the only hope of salvaging something from the season was in the cup. At the time Portsmouth were a really horrible team to play, and we drew them in the FA Cup. They had a nasty little piece of work called Mick Kennedy, who really irritated me. Lots of verbals. "I'll break your leg in a minute, Hodgey. I'm after you again tonight." We beat them after a replay and came up against Millwall.

I'd been picked to play for England in Cairo against Egypt in January 1986 and the Millwall game was important because if the tie went to a replay I'd miss the trip. My worst fears came true and I had only myself to "blame" because I scored to equalise right at the end and so forced a replay. I was gutted. This was the second time I'd missed out and so I called Graham Turner and asked if I could play for England instead of Villa. Looking back now, it was absolute stupidity. What was I thinking? I explained to the manager that this could be my first England cap. He said, "Leave it with me." He called back and said the situation with his job meant that he couldn't justify letting one of his best players go for a friendly when the club was having a bad time. The next morning Bobby Robson called me. Turner had phoned him and explained that I was on the floor about missing out. Bobby said, "If your form's good and you stay fit you will get your chance." It softened the blow, but I knew that most players never get that close or maybe sit on the bench once and never get a second chance.

Millwall were managed by George Graham and they beat us in the replay on a muddy pitch in a howling gale. I went through the game in a bit of a dream. At one point I went to get the ball for a throw-in and a cockney accent rang out from the terrace: "Eh Hodgey! Bet you'd rather be in Cairo than Cold Blow Lane, son!" I smiled back at them but deep down it hurt. I must have performed the quickest change of all time afterwards and a few cans of drink were thrown around in the shower area. Later I heard that Gordon Cowans, who had replaced me in the England squad, had scored a goal as England won 4–0. That made it even worse. The next day me, Andy Gray and a few friends went on a ten-hour drinking binge. At that point in my career I was as low as I'd ever been. We were in the bottom three, out of the FA Cup and my England replacement had taken his chance. My move to Villa seemed to have all gone wrong. I couldn't help thinking back to Brian Clough's words about my transfer request: "Everything that happens to you now is because of this letter."

Now on trips back to Nottingham people began asking me if I regretted leaving Forest. I'd always said "no", but now I was starting to wonder. The League Cup was our last chance to salvage something from the season. Would I get the chance of a Wembley appearance after all? We'd won through to the semi-finals and drew Oxford United. They had some good players like Ray Houghton and John Aldridge, but we were happy with the draw. We were held at home 2–2 and they proved to be a very experienced side and more streetwise. At the Manor Ground we lost 2–1. Afterwards as we sat in the bath we could hear them singing, "Oxford's going to Wembley! Oxford's going to Wembley!" Andy Gray turned to me and said, "You just don't know what you've missed." I was seriously doubting my move to Villa by now. Forest were doing quite nicely without me and were up around the top five while I was in a relegation scrap and Oxford United had just robbed me of a trip to Wembley. Things had just about got as low as they could, but the next day our season and my career was saved. We were called in to an announcement that we'd signed Steve Hunt and Andy Blair. That turned both my and the club's season around. They were two experienced midfield players and made their debuts at Forest three days later in a 1–1 draw, which was a decent point for us. The next time out I scored both goals in a 2–1 home win over West Ham and I was back to my old free role alongside Steve Hunt in the middle.

Before the end of the season I was approached by Gianni Paladini. Mr Paladini was often seen around Villa Park and was known to be an adviser behind the scenes. One day he asked me quite openly, "Do you fancy going to play in Italy?" At the time Serie A was *the* league to play in. "I can get you to Bari," he assured me confidently. I believed him because Gordon Cowans and Paul Rideout had gone there from Villa in 1985. I felt like things were going on behind the scenes that I wasn't privy to and I couldn't help but wonder if a move was being engineered for me. I hadn't asked for a transfer and I'd only been at Villa for about eight months. Even though it had been a disappointing start at the club I was prepared to see it out, so to start hearing things like this was unsettling. I don't know how much the Villa hierarchy knew about it, but I began to think they were going to cash in on their new international and my doubts about being at Villa intensified.

Capping off the season

On March 19th 1986, much to my surprise, the next England squad was announced and I was included for a trip to the Soviet Union. The previous month I'd been omitted completely as the national side played another friendly against Israel. I thought my withdrawal from the Egypt game was going to cost me and that it was now much too late to be in any World Cup plans. I just hoped that I'd get a real chance after the tournament and be included in the qualifiers for Euro 88 which seemed a long way off.

We flew out to Tbilisi which was still very much in the grip of communism and I remember being made to wait for ages at customs while they went through absolutely everything. We travelled in confident mood and there was a good spirit between the players. I was my usual quiet self, just easing myself into the England set-up and trying to get to know people's characters. I knew Viv Anderson, and vaguely knew Peter Shilton, but I took a deep breath to see that I was in pretty good company. I was the only one from the First Division relegation dog-fight. The others, like Gary Lineker, Glenn Hoddle and Kenny Sansom, were challenging for the championship, or at least a European place. I didn't feel out of place though. In fact, I felt that I should have been there a little bit sooner.

Our team hotel was far from glamorous. We were given pokey little rooms with no telephone and an old fashioned black and white TV which crackled out the communist news of the day. In training I tried to make my mark and I was pinging my passes really hard, full of confidence. Don Howe was chuckling as he watched me. Cloughie would always tell me to ping my passes and that day I really did. The late arrivals travelled separately from their clubs in Italy – Gordon Cowans, Ray Wilkins and Mark Hateley – reinforcing the quality that we had in the squad.

I would always read Bob Harris's column because the players knew that he had Bobby Robson's ear and what he wrote was most likely to be true. So when one of the papers took me out for a photo session by a statue of Lenin I hoped that they knew something that I didn't. On the morning of the game the team was announced and I was overjoyed to be on the bench. Bobby pulled me to one side and told me I'd be getting on at some point during the game.

Just walking into an England dressing room was an amazing feeling. Walking over to my peg was even better, because there was a beautiful white shirt with number 16 waiting for me. I had longed for this and now it was hanging in front of me. I felt justified as I pulled that shirt over my head.

The game was played in a huge old stadium, but the 60,000 crowd created an eerie atmosphere. People just clapped when there was a chance rather than let out a roar and there were guards armed with guns around the perimeter. The game was a tough one against Dasaev and Oleg Blokhin and the Soviets missed a penalty to keep things even at half-time. Ten minutes into the second half the gaffer told me to get warmed up. My heart really started to pound because I knew this was the moment I'd been waiting for. Gordon Cowans was looking tired and I replaced him. It was a great moment for me as I ran on and Ray Wilkins came over to me and said, "Good luck Steve, you're one of us now." That calmed me down because playing with new people is strange enough, but for your country, and for the first time, it was pretty nerve-racking. Ray's words helped me enormously and though I had a dodgy start I settled down and grew in confidence. I had a hard time believing that I was a full England player after all the near misses and withdrawals, but I just tried to get on with my role. Bobby had told me to make sure I got a good first touch, but I'd immediately lost the ball. Then I just kept things simple and worked up and down the left wing.

Chris Waddle scored and we became the first team to win in the Soviet Union for seventeen matches while keeping our own unbeaten run going towards the World Cup. Terry Butcher congratulated me as I walked off the pitch and there were buoyant scenes in the dressing room. I just sat back and tried to take it all in. I was delighted with the result and the way I'd played, and I was determined to enjoy the moment; it had been a long time coming. On the plane home as I was quietly reading a book the gaffer tapped me on the shoulder and said a few words, saying it was my first cap, to which the players all applauded in what was an England tradition. It was a really special moment and something which I'll always remember. When we got back to England I immediately drove back to my parents' house and presented them with my England shirt as my dad popped open a bottle of champagne to celebrate. All of those junior games, youth team trips and long hours had been worth it.

○ ○ ○

Back at Villa I got congratulations from all the players and Andy Gray gave me some light-hearted banter about England caps not being worth as much as Scotland ones. It was to his great credit that he always kept things light-hearted for the lads, even in the darkest moments. His infectious character could bring the meekest of souls out of their shell and he taught me the importance of always smiling no matter had badly things were going. There wasn't as strong a social scene at Villa as there had been at Forest but Gray, Gary Williams, Brendon Ormsby and Simon Stainrod could all be called upon to keep the team spirit going. Paul Elliott joined later and he had a great sense of humour. He'd take the Michael out of anyone, without a second's hesitation. These were the few positives in a disintegrating team – Graham Turner was showing signs in his face that the pressure was taking its toll. We went through a spell of games when all we could hear while in the post-match bath were demonstrators chanting "Turner must go!" and "Ellis out!" This was a whole new experience for me, having come from a club where the very thought of sacking the manager was inconceivable. Things did pick up at Villa and the side's improved form no doubt helped me get picked again for England duty, this time for a game against Scotland at Wembley.

When Bryan Robson pulled out of the squad through injury the press were speculating that I'd take his place. His shoulder kept popping out of its socket and though it could be put back in, it couldn't be relied upon to last ninety minutes. Obviously Bobby Robson was looking for an understudy to provide some back-up for Mexico. Now I was scoring goals again everything seemed to be happening for me at the right time. I found out on Ceefax that I'd been picked, though I didn't dare think that I'd be in the World Cup squad. I might be able to say that I'd played against Scotland at Wembley though, which in the mid-1980s was a massive annual fixture. While the papers seemed to think I'd be playing, I tried not to take much notice of the press while secretly hoping that they'd be right. I was ecstatic when the team was announced and I was starting. I phoned my parents and started making arrangements to get them to the game. In the build-up to the match all the talk was about it being the last chance for me, Trevor Francis and Dave Watson to stake our claims for the World Cup finals.

Despite the fact that a World Cup place was dangling before me, I wasn't nervous before the game, never have been really. I've seen people be sick and those who are hyper and can't sit down. Brian Clough had always drummed it in to me that, "You can't play if you're not relaxed". I was also very confident of my own ability, which relaxed me too. After a good afternoon's sleep we boarded the bus and arrived at Wembley with lots of flags and banners about, even though a capacity crowd wasn't expected. I went out for a walk on the pitch and the Tartan Army was in full voice. I stood in the centre-circle and took a moment to take it all in. The history was seeping out of every corner of the old stadium and I had to take some deep breaths while I stood there. In the dressing room the players were confident and everyone knew what an England–Scotland game meant. Scotland had also qualified for the World Cup and had some quality players on show that day – Graeme Souness, Richard Gough and Alex McLeish to name but three. There'd be plenty of fire and passion, and for me the ultimate prize was at stake: a ticket to the World Cup finals, every footballer's dream.

Viv Anderson came over and wished me good luck. "Get yourself on that plane," he said. It was a sincere comment coming from probably the biggest mickey-taker in that England team. This was my first game at Wembley and the sound as we walked out was tremendous, even though there were "only" 70,000 inside Wembley. I was determined to take it in and enjoy every moment because I had seen so many famous players walk out of that tunnel over the years and now it was my turn. The whole day was an experience that I'll never forget and it was very special for me when I sang the anthem for the first time as an England player at Wembley.

The game started and this time my first touch was a good one; from then on I felt at home and we started to get on top. I was fouled by Willie Miller at the edge of their area and Glenn Hoddle lined up the free-kick. The Scottish defence half cleared it up in the air and I raced in to head it back across the goal where Terry Butcher planted it into the net. I wheeled away as though I'd scored the goal! Ten minutes later we made it 2–0. I calmed myself from the euphoria at half-time, had a couple of cups of tea, no energy drinks back then, before the bell rang to send us back out again. They got back into things through a dubious penalty, and I took a kick on my ankle and went off after seventy-five minutes to a nice round of applause. At the final whistle we went up the famous steps to collect the Sir Stanley Rous Trophy. The lads all said they thought I'd done well and would be in the squad but I tried to blank out the words. I didn't want to believe it because it might lead to the biggest disappointment of my life. I had six days to wait before the World Cup squad was announced. I'd only got two caps and hadn't played a full game, but my fingers were crossed that I'd be involved in the biggest tournament in the world – it was all I could do.

My ankle kept me out of the next Villa game but we won and were safe due to other results going our way that day. I went down to the dressing room and everyone was celebrating but it dawned on me that we were celebrating a failure. A lot of money had been spent on a lot of players and we'd failed miserably as a team, but here we were congratulating ourselves. I hadn't signed to be a failure; I'd signed to be in the hunt for trophies and this just felt all wrong. It had been close to being a disastrous season. We could easily have gone down and I'd be a Second Division player. Instead I saw the news on Ceefax that I'd been picked for England. I was going to the World Cup! Someone told me before that 1986 World Cup to forget it and concentrate on the next one. I'm so glad I didn't take that advice! The sense of pride and pressure representing England at a World Cup is immeasurable. The players know that reputation and history are in the making, and while some players find it too much to take, I intended to love every last minute of it.

Living in a Dream

It was early one morning in the middle of May. I slowly woke up and wandered over to draw back the curtains of my hotel room. To my utter amazement it was snowing quite heavily outside. The Rocky Mountains were shrouded in cloud and couldn't be seen. I was staying at the Broadmoor Hotel in Colorado Springs with the England squad as we prepared for the 1986 World Cup. Training was actually taking place at the United States Airforce Academy, which had excellent facilities but was an hour away from our hotel. Training at altitude was necessary for the upcoming tournament and the recovery times from long runs were a problem. We knew we had to go through this torture but it wasn't really what we wanted at the end of a gruelling domestic campaign. Climbing the Rockies to prepare our lungs for a lack of air was necessary but it was really hard work. We played a practice match against the USAF and won about 20–0, then the Everton lads arrived after playing in the FA Cup final. Peter Reid was my room partner, a real social animal. I'd first met him in a queue at Stringfellows after a PFA night in London. He'd come over to me a little worse-for-wear saying, "You're a good player you! I rate you!" That was the night I'd found myself sitting next to Diana Ross in Langan's Brasserie in the West End! One night after Reidy joined up with us, I was having a kip and he came back to the room, literally bouncing off the walls before he crashed into the bed. I was never a big drinker and as we had some free time on our hands between training sessions, I started to keep a diary.

May 14th 1986
Today we played against South Korea at the Fountain Valley High School. The boss just about picked his first choice 11. RW [Ray Wilkins] and BR [Bryan Robson] were the starters in midfield. BR came off as a precaution and I got on for the second half. Only lasted five minutes, felt a sharp pain in my left ankle when I stretched for a ball. Couldn't run it off and had to be replaced after just ten minutes. Vernon [Edwards, the team doctor] says it's nothing much but I'm not so sure. There's no bruising or swelling which actually worries me more, because the pain is so sharp. Won't be doing any running for a couple of days. Can't believe I've got so close and might miss out.

May 15th 1986
Boss asked about my ankle at breakfast today. Don't think he was too impressed that I couldn't really tell him anything other than I would need a couple of days rest. I can see his problem, he needs to make a decision about me quickly. He said I'd have to go for a run with Fred Street in two days and see how it feels. Though he didn't say as much I know that if it isn't OK by then I'll be on a plane home before I even get to Mexico. I'm ready for the worst.

May 17th 1986
Rest of the lads flew to LA to play Mexico in a friendly, I stayed here. BR's shoulder popped out again in that game. I know if I can get fit I might be needed in the World Cup, his shoulder is obviously a big concern for the squad and I don't wish him any ill feelings but I have to be ready.

May 19th 1986
Relief! Fred Street called me down at 9 a.m. for a run on a patch of grass by the hotel. He put me through my paces for half an

hour. I knew that if I had to stop at any point I'd be finished, but though I wasn't 100 per cent I didn't feel any real pain. On the way in Bobby Robson came to ask how I was and I told him 'fine'. More importantly, Fred Street told him the same. Can't describe the sense of relief, it was great to tell the lads I was OK with a big smile on my face and I called home to say the same. Mexico here I come.

May 22nd
Fly to Vancouver tomorrow for another game.

May 24th
Played against Canada this morning. Bryan Adams sang on the pitch before the game. I got the start because BR has a hamstring twinge on top of his shoulder problems. The Canadians are also in the World Cup and were a tough team that matched us fairly well. I hit the post in the first half and then pounced on a rebound which led to Mark Hateley scoring the only goal in the second half. Felt strong and good, proved to the boss that I could last ninety minutes if necessary. GL [Gary Lineker] hurt his wrist and is now a major doubt. Will things ever start going our way? Thought it was fractured and he'd be out but X-ray showed it was only badly sprained, so he's got a chance.

○ ○ ○

The day after playing Canada we flew down to Mexico via Los Angeles. During our stop-off at LAX I wandered off to the shops, looking for a couple of sports biographies to read as there'd be little in English in Mexico. For the connecting flight I found myself standing at terminal 28 and it was close to flight time, but where was everybody? I was sure they'd said 28. Then a chap in an FA blazer came running around looking for me.

"We're at 33. Everybody is waiting for you!" So we had to run through the airport, which was really embarrassing. We had different tracksuits for training, different ones for dinner, and different ones for games. Sometimes I'd forget which one to wear so I got a bit of a reputation amongst the lads for getting things mixed up.

When we finally got to Mexico, I immediately knew I was in the big time. There were pressmen and police with guns everywhere and we were given a big presidential-style escort to our camp in Saltilho. We didn't get to see much of Mexico itself and for the most part we were entrenched in our camp. I didn't see any signs of the massive earthquake that had hit the country months before and any problems the country might have been having were well away from our thoughts. The police motorbikes lit up the Monterrey night as we drove to our base in the mountains. I got a lie-in on the first day as everyone was tired from travelling, then I had a look around our base. The camp wasn't too big and the closeness of the rooms helped give everyone a feeling of togetherness. We started out doing some gentle training, just to get us used to the heat. Most of the time we'd train quite early in the morning but we also did some sessions at lunchtime, which was when some of the games would be scheduled. We could watch CNN but there was very little English TV. We had our own chef serving familiar food like baked beans, bacon and eggs and cornflakes. Everyone had blood tests to monitor our sugars and iron levels once a week, so even back in the mid-1980s things were starting to get a little bit technical. We were provided with a new type of shirt that could "breathe"; it wasn't as advanced as today's but I could see that things were starting to change and we felt that we were being taken care of.

We trained on a local training ground, which wasn't great and had just one pitch. Bobby used to get stressed out because we had the sports press and the news press camped out watching

us. Obviously the news press was there in case anything untoward happened and he used to ram home to us the importance
of behaving properly. "I want no trouble," he'd repeat. "We all
know they're out there so if you go into town go in twos and
with an FA fella with you. These people are here for one reason
only so be ultra careful." Only one or two sports journalists
would watch us train, nothing like it is today.

I was still getting my body used to the climate; Gary Lineker
and Bryan Robson were training on their own with Fred
Street. Gary had his wrist in a cast; Bryan still had his dodgy
shoulder. On May 28th we played Monterrey, the Mexican
champions. I started alongside Ray Wilkins in midfield. I felt it
was a great workout and we won 4–1. Afterwards we were
called together to be told the news that Dr Vernon Edwards had
suffered a massive heart attack and was in intensive care. The
news certainly took the edge off our win. We sent messages but
he was kept in for ten days before being declared fit enough to
go home to England.

There wasn't long between our arrival in Mexico and our
first World Cup game. On paper our group didn't look too
difficult. Portugal, Morocco and Poland. Portugal weren't
the force that they are these days, Morocco were a bit of an
unknown quantity but we expected to beat them and Poland
were decent but not as good as they had been in the 1970s and
early 1980s. Bobby announced the team for the opening game
at a meeting in the team hotel. It was as we'd expected. Bryan
had declared himself fit and FIFA had granted permission for
Gary to play with a cast on his wrist. Peter Shilton was of course
in goal; the back four consisted of Gary Stevens and Kenny
Sansom as full-backs with Terry Butcher and Terry Fenwick in
the middle; the midfield was Ray Wilkins, Bryan Robson, Glenn
Hoddle and Chris Waddle; Gary Lineker and Mark Hateley
started up front.

Portugal

With the top two teams in each group progressing to the knockout stages of the tournament we were confident that we'd progress. I met Bobby Charlton before the game as some of the 1970 squad were out there with us. With limited TV, few English papers, and no mobile phones or email, we were cocooned from the world at large. Bobby Robson kept telling us about the messages he'd received from back home. He said it was a great chance to make our names. His passion and patriotism came through. He'd spoken to his dad on TV the night before the game and we were all confident. I was on the bench for one reason alone, Bryan Robson's shoulder, but I didn't think the balance of the team was right, with Glenn Hoddle playing wide on the right wing. Everyone knew he wasn't an athlete as such and playing wide right in those conditions dictated that you needed to be an athlete to be able to put the work in. There wasn't a huge crowd like there would be today and it wasn't a particularly nice stadium. It was the university's pitch and was very bobbly. It was a red-hot day which the Portuguese were better suited to than us. Nothing much happened in the first half and we came in at 0-0, a score line which both teams seemed to be happy with. As usual, Bobby was upbeat at half-time. We weren't flowing, but were OK. Bryan Robson was being as brave as a lion, getting stuck in, and I didn't expect to get on at any point during the second half. Then Portugal scored out of the blue. The England bench was deathly silent. We just couldn't believe it. I was frustrated to be sitting there and not being able to do a thing about it. Bobby eventually sent me and Peter Beardsley on to try and salvage something. I thought I did all right in my World Cup debut. I ran about a lot as usual, but we lost 1–0. It was the worst possible start. After the final whistle I went over to the England fans with Peter Beardsley and Terry Butcher to clap them but we just had to face a lot of the anger that was flying towards the team. Chants of "You don't know what you're doing" and "We want our money back" greeted us. What the press and fans didn't know was we'd had people gasping for air and using oxygen tanks at half-time. Players had been wearing cold towels on the back of their heads in the spartan dressing rooms. It hadn't been easy, but people did not want to hear that. The Portuguese scorer, Carlos Manuel, was really leery on the pitch after the match, I'm not sure if he was actually goading us or not, but some of our players weren't happy about him being so loud. It was a really flat atmosphere on the way back to our hotel. If we'd played well and lost we could have taken something out of it, but we hadn't. We knew we'd be hammered in the black and white of the press and could only hope that the next game would smooth things over.

Morocco

We only had three days to wait before facing Morocco. Though I thought we'd seemed to play as three separate units of back four, midfield, and front two which didn't really link with each other, we were keeping the same side for Morocco. I felt everything was too individualistic. Mark Hateley had been stifled in the air and produced few knockdowns, meaning Gary Lineker had nothing to work with.

Life at the hotel was leisurely. Bobby Robson would walk around with his Walkman on. He'd wander around the pool, tapping his sides to the music. I did wonder what he was thinking because I didn't think he was the kind of person who could relax very easily, especially at times of stress. I thought the Walkman was just for show while he deeply considered his options. The players who hadn't played trained, the others rested by the pool but by about 2 p.m. everyone was back to their rooms and out of the sun. We watched the other games on TV, phoned home and read the few English papers that could be rustled up.

The movie *Beverly Hills Cop* was big at the time and Kenny Sansom would wander round singing "The Heat Is On" from the film. One day Bobby Robson walked in and misheard Sansom singing. "The heaters are on?" quizzed Bobby, "Well, turn them bloody off!" The manager was well known for occasionally getting the wrong end of the stick. One day I was walking into breakfast with Bryan Robson when Bobby came towards us. "Morning, Bobby," said the manager. "No, you're Bobby, I'm Bryan," laughed the player. Bobby would sometimes call me Martin, confusing me with the Sheffield Wednesday goalkeeper, Martin Hodge. These little mistakes he made while he had a million things on his mind made him human and made you warm to him.

Bobby was loyal to the players that let him down in the first game. Bryan Robson had his shoulder strapped up in a big harness and I didn't think I'd get on again. We had no idea how Morocco would play but I knew that other North African teams like Tunisia and Algeria had done OK and so we should be more realistic than some of the fans who were expecting a hatful of goals. I don't think the management knew a thing about how they would play either. We just played our usual 4–4–2 and had to deal with whatever they threw against us. Having lost our first game the doubts were there and if we lost again we'd be out.

On the day the intense heat stopped us playing our high energy "English" game. It just wasn't happening for us and the Moroccans seemed to be happy with a 0–0 again, as they'd already opened their campaign with that score against Poland. To be honest, it was drabness personified. Then Bryan's shoulder went and I didn't even need to be told to warm up. As soon as he went down he looked to be in serious trouble. I kept an eye on the pitch and after a couple of minutes he was being walked off, with Fred Street holding his shoulder gingerly. Bobby may have wanted to change things but I was the only player who'd got up and in my mind that's the reason I was there and he called me over and sent me on. I went into the middle with Ray Wilkins, but within two minutes Wilkins was sent off. I was running back towards the halfway line when Ray rashly threw the ball towards the referee and out came the red card. Down to ten men, having lost our captain and having an hour to go in the heat, we were in big trouble. Morocco looked dangerous but weren't in any hurry to try and go and win the game. Luckily for us they seemed to think a draw would be enough, even though we were vulnerable and could be going home. For me, getting on in the absence of Ray Wilkins and Bryan Robson was strange, because if I'd had to pick two players I'd like in the midfield with me it would have been those two.

I don't know if it was Glenn Hoddle, Terry Butcher or the manager who called it but we went narrow in the midfield and had Mark Hateley come back to help a bit. We just sat three in the middle through to half-time when we went in shell-shocked. The dressing room was in turmoil. The captain was in the corner on oxygen, players' heads were bowed gasping for breath with cold towels covering their heads and Ray Wilkins was away in the shower area, upset at what he'd done. The manager must have been thinking, "We could be going out here." He looked like a worried man. The best we could hope was for a draw. Don Howe was trying to organise us. Bobby was telling us to "dig in". In the second half we did all right but were helped because they didn't go for it. In the last ten minutes both sides backed off and it ended 0–0. I really felt for the fans, as it would have been a big undertaking financially and some had left jobs that wouldn't be waiting for them when they returned. I just kept thinking that we weren't out of it. Bobby kept stressing that if we beat Poland we'd be through, so there was a great sense of relief that it was still in our hands. That night I went to bed really early. I was absolutely shattered.

Poland

The Poland game was scheduled for a different stadium which was about an hour from our base in the hills. It was more of a "proper" stadium with a big grassy pitch, which suited us better than the university setting of the first two games. Bryan Robson hadn't trained and Ray Wilkins was banned for two matches, but I didn't know if I'd be playing. We went to the stadium the day before the game and I did my usual routine of walking the width of the pitch. Bobby Robson came over to me. "Have you ever played left wing before, son?"

"Yes."

"OK."

Then he walked off again. I read into that brief exchange that I'd be playing wide left for the Poland game. Having seen some of the papers back home that had been absolutely slaughtering the players and boss, I knew that they were calling for changes, which gave me a chance. We played a light-hearted eight-a-side game during which he put me on the left, exactly where I'd been playing when I'd asked for a move from Nottingham Forest. He officially told us the team on the morning of the game. Peter Beardsley and Gary Lineker were paired up front and I felt we were a more balanced side. Peter Reid came in from nowhere. We'd been talking in our room and I knew he had a dodgy ankle but had played in the FA Cup final with it. Trevor Steven replaced Chris Waddle, and on paper we had more of a passing side.

I've always had a love of music – Elvis watch out!

Aged eight, dreaming of playing for England.

Another battle with cousin Paul. This time it's a water fight at Skegness as Dad looks on.

Me on a scooter at Granddad Hodge's house.

My first winner's trophy, as captain of Stanhope Junior School, 1973.

Stephen Hodge, who is almost 15 years of age, and is a local boy from Gedling Comprehensive is shown with youth scout Alan Hill and Committee member Derek Pavis after signing associated schoolboy forms with us recently

Signing associate schoolboy forms at Forest, flanked by Alan Hill (left)
and committee man Derek Pavis.

ABOVE: *"Young Hodge, go and show the trophy to our fans!" More orders from the great man. Not sure about my haircut, though!*

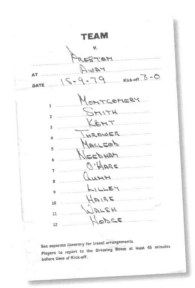

TEAM

v.

PRESTON

AWAY

AT

DATE 15-9-79   Kick-off 3-0

1 MONTGOMERY
2 SMITH
3 KENT
4 THROWER
5 MACLEOD
6 NEEDHAM
7 O'HARE
8 QUINN
9 LILLEY
10 HAIRE
11 WALSH
12 HODGE

See separate itinerary for travel arrangements.
Players to report to the Dressing Room at least 45 minutes
before time of Kick-off.

My first team sheet – ripped from the noticeboard in the main stand corridor.

Collecting a trophy in my first full season. The gaffer was saying, "Son, you might be the Player of the Year, but you still can't play!"

Johan Cruijff – that's me, trying to get near him.

Pre-season posing at the Acropolis in 1984. Left to right: Johnny Metgod, Colin Walsh, Gary Megson, me, Ronnie Sinclair, Chris Fairclough and Jim McInally.

My favourite goal: surely we were in the UEFA Cup final? Maybe not! (Bob Thomas/Getty Images)

Trying to drive Villa forward. Right club, but wrong time. (Colorsport)

The last England team to win a major trophy: European Under-21 champions.
Left to right: me, Paul Bracewell, Dave Watson, Mark Hateley and Nigel Callaghan.
(Bob Thomas/Getty Images)

Being challenged for the ball by the great Oleg Blokhin during my England debut in Tbilisi. (Bob Thomas/Getty Images)

First Cloughie, now Lenin. I seemed to be surrounded by dictators! (Bob Thomas/Getty Images)

Sir Bobby looking happy and relieved, me looking shattered, after England had just beaten Poland 3–0 during Mexico 86. (Bob Thomas/Getty Images)

Lineker scores the third against Poland. (Colorsport)

Take a deep breath. I'm number 18 and I could just see Maradona's mop of hair ahead of me. (Allsport/Getty Images)

This undoubtedly helped Gary Lineker, who had the biggest game of his career and changed his life for ever.

On the bus to the game I was quiet, thinking back to family and friends who'd be glued to their TV sets that night in England. I found it hard to believe that I was going to be starting in the World Cup. Fifteen minutes before kick-off the boss had to leave the dressing room in line with FIFA regulations. He took the last chance to say a few words and I could tell he was apprehensive and concerned. Terry Butcher was loud, telling us to have "no regrets ... Come on, Hodgey boy. Work, work, work ... " and then we started. Zbigniew Boniek had a couple of chances for them and Butcher made a really important tackle on him while Shilton made a save when it was still 0–0. Who knows what might have happened had they scored first? As it was, we scored first when Gary Lineker poached a goal inside the six-yard box. We really got moving when Peter Beardsley came short and sent me on a run deep into the Polish half. I just had to deliver the right ball at the right moment. In my years at Forest I'd been able to deliver a decent ball enough times and I caught this one just right. I knew immediately that the defender was beaten and Lineker got there first. It was a great finish that looked easy but wasn't. At 2–0, I knew then it was our day and we all piled on top of him. Peter Beardsley had the link play, the imagination and the ability to make our 4-4-1-1 formation work. Glenn Hoddle gave Lineker the confidence that a pass would come at the right time and with the right weight. We generally had more options and with Peter Reid sitting back in the middle it allowed myself and Trevor Steven to get forward on the flanks. It was a well-balanced side. The third goal came from a corner, six yards out again, job done. My only regret is that I scored a goal at the back post from a Trevor Steven cross bang on half-time. It would have been 4–0, and I celebrated even though the flag was up. I was maybe half a yard off, but I've seen them given. The players were ecstatic at half-time. The calmer heads were telling people to steady on, we still had forty-five minutes to go. Bryan Robson just said, "We've got what we wanted." In the second half we kept the ball well and could have scored a couple more but it petered out. The point against Morocco had proved to be vital and was made even sweeter when we heard that Portugal had gone out. They had been sent packing after a 3–1 loss to Morocco and I was delighted because they'd started all of our problems in the first place. Just days earlier they'd celebrated like they'd won the World Cup when they beat us, but now we were going through and they were going home.

Paraguay

In the round of 16 we faced Paraguay, which was one of the best draws we could have had with the likes of Brazil, Italy, France, Spain, West Germany, Denmark, Belgium and the hosts all safely through. We respected Paraguay, but we certainly didn't fear them. The match was to take place at the massive Estadio Azteca in Mexico City. We flew to the capital and checked into a hotel which was located by the main motorway running through the city. I don't know who at the FA decided that would be a good place for us to stay, but the players couldn't sleep and it was causing unrest. We had a meeting and told the staff that we wanted to move. So two days later we moved to a Holiday Inn in a much quieter area. The Italian squad was staying in the same hotel, which probably wouldn't happen today, and it was a little surreal for me to be walking past the current World champions while I'd played a total of one full game in the World Cup. I saw Gary Lineker in his room; he'd just become the first Englishman to score a World Cup hat-trick since Geoff Hurst in 1966. He told me that he'd had a call from Barcelona about signing for them. I said he couldn't turn down a chance like that. He'd had a great season with Everton but that World Cup enhanced his career and gave him worldwide fame.

We had seven days to prepare for Paraguay and again we didn't do much tactical work. Howard Wilkinson and Dave Sexton had been scouting the other games in the tournament and they reported back to Bobby Robson about Paraguay but he never once mentioned to us about how the other teams played. We did lots of crossing and shooting, a few six-a-sides, but nothing too hard – we couldn't afford any more injuries. I found myself really having to take lots of air in to recover in the high altitude, a real contrast to the problems of the heat in Monterrey. When we visited the stadium on the day before the game it was the biggest thing I'd ever seen. This is where I'd watched Pele score in the 1970 World Cup. The pitch was wide but the playing surface poor. The grass was very loose, not established in the soil, which made changing direction quite tricky, as it would move under your feet. Our only change was Alvin Martin, who came in for the suspended Terry Fenwick.

Paraguay made a good start. Their grey-haired captain Nunez could play but when we got Glenn Hoddle on the ball we started to play too. Glenn put a great ball across the box which everyone missed. I'd always been taught to get in at the back post, so I collected the ball but was at too sharp an angle to shoot. Everyone had been beaten by the quality of the ball in. I saw Lineker in the six-yard box but I had to beat the keeper across the face of the goal. I reacted sharply and passed the ball quickly to Gary, who had a tap in. I was enjoying the game and had a header at goal but the keeper made a great save. We were playing well again, like a team with confidence, and Peter Beardsley was at the centre of everything. I can't describe how good a player he was. He got a well-deserved goal in the second half when he capitalised on a rebound from a Terry Butcher shot to make it 2–0. Gary Lineker got an elbow in an off-the-ball incident. The South Americans were renowned for that sort of thing. Now they were losing their heads a bit and we knew if we stayed calm we'd win. Gary got another one to seal the win and take his personal total to five goals in two games. Bobby Robson was cock-a-hoop after the game and with consecutive 3–0 wins it was a case of "bring on the next one". The next one, we knew, would be Argentina.

Argentina

This was really the big time now. Only eight nations still had a chance to win the World Cup, and we were right in there. In fact, by the time we kicked off against Argentina there were only six teams left, as both Brazil and Mexico had lost their quarter-finals on penalties.

Before the game we were to have trained at the Azteca but when we arrived I was surprised to see that the pitch was unusable. It was in a terrible state, much worse than the TV cameras had indicated. It was hot that day, but the altitude was the immediate difficulty. As you ran up and down it was hard to take in air to your lungs and as the day got hotter the two things combined to be a problem. As we lined up for the anthems I remember looking across at Bryan Robson, who was taking photos of the team, and thanking my lucky stars because I was only standing there because he wasn't fit. At the time he was England's best player. As the anthem played it was a bit of a tingly moment for me. This was only my fourth start for the national team and I'd almost been relegated a few weeks earlier. We'd only escaped by four points! I also thought back to a low point in January when I'd been knocked out of the FA Cup at a freezing Cold Blow Lane. These things flashed through my mind. I always sang the anthem quietly. Some are embarrassed to sing it on TV but it doesn't mean any less to them, they don't want to win any less badly.

As we broke away I did my usual routine of six sides across the pitch to get my lungs going, running at three-quarter pace.

Running was my game and I had to be ready to be at them from the first second. Terry Butcher went around everyone individually. I was one of the youngsters and I looked over at Peter Reid, my roommate. We'd spoken at length about the game and where he'd come from at Bolton. He had a dodgy ankle on the day and knew it wasn't great, but he wasn't about to miss out on this match for anything.

Everyone in England played with a 4–4–2 formation and wasn't used to playing against teams who employed other formations and tactics. On this day their full-backs marked myself and Trevor Steven really high up the pitch so whenever we got the ball we found it difficult to get going at them. I think Bilardo, their manager, had really done his homework and outsmarted us in the way he nullified our threat. I also think we perhaps gave them too much respect and didn't impose our own game on them. I'd been booked against Paraguay and knew a yellow against Argentina meant I'd miss a potential semi-final. Early in the game I brought Maradona down but I picked him up straight away; we always did that at Forest. I picked him up and they had a free-kick at the edge of our box. He took it and dinked it wide of our post. Me and Kenny Sansom had been a good combination on the left but we never really got forward in the first half and it was the same story for Trevor Steven on the right. They packed the midfield but there were flashes of brilliance from Maradona. Terry Fenwick got booked for fouling him but it wasn't a good pitch for dribbling on and we hoped he wasn't about to do something special. As half-time approached we realised that we were well in the game. They weren't a fantastic team but we wanted to cause more of a threat. Gary Lineker hadn't had a sniff and we hadn't had enough possession to do them any damage. Everyone on both sides was scared to make a mistake so it wasn't much of a spectacle for the 115,000 fans. We'd closed them down pretty well and it was a 0–0 stalemate, but things were about to change.

The second half was hotter and maybe it affected us a little bit more than it did them. The game was there to be won. The big pitch meant that we all had to work hard to close each other down. As the game progressed everyone found that they had a little more time and space. Five minutes into the second period it all changed.

Looking back, I wonder what I was doing on the edge of our own box with Jorge Valdano tugging on my shoulder. Maradona had the ball and as he approached the "D" at the edge of our area we had eight men behind the ball. He was looking to do a little one-two with someone or looking to be brought down – he was just a little guy and he'd go down very easily. As he moved in, our defenders began to narrow off the area so he didn't have so much space. He flicked the ball; I think he mis-hit the pass, and it bobbled off to my left side. The ball was spinning behind me and Valdano was leaning on me, probably hoping he'd make me put it out for a corner but the ball spun just perfectly for me and I wanted to knock it back to Shilton. I caught it perfectly. I just knew I'd caught it nice and high and I turned around thinking, "That will be Shilton's." I hadn't seen Maradona run into the box and when I saw them both going up for the ball I just thought, "Why is he there?" There shouldn't have been anyone near Peter Shilton; there had been a big space between the back four and the keeper. As I watched, the ball somehow looped over Shilton and straight away I was thinking "Jesus, have I made a mistake there? Shit, that was my mistake!" With certain back passes you know you are taking a risk by doing it, but with that one I never thought for a second that it would turn out that way because back then the goalkeeper was allowed to catch it.

I was dumbfounded but we didn't really have time to think how it had happened. I hadn't seen his hand at all, but I knew something was wrong because the ball hadn't gone like a bullet – if he'd headed it, it would have gone with some pace into the net. The ball had just bobbled into the net. I wondered if Shilton was just claiming hand ball to try and get the goal disallowed and that the others were just backing up the keeper. I hadn't seen a hand of God. Maradona ran over, celebrating, towards the linesman and the linesman's head was down, running back to the halfway line. The linesman should have had the best view of the incident but in his defence I have to admit that I was just a few feet away and I didn't see Maradona handle it. I know there was a lot of colour in the background and a lot of noise so I can understand that if he wasn't 100 per cent sure then he wasn't going to raise his flag. I think the referee looked at the linesman for some guidance but didn't get any. It's something that should never have happened but he took a chance, he cheated, and he got away with it. In today's game he might not have tried it because he might have got a red card for it. I've since read that he'd done it before in Argentina and it was just seen as being a bit cheeky.

On the BBC commentary Barry Davies said, "Steve Hodge must be in turmoil," but I wasn't. My upbringing in football had taught me to concentrate on the now and try to repair the damage, so I was just getting on with it. Then four minutes later we were hit with another one. I remember Kenny Sansom bombing past me and I was thinking: "Hang on a minute, we've just gone a goal down." Maradona picked the ball up in his own half; he had his back to me about four or five yards away. He did a drag back to take out one player and he scarpered away and it was one of the rare times when I didn't have another gear to sprint back. I was going at one pace. I thought I'd tuck in and work my way back and we'd smother it. On the bad pitch he had a long way to go to our goal. I thought Terry Butcher and Terry Fenwick could deal with it until Peter Reid and I got back, but I just watched him dance past Fenwick, who'd been booked earlier and didn't want to get another card, then he was in the box and I was thinking: "There'll be a bobble somewhere and someone will be able to get a toe in."

As Shilton came out I thought he'd try and curl it left footed around Shilton's right hand into the far corner, but he sent him a dummy and went down the narrow side which was not easy to do, especially with Terry Butcher all over him. By now I was back to the edge of the area and I could only pray he'd make a mistake, but he hadn't made a mistake while dribbling the ball for fifty yards. He finished it nonchalantly and all I could do this time was hold my hands up and say it was too good. Not many people did Shilton like a kipper, but he did. That was when I thought: "We're going out. They're on fire and they might even get a third." But there was still some hope because we still had our in-form striker.

At 2–0 they threw some water bags on for the players during a stoppage and Maradona had two or three to himself. He whistled over to me and motioned did I want one, so he gave me some water. Perhaps he thought I was flagging and needed a drink, but it was kind and I did need it. Was he just trying to keep us happy and not wanting to rile us up? He'd got what he wanted; he'd got his victory. If we'd been winning 2–0 I don't think he'd have been quite so friendly. With twenty minutes to go Chris Waddle and John Barnes came on. Bobby moved me into the middle with Glenn Hoddle and we had to try and get the ball to the wingers. Just nine minutes remained when I managed to get the ball to John Barnes on the left. I watched him do his bit and, as I ran into the box, Gary scored.

I ended up in the back of the net with their keeper Pompido

and he wouldn't give me the ball back. We exchanged words and tussled a little bit. We had ten minutes to get a second. We had to push forward and very late on Glenn lost the ball and I saw number 10 flash away from me. I heard Brian Clough's voice echoing in my head – "Get the ball back" – so I got my head down and sprinted back to slide in on the halfway line and get the ball back. We worked it to John Barnes again and I just did everything I could to get into the box. I'd just run forty yards to get the ball back in the last minute and I immediately spun round and tried to get back into their box. The ball arrived and I was looking at Gary as he'd found a little bit of space and in my head I thought, "Yes! He won't miss from that range," but the lad flicked it away from close in with some brilliant defending. It just wasn't our day. With seconds to go in a big match when you are losing, you start preparing for it mentally, and then the whistle blew and they went mad, screaming all around us. Maradona was running around celebrating in his shiny shirt.

Hate Figure

I was soon back down to earth and back in training with Aston Villa at the start of July, having had just a week off since returning from Mexico. Graham Turner had tried to strengthen the squad and had bought defenders Martin Keown and Paul Elliott and striker Gary Thompson. I think Martin Keown, like myself, realised quickly that he'd left a club with great stability and a strong, legendary manager, and arrived at a club that was about to go on the slide. He seemed uncomfortable. He was also young, and though he hadn't been able to force himself into the Arsenal side, he was too good for the Villa team at that time. He soon moved on to Everton and then back to his spiritual home of Highbury where he played the best football of his career and became an England international. Another addition to the squad was Neale Cooper, the funniest man I ever met in football. He'd been part of Alex Ferguson's brilliant Aberdeen side but after he came to Villa it all went wrong for him. He constantly got injured, his car broke down, his house was burgled, then the ceiling in his house collapsed – you name it, it went wrong for him. But his spirit and character never changed and he eventually moved back to Scotland. Just seeing his face and smile made you laugh and it's good to see him in management with Peterhead.

Before long I was back on a plane again and flying to Italy for a badly organised preseason trip. The whispers around the camp were that we only made the trip to showcase players to Pisa. Later on Paul Elliott would move to that club for £450,000. Despite the additions our preparation was bad and we started terribly with a 3–0 thrashing by Spurs. At one point in the game Chris Waddle walked past me laughing. "How's it going?" he chuckled. "Here we go again," I replied. We lost to Wimbledon and soon we were bottom of the league. The abysmal performances contributed to crowds shrinking to 14,000, which looked very sparse rattling around in Villa Park. I decided that I had to do something after we lost at home to Oxford. As I trudged off I saw my dad standing by the side of the tunnel. I was shocked that he was even there. I thought, "What are you doing here?" He just said to me, "Sort it." I think he could see what was going to happen. Being in a losing team every week affects your England place.

I went to see Graham Turner and told him that I wanted away; he wasn't happy. Days later I was off to Sweden on England duty. We lost 1–0 but I remember that night Bobby Robson told John Barnes to have a real go at their young full-back Roland Nilsson because he was "vulnerable". Well, that young lad went on to gain over 100 caps for Sweden so he wasn't that bad! When I got back to England all hell broke loose. My transfer request had been leaked and it was in all the papers that I wanted away. The two Birmingham radio stations were having phone-ins about me and I was told to stay away from the ground. I wasn't in the squad for the upcoming Forest game on the Saturday and the manager didn't want me anywhere near the club. I went along to watch the Forest game at the City Ground under my own steam and sat in the stand while keeping a low profile. Forest tore Villa apart that day and won 6–0, but it could have been ten. Certainly a good game for me to miss. Forest were top of the league and we were in the bottom three again. The next day Graham Turner was sacked.

The club moved quickly to bring in Celtic legend Billy McNeill as Turner's replacement. On his first day he gave us a speech about his footballing ideals. "Football is simple," he explained. "You get the ball, get it out wide, cross it and score – bingo!" From then on the players referred to him as Billy McBingo.

My worst day as a Villa player came when we hosted Norwich City. It was only our fourth home game of the season and the grass was very lush. About ten minutes in I was chased back towards our own goal by Mickey Phelan. I played a back pass to our keeper, Kevin Poole, but the ball slowed up in the long grass. As I played it I slipped and watched it fall short as Phelan nipped in and scored. The boos came cascading down. It was clearly my fault, and at the Holt End of all places. Allan Evans came over and spoke to me, tried to pick me up. Then five minutes later I was caught in a tackle and went down. My own fans started singing, "Let him die, let him die, let him die" and I was booed with every touch. It became the hardest game I ever went through and we lost 4–1, but I kept running and tackling just like Brian Talbot did for Arsenal years earlier.

I sat in the stand to watch one game and got some vicious verbal abuse from my own fans. When we played at Reading in the League Cup I was booed by the Villa fans during the warm up. Irving Scholar and David Pleat from Spurs were in the stands that night and I scored. Billy McNeill wanted to keep me. He was a likeable chap but I needed to move. We drew 3–3 at Liverpool, where I scored again, and then we won at Coventry. McNeill had got us playing well and moving up the table, but I hadn't heard of any firm interest in anyone buying me. Liverpool were mentioned in the papers and it was an unsettling time for me. The other players were OK, but I didn't know what they were thinking. Was I the rat leaving the sinking ship? In early December we drew 3–3 with Manchester United and I scored again. That night I got a call to say that Villa had agreed a fee with Spurs. I was to go and meet David Pleat the next day. As usual, the player was the last to know; it had already been done between the clubs. Doug Ellis was there at the Coventry Posthouse. "We've agreed a fee," he said. "Do you want to know what it is?" The fee was £650,000, so Villa had made £200,000 on me in just over a year. I travelled down to London and that was it. I'd known David Pleat for a while. He was a Nottingham lad and had often been at the City Ground when he came to see Brian Clough. On one occasion Pleat pointed out that I was the highest scoring midfield player but Brian Clough put me back in my place with a swift, "He may be, but he still can't play!"

On paper, Spurs had some good players, were winning trophies and so I couldn't really refuse. What I didn't realise was how much of a problem it would be, moving to London. Though they were safe when I left, Villa went on to be relegated and I got a lot of letters calling me a "Big Time Charlie", saying that I shouldn't have left, and lots and lots of verbal abuse. The *Birmingham Evening Mail* did a piece to have a go at me and the hate mail continued long after I'd signed for Spurs. Even in the last couple of years the shadow of leaving Villa has still fallen over me. I went back to watch a game at Villa Park quite recently and was greeted by a steward, who said, "You're brave coming back here, aren't you?" Then on another occasion I was at the airport when a middle-aged chap walked up to me and in a heavy brummie accent asked me, "Why did you leave the Villa?" I was taken aback, but before I had a chance to give any kind of reply he turned on his heels and walked away.

When David Pleat became Tottenham's manager in July 1986 he set to work on assembling a team to challenge for the major honours in the game. With Ray Clemence in goal, he paired myself and Richard Gough as the central defensive partnership, added a thrilling midfield of Ossie Ardiles, Glenn Hoddle, Chris Waddle and Paul Allen and played Clive Allen as our lone striker. The vision was to have a formidable five-man midfield to supply ammunition and support for Clive up front. Steve's signing from Aston Villa was the final piece in the puzzle. Steve was a naturally left-footed midfielder, equally comfortable in a central or wide position and he quickly found his place in Spurs' vibrant attacking midfield. He was a rare commodity in the game: he had a knack for scoring goals at one end and working hard defensively at the other.

Despite all of Steve's achievements in the game he has always been a very modest and unassuming gentleman and a good friend.

Gary Mabbutt MBE

Big City Lights

Harry Harris, the *Daily Mirror* columnist, called me just after I'd signed for Spurs and said, "Welcome to England." I didn't know what he meant at the time but it soon became apparent that London was where everything happens. I did a piece with him, thanking Mr Clough for all he'd taught me about football, and for the second time in just over a year I found myself apprehensive about meeting a new squad of fresh teammates. I knew more of the players this time, with Glenn Hoddle, Clive Allen, Mitchell Thomas and Gary Mabbutt all people I'd met via England duty at one time or another. I roomed with Gary Mabbutt for a while and I remember being shocked the first time he pulled out his bag of gear to deal with his diabetes. He had to check his blood sugar levels four times a day and seeing him take out his syringes, sugar level readers and watch him analyse his blood was a real eye-opener. I could do nothing but respect the organisation he had to have on a daily level, and the fact that he had a long career at the top of the game is testimony to his skill, determination and dedication. I reported for training at the old Cheshunt training ground and things were pretty smooth. Unlike today, when players have all sorts of PAs and club officials helping them, I was left to find a house and sort a mortgage out after training, so for the first few months I was ensconced in the West Lodge Park hotel near Potters Bar. It was a quiet place, perhaps too quiet, and tucked well out of the way.

My Spurs debut was going to be on Boxing Day, at home to West Ham. On Christmas Day night I went to White Hart Lane to have a look around the ground. I walked on to the pitch and visualised scoring a goal in the bottom corner. As usual I walked the width of the dimly lit pitch to get a feel for my surroundings.

The next day I got a great ovation when my name was announced over the tannoy, which gave me a boost because I was feeling the pressure of what would be roughly the equivalent of about a £9 or £10 million fee today. Despite the early start we drew a full house of about 45,000. The passing and movement in the side was a joy after the previous eighteen months at Villa. I was surrounded by talented top-notch players and, to top it all, I scored just like I'd visualised. My goal made it 3–0 and I was in ecstasy as I turned Alvin Martin and pinged it past Phil Parkes. As I ran, arm aloft towards the "shelf" I knew I'd made the right choice to join Tottenham, or so I thought, and I was relieved that it had all gone so smoothly for me. Next up we lost a fantastic game 4–3 at Coventry. They became our bogey team that year, a big strong side. I knew I'd joined a huge football club by the size of our team bus: a double-decker with TV, hot food and a chef on board. No soup and rolls here!

Life in London was very different to what I'd been accustomed to and the size of the city could make you feel quite lonely. We'd train at Cheshunt and then the players would shoot off to Luton or Harlow or wherever they lived around London. For me it was back to the hotel or I'd wander around Southgate or Enfield. Niall Quinn recently told me that he remembered seeing me around the snooker halls of the area when he was just a kid starting out at Arsenal. I'd often go for a game with Mark Robson and I didn't have much else to help me while away the hours.

Back at my hotel I saw Spike Milligan in the restaurant one night. He was having a family meal and when he had a quiet moment we had a little chat before I left him in peace. He looked old and frail and I'm not sure that he knew who I was, even though Spurs had quite a few famous fans.

The routine of the hotel wasn't too bad, at least not yet. Unlike at Forest, and to a lesser extent at Villa, the Spurs players didn't socialise that much, but on the pitch the first five months were absolutely fantastic. The football was great and it was easy. Four weeks after signing for Spurs we hosted Aston Villa at White Hart Lane. I made sure that I kept out of the paper in the week leading up to the game and declined all interview requests. I took only a short warm-up and noticed that there were lots of away fans. I scored in the first half but kept relatively calm. In the second half we were attacking their end and they were loud. Their whole end was singing, "Hodgey lost the World Cup" really loud when Chris Waddle sent in a diagonal ball towards the "D". I glanced a powerful header across the goal that looped into the top corner of the Villa goal from about sixteen yards. I thought for a second, "Should I?" It was 2–0 and I'd got both, but I ran to the corner flag instead, got mobbed by my teammates and then turned away from the Villa fans. There are certain points when I defy anyone not to react to what the fans are saying or singing, but on that day the two goals in a 3–0 win was ample compensation for the abuse I got.

Since I'd arrived we'd won lots of games and I was scoring freely. We didn't have a defensive midfielder as such; it was a team designed to attack and score goals. Chris Waddle patrolled the right, I was on the left, which left Glenn Hoddle in a free role which he relished. Clive Allen played on his own up front but the midfield was quick to assist him. Ossie Ardiles was the artist in the centre alongside the workhorse Paul Allen. Ossie was the only player I ever knew who would wear rubbers in all conditions. He never ever wore studs because he could glide over the mud, the ice, or whatever the conditions were. It was great to play with a World Cup winner and I remembered watching his debut in England at the City Ground back in 1978. Despite our good run I wondered if the players really trusted and believed in the manager. Many of them had been students of the Keith Burkinshaw/Peter Shreeves school. Some players would question David Pleat at half-time. Why was such-and-such playing in this position or why wasn't so-and-so pushed up here? Should we change the formation or bring someone on? At Forest the manager was never questioned, and at Villa the players were too young to question the manager, so this was all new for me.

The success I was enjoying with Spurs meant I was right in the centre of Bobby Robson's England thoughts. The previous autumn, when I'd still been with Villa, I was lined up in the tunnel at Wembley as we were about to play Northern Ireland when Bobby walked past and said to me, "Hodgey son, you're playing for your place you know." I didn't need that as I was about to run out! We won 3–0 and I made two goals so perhaps that was his way of man management: he was letting me know. I was in a good run of playing in nine consecutive England games and though I was stretchered off against Yugoslavia at Wembley when I clashed heads with Glenn Hoddle, I played in the next game away to Spain. By now Gary Lineker was a Barcelona player and he scored four that night in the Bernabeu as we won 4–2, another career highlight for me. At the end of the game Bobby said to me, "Well done, you covered every blade of grass tonight," which made me feel content because that was my job. When Bobby gave you a "Well done", you knew he really meant it.

○ ○ ○

I was cup-tied in the League Cup but got to see the real hatred between Arsenal and Spurs in the semi-final from a place on the bench. When David Rocastle scored to seal the Arsenal win we had fans climbing over our dugout and running on the pitch. At the final whistle it was even worse. I feared that someone might get hurt as the players tried to leave the pitch. Afterwards, in the players' lounge, one of the younger Arsenal players came in. It was mainly filled with Spurs' players' wives and naturally the atmosphere was subdued. "Has someone died in here?" the young Arsenal player called out. He'd done it for maximum effect.

We were still doing well in the league and progressed in the FA Cup, despite a shaky start. We only just scraped past Scunthorpe, then faced Wimbledon, my old nemesis, away on a Sunday afternoon and live on TV. They hit us in usual route-one fashion. John Fashanu and Richard Gough spent the afternoon battering each other and it took a couple of bits of class to settle the tie: a Chris Waddle screamer and a forty-yard free-kick from Glenn Hoddle. It was really nice to beat them for the first time. Glenn Hoddle dedicated the win to Danny Thomas, our young full-back who had had his knee mangled. I watched him try to train and get back every day but he never made it and the day that he told us he was retiring was really sad. It made you think that that could be you. Football could be a very short career and Danny's was over at just twenty-five.

In my first fourteen games at home with Spurs we'd won every one. One player having the season of his life with us was Clive Allen. Clive didn't contribute too much outside the box, but inside the area he was lethal. He scored forty-nine goals that season. He grabbed three in about nine minutes late in the game against Norwich and it was game over. Give him a chance and that would be it.

Our FA Cup semi-final was against Watford, at Villa Park of all places. In the build-up they'd lost first-choice goalkeeper Tony Coton and his back-up and bizarrely signed up their chief executive's son, Gary Plumley, to play his one and only game for Watford in goal. He had a poor match but was left exposed by his defence too often. I scored twice and we were 4–0 up after an hour. It was great to see the Holt End filled with cheering Spurs fans after what I'd endured there six months earlier. Watford were a decent team but everything went our way that day. It was good to see all the cars on the way back down the M1 with scarves hanging out of their windows. We all went back for a party at White Hart Lane, which got a bit out of hand as we trashed the offices and threw stationery around. It was completely alcohol fuelled and was especially encouraged by some of the older players. The players were throwing around bins, stacks of paper, pens, basically anything they could get their hands on!

Back in the league we pulverised Manchester United 4–0 to ensure that we'd finish third in the table and then the manager rested the entire first team during our last league game at Everton, who had already been crowned as champions. We drew 1–1 anyway.

Back in 1987 the FA Cup final was still very much the biggest day in the football season. We had a busy week leading up to the game against Coventry City, with a celebrity golf day (the celebrities being Cliff Thorburn and Russ Abbott). We sang our song ("Hotshot Tottenham") with Chas and Dave on *Blue Peter* and had a press day which was centred around the final being Glenn Hoddle's last game for Spurs.

We trained until seven-thirty on the Friday night in pouring rain, practising set-pieces. Someone said, "What signal do we give?" at a certain set-play and because people were so pissed off we started doing Cowboy and Indian whoops with our hands over our mouths. It was all a bit silly to be out in the rain before such a big match.

At eight-thirty the next morning I went for a walk to clear my head. There were TV crews around our hotel and the whole day was a big extravaganza. Going down Wembley Way and seeing all the scarves was pretty spectacular. I'd seen it on TV many times but to be on the coach and have it all stretching out a mile ahead of me made the hairs stand up on the back of my neck. I thought back to Ian Bowyer's words before playing in the third round years before, "The Twin Towers are beckoning," and "The first game is sometimes the hardest," which Scunthorpe had been for us that year.

I was totally at ease when we walked out to look at the pitch in our Top Man suits. When it came to our playing kit I'd been superstitious that year. I'd worn the same pair of shorts since round three and before the final I'd seen the kit man and said I wanted them for the final but, "No, we're in a brand-new kit," he said. We were lined up to uncover a new design for the final, but when he turned his back I nicked them and put them in my kit bag. So for the FA Cup final I wore jockey shorts, my old shorts and the new pair on top! There was trouble with the new shirts, as some had the sponsors, Holsten Pils, printed on them and some didn't. The sponsors were fuming, but the cock-up was given so much publicity that they got more coverage than they could have hoped for.

Coventry were a tough, rugged, streetwise team but we were confident and we got the perfect start when Clive Allen headed in after just two minutes. However, when they put a ball into our box there was confusion between Mitchell Thomas and Ray Clemence which allowed Dave Bennett to nip in and score. I tried to get across the line but couldn't stop it. We'd let them back into it too soon. We were an attacking team, good to watch, but we did concede goals.

Our midfield had great flair, balance and a good work ethic. Chris Waddle was the dribbler; Glenn Hoddle was allowed to play in a free role which allowed his imagination and technique to damage any opponent; Ossie Ardiles hardly ever gave the ball away and kept us moving quickly; Paul Allen was a grafter with drive and enthusiasm; I patrolled the left and had both to score and make goals while also helping out with defensive duties. I would have loved to have been able to watch that Spurs midfield take on the Leeds championship midfield of 1992 or a Forest midfield of Garry Parker, Neil Webb, Roy Keane and myself. They were three quality midfields.

Back in the cup final, we regained the lead when a Glenn Hoddle free-kick was flicked on first by Gary Mabbutt and then by Brian Kilcline. I could have got a touch if I'd dived in but although I thought about getting a goal in the cup final I might also have messed it up and it was going in anyway. So I just ran in and let it roll across the line. We went in at half-time 2–1 ahead. We weren't too happy with the way we'd played but we led. We thought we'd get more chances in the second half and expected to score again. Things didn't go to plan though.

After an hour Cyrille Regis got a flick-on to Dave Bennett and I kept shouting to Mitchell Thomas, "Stop the cross! Stop the cross!" but he backed off a wee bit and the cross came in for Keith Houchen to head a spectacular equaliser. For a neutral, that kind of diving header deserved to be in a cup final, but from our point of view it was a preventable goal. We wilted a little bit, not badly, but they were strong and they got a bit of luck with a deflection off Mabbutt for 3–2 and I was thinking that this wasn't going to be our day. They had Dave Phillips at right-back, who was a tough defender, quite strong and quite quick, and I didn't have a massive impact on the game.

One of the worst feelings in football is when you're losing in the last minute of a cup final and the opposition have the ball in the corner flag; you're mentally preparing for what's about to happen. You're secretly hoping for a miracle that somehow you might get the ball back and go down to the other end, but deep down you know it won't happen. At the end I shook hands with Brian Kilcline; in a funny way I was happy for him – after all we went right back to school days together. I was flat on the grass for a few minutes, lost in my own thoughts. Then we had to go up for our medals and walk past the cup. The Duchess of Kent was handing out the medals and she told me that we'd been unlucky and that no one deserved to lose that game, which was all she could say really. We had to walk around the fans and I felt we'd let them down. I'd have rather have won a crap game 1–0 than lose a classic.

That night we went back to a marquee on the White Hart Lane pitch, but it was all a bit flat as you can imagine. I chatted to Bill Nicholson and David Pleat about his days back in Nottingham, and Chas and Dave tried to liven things up, but it was a sad end to what had been a very promising season.

The following week we flew to Miami for a short end of season jaunt and we lost 1–0 to a Columbian team in the Orange Bowl. Most of the players took the chance to take a boat trip to the Bahamas but it was going to be five hours to get there, a one hour stay and then five hours to get back and I didn't fancy it. A few of us stayed in the hotel bar which had a lovely long glass wall that overlooked the ocean. We were hanging out there through the afternoon, but some minor disagreement suddenly turned into some nasty verbals with a group of locals. It eventually calmed down but later that night Mitchell Thomas and I got a call in our hotel room which simply said, "We know where you are. We know what room you're in and we're coming to get you!" We absolutely shit ourselves. Everyone else was away on a boat and we felt very vulnerable. We called down to security, but they just made a note of our complaint, and we kept very quiet in our room; this wasn't something I'd experienced before. Half an hour later there was a knock on the door. We kept deathly quiet, but it was just the rest of the players coming back from their trip. We hadn't known who these guys were in the bar – they could have been anyone. Luckily nothing came of it.

I was really tired, having had two long seasons and a world cup with just two weeks off in almost two years. The previous year I'd gone from the low of losing a semi-final at Oxford to the high of the World Cup finals and this season had gone from being booed by my own fans to an FA Cup final. I'd had to fight back in both seasons, and though we'd ultimately won nothing, I thought the future for me at Tottenham would be bright.

All Change

As I prepared to report back to training at Spurs in the summer of 1987 the club was embroiled in newspaper allegations about David Pleat. David was such a stickler for discipline and good conduct that the stories were all the more shocking. He soon called us all in and told us that a lot of rubbish had been written in the press and that we weren't to believe a word of it. After some preliminaries in England we headed to Scandinavia. The manager arrived late for our tour of Sweden because he'd been away for a holiday with his wife and when we saw him next he'd had a drastic haircut which caused much amusement with the players. He joked that he'd done it so that no one would recognise him but behind the jokes I think he knew it would take a lot of courage for him personally to survive at the club.

During the summer there had been a fair bit of player movement with Danny Thomas retiring, Richard Gough going back to Scotland and Glenn Hoddle signing for Monaco. Two newcomers were especially friendly faces to me: Chris Fairclough and Johnny Metgod from Nottingham Forest. Johnny had a hernia in the preseason and never really got fit while Chris was a good friend who I could spend some time with. I'd bought a house over the summer but it was almost an empty shell as I hadn't got much furniture yet. Still being single, I soon found myself rattling around in it.

We started the new season just like we'd finished the previous one, with a loss to Coventry. Though we never reached the heights of the previous year, we did reel off a seven-game unbeaten run which took us to second in the table. I was acutely aware of the effect on the team of the loss of Glenn Hoddle's sublime talents. He was a genius with the ball at his feet and I'd been very disappointed when he left for Monaco, as he made our whole attacking style tick along with his brain and his passing. Nico Clausen was playing up front with Clive Allen, with myself and Chris Waddle in the wide positions. I still felt weak with the after-effects of a bug I'd picked up in the summer while on holiday in Tenerife.

In early September we beat Oxford 3–0 but I caught another flu bug and was in bed for two days. On the Friday before playing Everton I said I wasn't going to play, but I was asked to travel and see how I felt on the day. Bright lights were affecting me but I started the game. I had little energy in reserve and I was happy to be substituted after an hour. I also travelled midweek to Germany with the England squad but I was too ill to play. Back in England we were getting ready to play Nottingham Forest – my ex-clubs always seemed to crop up at pivotal moments in my career – when more allegations broke in the press about David Pleat. On the Thursday David had come into the canteen at the training ground and put a hand on my shoulder, "You all right, son?" he'd asked. I wondered why he'd made a point of doing that, but it soon became apparent that he was going around saying goodbye without actually saying it. The next morning when I arrived at the ground to travel up to Nottingham the papers were full of it again. We travelled up without the manager and were told that an emergency board meeting was taking place. We soon found out that he'd lost his job. I really felt for him and his family but there was nothing anyone could do.

It was a blow to lose the manager who bought me and who had been supportive of me. I think most of the players pretty much knew he'd be going, he was a high-profile manager so anything negative in the papers was big news and bad for the club. Pleat's sacking was the first nail in the coffin as far as my London career was concerned. Without the backing of the manager who signed me, London seemed a lonelier place than ever.

I was spending more time nipping back to visit friends and family in Nottingham and I was getting increasingly despondent about my off-field life. After 1.30 each day I basically had nothing to look forward to but an empty house. The players all shot off home and though Chris Fairclough lived fairly close by, he had a young family and I couldn't keep going around – they had their own lives to live. I'd still spend time at the pool hall. Neil Ruddock would be there for a game – he was just a young lad coming through the ranks. The days were long and I'd sit around alone, playing *The Joshua Tree* over and over. It was a lovely part of the world but not ideal for a young single lad on his own. Things got worse when I missed a few games with injury, so I wasn't even training with the rest of the lads, just going in for treatment then going home again. I sat in the stands for a League Cup game against the now Second Division Aston Villa at Villa Park. Someone called out "Hodgey!" and when I turned around this chap stood up with his mate. They had venom in their eyes and gave me a massive volley of verbal abuse; I was quite taken aback.

We found out that Terry Venables would be taking over as manager but it would be a while before he arrived as he had to sort out a settlement with Barcelona. We were left with the incredible situation of the players picking the team for four top-flight matches in a row. Something like that would be unthinkable these days. Ossie Ardiles, Ray Clemence, Chris Waddle and Gary Mabbutt ended up picking the team. I assume they went to the board but I don't know how it came about. I wasn't playing well but was picked most of the time when I was fit. In the four games we managed no wins and just one goal. There was a massive sense of being leaderless and the whole thing was a mess. I really questioned whether I was suited to living in London. I started going back to Nottingham at weekends after Northern away games and then had to face a long drive back to my empty house at midnight on a Sunday for Monday morning training.

Before a game at Norwich there had been a bit in the paper about me not being very happy in London and I received a few boos from the Spurs fans before the game. David Pleat had hinted to the press that I wasn't very happy just before he'd gone in early October and my unhappiness was getting to be a real problem for me. As soon as Terry Venables arrived he called us in for a meeting one by one.

"Pleased to meet you. What are your opinions about why the team are struggling at the moment?" he asked.

My reply seemed to shock him a bit. "Before you start, Terry, I need you to know that I want to leave the football club," I said. It was a relief to get that out. I knew I really needed to move on. I wasn't going to be living like that for the rest of my three-year contract, though maybe with a wife and kids it would have suited me better. He accepted my comments though he was very keen to keep me. I also spoke briefly to the press about my wish to move on. That was a big mistake. What I thought would be a small column about wanting to go back to the Midlands turned into a double-page spread in several papers. The rest of the season was going to be tough for me.

Terry's first game in charge was at home to Liverpool in November. He'd done a lot of work with his number two, Alan Harris, on zonal play. All through my career it had pretty much always been 4–4–2. I'd never heard of zonal play, something that's quite common now. Terry was a tracksuit manager; he was energetic and enthusiastic. On the training pitch he'd cone off the zones – you couldn't run past this cone, or go past that one. He used this system for general play and not just for set-pieces. I had to stay on the left and couldn't roam at all, not even a little bit. The Liverpool game was a big media event with Venables' return to England and 47,000 crammed into White Hart Lane. My season took another turn for the worse when I elbowed Ray Houghton and he went down. Steve MacMahon hassled the referee and I got a straight red card. I'd actually turned to go back to my zonal position having not looked at the colour of the card when the referee called over, "You're not going that way Steve, you're going that way," as he pointed to the tunnel. We lost the game 2–0, having to play with ten men for seventy-odd minutes. This was just another of the many bad situations that seemed to be happening to the club and to me. I knew I'd let the players, fans and manager down and got away very quickly at the final whistle.

We won a few games over Christmas and into the new year and I was reinstated to the team for a game against West Ham. There had been more in the press about me not enjoying London. Johnny Giles had a pop at me, but he'd never played in London. Even tabloid editor Derek Jameson did a piece about me, the usual "He's earning thousands of pounds a week, he shouldn't be moaning" kind of article. Against West Ham some young kid turned to me and said, "Fuck off, you homesick bastard!" His name was Paul Ince. I thought, "Jeez, even the kids are having a go now!" I never reacted to those verbals or had a go back – there was no point.

At Oldham I twisted my ankle on their awful plastic pitch and missed about ten games, which I really didn't need. I was back in the treatment room again and the club were struggling. At Port Vale in the FA Cup we played with four centre-halves, two at the back and two in midfield. I thought this gave the message to Vale that we were scared of them. I had always been told you should pick your best side, but on his occasion we hadn't. We went behind 2–0 in a dreadful first half and we eventually lost 2–1. We were going from bad to worse and watching from the stands was difficult. As the season progressed I asked Terry if anyone had bid for me, but being injured there was nothing happening. The months dragged by, and boy, did they drag. By March I'd put my house on the market because I was adamant I'd be leaving. I didn't tell Terry but I'm sure some of the players had mentioned it. After playing at home against Forest I was driving out after the game, and I drove out on to the M25 and then the M1 and pretty much followed the Forest team bus back to Nottingham. I might as well have been on it.

I finally got back into the first team at Queen's Park Rangers for a morning game after being out for two months. I was suffering with tension headaches and getting away from London was always on my mind. Each day I'd wake up and think, "Is this the day when I'll get a phone call?" At QPR all the stresses and problems came to a head for me. As the game started I began to sense that something was amiss. When I went to close down a Rangers' player with the ball, I seemed to be moving out of sync with reality. I'd be facing someone in midfield, but when they played the ball past me my eyes would remain transfixed on his leg even after the ball had gone. It took me a second or so to register that the ball was no longer there. It was surreal: I couldn't concentrate and the tension was affecting my performance. I didn't know what was happening to me. I was in a daze. After ten minutes I just couldn't follow the ball and I wasn't exactly contributing much.

At half-time Terry Venables asked if everyone was all right. I said, "No, I need to come off. I'm mentally drained," and to this day whenever I bump into Paul Walsh he calls me "mentally drained". I can't imagine what the other players were thinking of me when I said that, but they didn't know how it was affecting me. I just had to get off and Terry substituted me. I knew that it was the culmination of all the stress that had been building and that I'd done nothing about so I went to see a doctor at an Enfield hospital and was told that I was mildly depressed. He asked what I thought the solution could be. I knew exactly what the solution was and it was time to act on it.

Once the intensity of the game was away I was fine. I was back in for the next game and things were OK from then. I decided to make a call myself. I told an intermediary that I was going to leave Spurs and that I wanted to get a message to Brian Clough through Liam O'Kane. Would he be interested in me? Forest hadn't missed me. Neil Webb had done well and they'd come third in the league, so there was no guarantee that I could go back. There were other options because Sheffield Wednesday were still in my mind from their earlier interest and I could commute there. Coventry City were also mentioned. Two weeks later I heard that, if the price was right, Forest would take me back. By then I was sleeping on the floor at Mitchell Thomas's flat because I'd sold my house pretty quickly.

Terry Venables said they wanted the £650,000 back for me but I said, "I've been out injured and you won't get that much for me, that's just the way it is." I thought £500,000 was more realistic. He replied by saying if John Barnes was injured would his value drop that much? I said probably not. "Well, there you go then." Eventually I was priced at £550,000. He was just trying to get the best price he could. He also asked about a swap with either Des Walker, Nigel Clough or Neil Webb but Cloughie didn't want any of that. Then Spurs signed Paul Gascoigne and I knew I'd be going.

Gazza and a Good
Tournament to Miss

Paul Gascoigne was a natural comedian and always the centre of attention. When he signed for Tottenham I saw him in a pub near the ground. He was with his father showing people card tricks. I'd first met him in May 1988 with the England squad in Lausanne, Switzerland. My England career was on hold and, after missing the Germany game through illness in the autumn of 1987, I was out for most of the season until I was picked out of the blue to play in an England XI in Alan Hansen's benefit game. The 1988 European Championships were fast approaching and my mind went back to my late inclusion in the Mexico World Cup. I was asked to report to Bisham Abbey and then watched England play Scotland at Wembley then Colombia. Though I didn't get a game I was part of the squad and flew with the team to Switzerland for the last game before the Euro 88 squad was announced. On the banks of Lake Geneva I watched the game from the stands. The Under-21 team was also out there and this kid sat next to me and said, "Do you want a bit of me Mars bar?" I didn't really know who he was but he had a broad Geordie accent. Afterwards in the changing rooms Bobby Robson named his Euro 88 squad and as he read through the list I was thinking, "Why am I out here? Has someone got an injury I don't know about?" He read out the first twenty and then I knew I wasn't going. In the room, only me and Mick Harford weren't in the squad, which was embarrassing but not entirely surprising.

Bobby Robson asked if I was surprised, but deep down I wasn't. He added that I was still in his thoughts, which was a bit of a boost. Naturally he had to pick the in-form players and looking back it was a good tournament to miss as England were annihilated. It wasn't a good experience for the players who were there and, perversely, it would help me get back in.

My escape from Spurs was still dragging on and I had to report back with them for preseason training. A big cheer went up when I walked in the door and lots of humorous clapping. Everyone asking what I was doing there. Bets had been taken about whether me or Tony Parks would be sold first. We had a crazy dressing room. Lots of young lads who were all take-the-piss merchants: Neil Ruddock, Vinny Samways, John Moncur, David Howells, and then came Gazza. It was a tough school in humour and they were as sharp as nails. I couldn't cope with their wit and instant banter. Chris Waddle would call me when I still had the house and I didn't have a lot of furniture and he'd say the call was echoing and he called it Echo Palace. That stuck. I wasn't on the team photo and they went on tour without me. I was still waiting.

I was told that Forest were just £50,000 short of the asking price, which was so frustrating. Then Roy McFarland called me at Mitchell Thomas's house and said that Arthur Cox wanted to sign me. He wanted to make Derby the best club in the Midlands again and outdo Forest. Cox wanted to talk to me and so did their owner, Robert Maxwell. He wanted to tell me about his plans. I spoke to Cox. They had Mark Wright, Peter Shilton and Dean Saunders and I met him out of courtesy, but I didn't really fancy it. The next day a fee was agreed with Forest but Terry wasn't being very warm about it. He told me the news in his office at the Mill Hill training ground. I got up to walk out but I didn't want to fall out with him so I turned round and we shook hands, but he didn't smile. The next time we shook hands would be on the pitch at Wembley after an FA Cup final.

I drove up to meet Cloughie with my adviser, Alan Baines. I'd been introduced to Alan by Viv Anderson. He'd been representing Viv and by now I thought it would be a good idea to have an adviser, as a few of the players were starting to use them in contract negotiations. I knew it would be difficult to negotiate with Cloughie because I was a local lad and he knew I was keen to move back home, so he was bound to use it as a bargaining ploy.

At the City Ground, Cloughie sat me down and I thought, "Right, be ready to discuss the contract." He opened with "Son, are you a homosexual?" I wasn't ready for that! I was about to barter the terms and then that came at me out of the blue. Maybe it was because I was still single there had been unfounded rumours, and I was coming back from London in my mid-twenties. "No," I said. "I'm just a shy lad who can't pull a good-looking bird." He said that was OK, and we moved on. Clough said that although he'd agreed a fee it wasn't a done deal until we could agree personal terms. I knew that could be a problem and that he had me where he wanted me. I was more concerned about getting a fresh start and I asked for a four-year contract. He offered decent money but not great, and he said, "I'll talk to your agent now. Go for a walk around the pitch with Alan Hill." So I went out for a walk and Alan asked me what I really wanted. I said, "I want to settle back in Nottingham and concentrate on my career. That's why I want four years. I'm still pretty young." I knew that local lads were always offered less money and that he'd obviously been primed by Cloughie when he said, "Well, you might have to accept a bit less than you were on at Spurs. We're not flush with money here." When I went back to the office I saw Alan Baines outside and he said, "You're looking at a man who's just been pinned up against the wall!" The offer was a lot less than I'd been on at Spurs and I said, "No, I can't sign for that. I can offer a lot to the club over the next few years and I need to know that the club values that." Clough was adamant and said the offer wouldn't change. I was in a difficult position. I'd said my goodbyes at Spurs, but I told him I'd have to leave it.

Derby were still sniffing around and that was my back-up position if I needed it. I drove back to my parents' house but I'd only been back ten minutes when the phone went. It was Brian Clough. "Son, what are you doing? What do you want?" So I explained what I'd already said to Alan Hill and he said, "Get back here now." When I arrived, the club secretary Paul White was there and they'd drawn up a three-year contract. "I'm going to put you on more than you were on at Tottenham Hotspur," said Clough. Somehow he must have known what I was on. It wasn't much more, but it was more. They were getting a player whose heart would be really in it and I had a point to prove. I signed it right away. That night I called Arthur Cox and said I wouldn't be signing for him. It was good to be home.

Wemb-er-ley! Wemb-er-ley!

Nottingham Forest had finished third in the league the previous season and reached an FA Cup semi-final. Unfortunately English clubs were still banned from Europe after the Heysel Stadium tragedy – it's a massive regret that I missed about five years of European football because of that ban. I was lucky to be playing for England but that was it. Another thirty or forty European games would have been great.

Things were much the same as they had been during my first spell at the club. The new faces included goal-scoring midfielder Garry Parker and hard-tackling right-back Brian Laws, and youngsters like the speedy centre-half Des Walker and goalkeeper Mark Crossley had come through the ranks. Darren Wassall was another youngster coming through and he often felt the wrath of Cloughie's humour. Wassall had a poor complexion at the time and during a team meal he was sitting near to the gaffer who asked him if he was going to finish the vegetables on his plate? "With a complexion like mine I think I need to eat a whole plateful," the youngster joked. "No son," said the manager, "with a face like yours you need to eat a fucking lorry load!"

It was the usual preseason at Forest with lots of games, ten this time. The pattern of play was exactly as I remembered it and I fitted back in right away. I did feel some extra pressure because they had done so well the previous season: I had to try and make them even better. The league campaign started away at Norwich and the gaffer was soon up to his unpredictable tricks. This time he made the team coach pull up about a mile from Carrow Road and told us all to get off and walk to the ground. So there we were, mingling with the fans as we strolled to the game. At half-time he said to me, "Harry, when you get the ball give it to Neil Webb because he's a *good* midfield player." That really made me feel inferior. He meant: you're back but there's a better player now and it didn't exactly boost my confidence. Early in the season we went to Everton and as we arrived he told me, "Don't worry, son, I'll get you back in the England squad one day." We drew 1–1 and the next day I was out in Gedling watching a local game when I was told that England had called and I was to report immediately. I raced down to Bisham Abbey thinking: is he a genius or had he been tipped off by Bobby Robson before we went to Everton?

Bobby Robson spoke at a team meeting that night. There was a table of Forest players, a London table, and so on. Bobby was at the top table, almost like at a wedding. He welcomed us all and dished out a few caps from previous games. He turned to me and said, "Hodgey, I said I wouldn't forget about you, son, and you've deserved to get back in. I'm a man of my word." He made sure that everyone else knew he was a man of his word. I was not just back in the squad but back in the team against a good Denmark side. Neil Webb scored and we won 1–0. But I was shocked to be playing even if it was "only" a friendly.

The next England gathering would include a Concorde trip to Riyadh in November. Our last Forest game before the trip was at West Ham. We were 3–1 up when Stuart Pearce gave the ball away and they came back to 3–3. Clough took Pearce off right away. He was furious. He came to me afterwards and said, "Hodgey, you're not your usual self. I'll pull you out of the England squad. It's only Saudi Arabia." He tried the same on

Pearce but Stuart stood his ground that day and insisted he was going. I regret not getting a flight on Concorde and I wanted to play as badly as Pearce, but he was the club captain and had a bit more power to stand up for himself. I'd seen what could happen in the past when players went against Brian Clough.

I was picked again for an away game in Greece and again in Albania, which was a bit of an eye-opener. There was a lot of poverty on our doorstep and Gazza was his usual stupid self. I saw him hanging out of his hotel window, tossing down chicken wings to kids in the street who were scrambling around for them and eating them, which he thought was hilarious. But he looked to be a really good player and was comfortable in the company of the other England players. He got on well with Bryan Robson, who I still thought had an aura about him, but he was matey with Gazza straight away. I could never really get pally with Bryan Robson. I still looked up to him too much, but Gazza and he were two Geordies together and Gazza just didn't give a shit.

○ ○ ○

With myself and Neil Webb in the centre of the Forest midfield we were very attack-minded but we had a great defence behind us. Des Walker, Stuart Pearce and Brian Laws were strong and good on the ball. I got my first goal back at Forest during a 6–0 drubbing of Chester City in the League Cup. There was no resting of players. Clough would put out his best XI no matter who the opposition. Afterwards, in the dressing room, he announced, "Harry, well done for getting your first goal back," before adding, "no one will know in ten years that it was just a tap-in from five yards!"

We had a slow start in the league and ultimately it could have cost us the championship. We drew five in a row before finally beating Queen's Park Rangers in October. We weren't clinical enough around goal but once we got on a good run our confidence blossomed. Lee Chapman was brought in and his goal record was brilliant everywhere he went. He was a great foil for Nigel and soon he was playing the Forest way. I roomed with him and every morning on trips I'd get *The Sun* and he'd get *The Times*.

Mark Crossley was another new face and was given his debut against Liverpool at home. Crossley was another player who often got the rough end of Cloughie's mickey-taking. The manager often referred to him simply as "Ugly Man". "Come and sit next to me," he'd say to the keeper. "You make me look good!" Or he'd ask him, in front of the whole squad, "Have you got a girlfriend yet? Well, make sure you keep hold of her because you won't get another one!" Crossley had said before the Liverpool game, in his thick Yorkshire accent, "I'm all right, me. I'm the future." From then on he was known as "The Future" but later that changed to "Norm" because someone thought he resembled Norman Whiteside. I was still known as "Harry", which echoed back to when I first broke into the side at Forest. Ian Bowyer had seen a programme on TV in which there was a supergrass called "Harry the Rat". I was already known as being a bit of a rat, popping up everywhere on the pitch, so I became "Harry the Rat" and then just "Harry". We beat Liverpool 2–1 that day. The games against Liverpool were great games to play in, especially by the Trent. We were never scared of them: they were a top team but we could beat them. The fans loved it because it harked back to the epic games between the sides in the late 1970s and early 1980s when both teams had been champions of Europe.

Though Liverpool failed to scare us, we always had trouble with Arsenal. Steve Bould and Tony Adams would just kick Nigel Clough to nullify him and their set-pieces always caused us trouble, partly because we never practised them at all. This time they thumped us 4–1 in Nottingham. We were still inconsistent during the autumn of 1988. We ended up drawing thirteen games that season, but if we'd only drawn nine we'd have been champions. Just before Christmas the manager decided to take us away to Cala Millor for a break. We had a few drinks and relaxed before a live TV date at Manchester United. Stuart Pearce was suspended that day and we wondered who would be made captain. The gaffer told Des Walker to lead the team out "because Webby will be leaving us". Neil Webb hadn't signed a new contract and the manager saw that as a sign that he wanted to get away. It certainly affected his play that day. Garry Parker was left out and told me he was going to ask for a transfer but I told him not to be so hasty. We actually lost that game 2–0 but Clough said we'd feel the benefits of the break later in the season, and he was right. After Old Trafford we went on a run of eighteen games undefeated, including ten straight wins. Garry Parker was given a starting role on the left, but he was dangerous because he could come inside and shoot with his right-foot. Brian Laws claimed the right-back position as his own and we were off.

There was a lot of excitement at the club as our run kept getting longer and longer. We faced Queen's Park Rangers in the fifth round of the League Cup and we hammered them 5–2. Lee Chapman scored four of the goals past David Seaman. Afterwards some fans ran on the pitch, celebrating the win, and I saw the gaffer looking quite angry but I just carried on into the dressing room. Later I was shocked to see the TV footage which showed Cloughie slapping a couple of fans and pulling them off the pitch. He was very protective of the pitch. It was another example of Clough treating the pitch as his place of work and he only wanted players and officials to walk on it at the best of times. There was some real concern for a day or two about what sanctions might be imposed or that he might even have to leave. The club gave him a ticking off, he received a touchline ban, and in true Clough style he engineered a photo call where he gave the two lads a kiss and got them to apologise to him!

Father and Son

In my second spell at Forest there was a lot of press attention on the father and son scenario at the City Ground. We had a legendary manager and a top-scoring son at the same club and I felt that Nigel Clough dealt with the tricky situation of being the manager's son very well. I hardly ever saw Nigel answer his dad back, though in the early days when they shared a car ride to and from training I can't vouch for what was said! I'm sure there were plenty of debates about players and games.

Nigel was one of the players who rarely got any stick in the changing rooms, most probably because he played some excellent football for Forest. His position was pivotal to the way Forest played and the team ticked along because of his passing and positional qualities, but he needed good athletes around him to allow him to show the best of his abilities. With the ball zipping across the grass to his feet he could spot and deliver the right pass, with the correct weight on it, into the right space, nine times out of ten. He was also as brave as a lion – and remember this was a time when rock-hard tackling from behind was an accepted and bruising part of the game. He would often take a battering but just pick himself up and get on with it without complaining. He could also score goals, his finishing was clinical and he was excellent with free-kicks and penalties. Whether it was league games or in semi-finals and finals, he handled the pressure, knowing that on top of everything else his dad was the manager and wanted badly to win every game. "Go and tell the number 9 well done," the gaffer would say to me. "It's not easy taking a penalty."

There were times when I felt Nigel needed a break; he might have looked a bit sluggish and a bit weary, he was played in every game in a tough position and I think it would have done him the world of good to allow him a short rest. Of course, we had a small squad and rotations were unheard of – the thought of Brian Clough dropping his son would have made newspaper headlines and so he played on. Another problem was that we didn't really have a replacement for Nigel, certainly not anyone who could play the Nigel-role as well as Nigel did; it would have been different in today's game and he would have got some rest.

I often wondered if any of the dressing-room banter would get back to the gaffer through Nigel. I'm sure that some players were cautious when Nigel was around but I never had the impression that he was going back and telling his dad what was being said. If anything had come out it would have been obvious who the source was and it would have caused big divisions in the dressing room, but that never happened.

Brian could also be very supportive of Nigel when it came to England duty. Whereas he would sometimes pull Forest players out of an England squad, I saw him fuming when Nigel was dropped one time. "I'll phone that shit, Robson, tomorrow," he ranted.

Nigel's best work undoubtedly came at Forest and his spells at Liverpool and Manchester City were less successful because their systems were different. At Forest his dad had decided on a system that revolved around Nigel and produced great results for the club. Nigel was also helped by the fact that Brian had been a striker and Clough senior always backed up his strikers; "Scoring a goal is the hardest thing in football," he repeated over and over, but it was something that both Cloughs managed with relative ease.

Medals

We were playing a heck of a lot of games with all of our cup involvements (we ended that season having contested seventy games and I played in fifty-seven of them) and I was beginning to get calf strains. My gait was changing and giving me calf trouble. Clough asked if I was OK before one game and I replied that I wasn't sure but when I arrived before the game my kit was laid out and that was it: I was playing. I struggled through to the end then afterwards he said, "Harry, don't you ever, ever do that to me again!" He thought I'd been conning him, but I hadn't. I'd actually thought I might get some praise for playing when I wasn't 100 per cent fit. You can't see anything with a calf strain but you feel it, even walking can be hard, never mind running.

Our next big game, and the first of many that season, was a League Cup semi-final against Third Division Bristol City. After the Oxford disappointment with Aston Villa I was desperate to get back to a cup final. I marked Steve McClaren in midfield and they had Joe Jordan leading their line. They were there on merit and proved to be tricky opponents during the first leg at the City Ground. We needed an own goal near the end to rescue us and ensure a 1–1 draw. In the big bath afterwards I was on my own. Sometimes I'd really ponder on things after a game and worry about why things hadn't gone right and I really thought we might get beat in the second leg. Cloughie came in and said, "Harry, come on darling, you can't do anything about it now. Soon be Saturday." That was one of his stock phrases if something hadn't gone well in midweek: there was always another game coming along quickly in which we could make things right. That weekend we were live on the BBC at Watford in the FA Cup, a tie which we won comfortably 3–0. Then we had another cup game. We'd entered the Simod Cup, which at the start of the season was seen as a bit of a joke among the players but the manager took it as seriously as ever. We'd beaten Chelsea and Ipswich and now faced Crystal Palace in a one-off semi-final at the City Ground. If there was any doubt that this cup didn't mean anything to the fans it was dispelled when we ran out and over 20,000 were waiting for us.

Ian Wright looked like a good player that night and I remember him giving his wingers an unbelievable amount of stick about the service he was getting; he showed real venom. They also had future England players like Nigel Martyn and Geoff Thomas playing but we turned them over 3–1 and qualified for Wembley. It was nine years since the manager had been at Wembley and he was ecstatic. Just a few days later we travelled down to Bristol for the second leg of the League Cup semi-final. It was really cold and really wet. Clough was in the stands, still banned from the touchline, and the old-fashioned ground was packed and noisy. They hit the post right at the end of normal time before Garry Parker scored – in hailstones and a howling wind. We were booked for Wembley again and became the first side to qualify for two Wembley finals in the same season.

Brian Clough would sometimes have a bath with the players after a game and then dust himself down with a copious amount of talcum powder. On away trips it was Liam O'Kane's responsibility to make sure the talc was packed along with the rest of the kit. On one particular trip to London, O'Kane realised that he'd left the talc back in Nottingham and compounded his mistake by telling the manager about it during the bus ride down on the Friday evening. Clough's response to this seemingly minor bit of news was swift and decisive. "Albert!" he called to our ever-present bus driver. "Stop at the next services would you. Liam's going to be getting off!" So we pulled up at Watford Gap and Liam O'Kane had to get off. The bus pulled away, leaving him in the car park. These were the days before mobile phones so he had to get some change to call his wife back in Nottingham, and she had to drive down and collect him, then they went to find some talcum powder from somewhere and then she took him down to London to join the rest of the team before driving all the way back to Nottingham!

We were rapidly moving up the league table too and we went and beat Arsenal 3–1 at Highbury to keep us in touch with the leaders. We were playing virtually the same players in all of these competitions and some tiredness began to creep in. We disappointingly drew 1–1 at home to Newcastle (they were relegated that year) before the next big game – an FA Cup quarter-final at Old Trafford.

Before most games the chairman, Maurice Roworth, would pop in for a couple of minutes before kick-off. Cloughie would tolerate him for a couple of minutes then say, "Thanks for your thoughts, now piss off, ta-ra." Before the United cup tie he'd popped in then disappeared towards the loos. At about ten to three I nipped in to go to the loo and heard some gasping coming from one of the cubicles. I pushed the door back and he was on his back struggling to breathe. I discreetly called in Graham Lyas the physio and he opened his collar and loosened his tie – he was having an asthma attack. Soon the other players were gathered round and then Cloughie casually strolled into the toilets. He peered over the crowd and said, "Chairman, if you're going to die, hurry up! I've got a game to play in ten minutes." Then as he walked away, Clough jovially added, "Quick lads, go through his pockets!"

Gordon Strachan said afterwards that it was difficult to play against a team who get ahead and then defend so well, stay on their feet and are intelligent. And that summed us up perfectly. Franz Carr worked a great chance that Garry Parker converted and that was all we needed. Des Walker explained that playing against Mark Hughes he always tried to not get him riled up and to stand off him a little bit. Des was superb that day. I helped out the defence by clearing one shot off the line with my shin. We were in another semi-final and still going for an unprecedented four trophies.

I was seeing a Brian Clough that was often mellower than the one I'd played for in the early 1980s. He was a very proud grandfather and he'd always make a fuss of any mascot who came in the dressing room before the game. "Come and give granddad a kiss," he'd say. "Who's your favourite player? Oh, he had a nightmare last week, he's not that good." The chairman would still pop in for a few minutes, but one time Cloughie put Maurice Roworth in his place. "Chairman, you should knock before you come in my dressing room," he called out. So the chairman turned around, left the room and closed the door behind him. Then we heard a knock at the door and Cloughie shouted, "Yes, who is it?" "The chairman," came a muffled voice. "OK, come in."

We were bound to lose eventually and one of my former clubs, Spurs, inflicted the 2–1 defeat. I chased Chris Waddle about sixty yards back to our goal before he passed for Vinnie Samways to score in the ninetieth minute. We soon bounced back against Derby where I scored past Peter Shilton in what was a big local game. Clough was always cock-a-hoop when we beat Derby. We then beat Manchester United again, this time in the league, and Cloughie impressed upon me that, "Young [Bryan] Robson's legs have shot it. I want you to run him and run him again. He's gone." I did run him and we tonked them 2–0; it should have been 6–0.

Our first appointment of the season at Wembley was in the League Cup final against Luton Town, the holders, who had beaten Arsenal a year earlier. We, in what would become a tradition, stayed at the Post House Hotel near Potters Bar. We'd had a pretty settled team since Christmas but when I saw the team for the final I was shocked because Clough chose young Lee Glover as a substitute. He'd get a £10,000 bonus if we won, but Brian Rice had played in five games on the way to Wembley. I was gutted for Ricey, we all were. It just wasn't fair, but Glover was definitely one of Cloughie's favourites.

The day of the game involved lots of hanging around. I went for a walk, had lunch, and sat around with my suit on, waiting to go. Luton were decent, but I was confident that if we played anything like we could we'd win. Early on I said to Chappy, "Come on! Get with it! Don't let it pass you by!" We were all sluggish and Mick Harford scored a header to give them a half-time lead. Not a lot was said at half-time, just that we needed to up the tempo, get some quick passes going between red shirts. I was told to get further forward more, and early in the second half Nigel Clough came deep and left space in behind which I went for and Neil Webb put me through in the inside-right channel.

We'd played at Luton a month before and Les Sealey had come out and brought me down. In the Wembley Final he did exactly the same. I didn't think there was any need for him to bring me down this time, I just thought, "Get in the box and you're in control." As he came out I knew there'd be an impact because he came out so fast and so I leaned in to him a little bit and he took me down. Penalty. I went to get the ball for Nigel. The gaffer would always say, "Someone go and get the ball for him. He's got the hardest bit to do yet. You go and get the ball and let him prepare." So I fetched him the ball and got ready for any rebound. Nigel must have felt under immense pressure. His team was losing 1–0 at Wembley, his dad was the manager and he had to take a penalty with 76,000 inside Wembley and millions more watching on TV. He coolly slotted it into the corner and we were back in the match. Years later, not long before he died, I met Brian Clough and he said, "I remember you got me that penalty and got me back into it at Wembley. People might have forgotten that but I didn't." Neil Webb put us into the lead and then Nigel scored again to make it 3–1. Game over. I didn't milk it because I knew what it was like to lose at Wembley, but it was a great feeling going up for the trophy and I felt some vindication for coming back to Forest. In three seasons away I hadn't won anything at Villa or Spurs but there were no big celebrations after the game: Cloughie had proved that he could produce a new young team of high quality and he'd done it without Peter Taylor. Plus, we still had three trophies to contest and six weeks of the season to go.

Harry and I played together for both Forest at club level and England. He was an attacking midfielder and had the ability to time his runs to perfection with great energy. A real box-to-box player who once arriving beyond the opposition back line was a composed finisher and match winner.

Having been to the 1986 and 1990 World Cups and having played for Forest winning trophies and playing in Europe, and enjoying years working with Brian Clough, he has a wealth of footballing experiences.

We both shared a love of music and watched many live gigs in our Forest days, but I was unsure about which way he was going musically when he started to listen to Kylie Minogue!

Best Wishes
Stuart Pearce

Stuart Pearce – Captain Pyscho

More than any other captain I played with, Stuart Pearce led by example. When I went back to Forest for my second spell I was a little apprehensive about how I'd be welcomed by some of the players. Would they think I was a big-time Charlie who'd left to seek his fortune, only to return? As it was, I was feeling good about coming home and it seemed as though I'd been accepted back into the dressing room. When I was invited over to Stuart Pearce's house for a meal it confirmed that I was back in favour.

When you arrived at the home of Stuart Pearce you were left in no doubt that this was the house of a passionate Englishman – he had a thirty-foot flagpole in his front garden proudly displaying the red cross of St George. I hadn't been there very long when he openly said, "Harry, you know what, I told Liz I wasn't sure about you but last week I came home and said I liked you, I think you're all right!" Knowing I had the captain's support meant a lot but the conversation quickly moved on to the more mundane matter of what our next gig would be. Even though Stuart's main musical passion was punk, which I never really took to, our shared love of music meant we had many nights out going to shows.

I enjoyed the captain's cockney banter and sense of humour and myself and Pearcey would always be at the centre of organising trips for a group of players to see concerts around the country and closer to home at Nottingham's Rock City. We saw Depeche Mode at the NEC and ended the night playing table football with the band, backstage. We also went to see the Cure at Rock City and hired a minivan which we filled with beer for a trip to Leeds to watch Big Country. Unfortunately bad traffic on the M1 meant that we only got there in time to see the last three songs but we did meet the late Stuart Adamson.

April 15th 1989

Forest had played Liverpool in the FA Cup semi-final at Hillsborough the previous season on April 9th 1988. Liverpool won 2–1 that day, but otherwise the game passed without too much incident. A year later the same two teams played in the same stage of the same competition at the same venue and it was very different. I remember our team coach going down the hill to Hillsborough in Sheffield on a beautiful spring day. When we went out for a warm-up I noticed that their end behind the goal was quiet but our end, the big kop, was packed and really loud. A couple of the lads said to me, "Where are their fans?"

The game kicked off and it was end-to-end right away. Peter Beardsley hit the bar in the opening seconds and then we broke away and got a corner at their end. There was some disturbance among their fans behind the goal and my mind flew back to Newcastle in 1974 and Celtic in 1983. I was half expecting that the whole lot would come spilling out on to the pitch. I just thought, "Jeez, we've only just started." Then someone ran past me on the pitch and shouted, "I'm sorry, Steve, but there's people dying in there!" My immediate reaction was that he was being a bit over-the-top. Maybe people were struggling but not dying. Seconds later the referee blew his whistle and said we had to get off. I was only about fifty feet from it and could hear screams and people bellowing for people to move back. I looked across the

Leppings Lane terrace and saw people being tugged up into the upper tier by fans in the seats.

We were quickly moved away from it, down the tunnel and into the cocoon of the dressing room. It was a surreal environment. We could hear booing and then it all went quiet. The manager was telling us to stay relaxed, he said, "Do whatever you have to do." Some players were lying on the benches, some with towels over their heads, a few were prone on the floor, keeping their legs stretched while others just sat blankly. Now the noise outside the dressing room was rising and it sounded like pandemonium outside. People shouting, ambulances wailing. Alan Hill went outside and when he returned he just said to me, "You don't want to go out there!" Then Brian Clough, along with Liverpool manager Kenny Dalglish, went out to see what was happening. When he came back he was quiet, he didn't say a word.

The FA's Graham Kelly came in to see the gaffer and said, "Brian we've got a problem out there but the game will be played today." We still expected that any delay would be temporary. Lee Chapman knew some of the stewards from when he'd played for Sheffield Wednesday. After about half an hour, he popped out and came back to say that two people had died. Brian Clough's reaction was, "Son, don't tell me I don't want to know." Graham Kelly appeared again to say, "Whatever happens the game has to be completed today." But by now we'd found out that a few more had died. I went out and tried to get a look down the tunnel; I could see people using advertising hoardings as makeshift stretchers but I couldn't really see much else. Kelly, of course, may have been unaware of the extent of the disaster unfolding outside but the gaffer was having none of it. "Graham, we're going home," he said. "There's no game today. Lads, get changed. We're off." It was pretty quiet; we were just waiting for news about what was happening outside. Then it was reported that five people had died – the numbers kept rising. Before then we were wondering if there'd be a replay or what would happen but by about 4 p.m. we were all changed and any thoughts of football had gone. We could still hear ambulances outside but things seemed to be quietening down.

It was all quiet outside when we were finally told that the coach was ready and we'd be leaving soon. Before we left I was able to get outside and walked on to the pitch unobstructed. It was getting on for about 5 p.m. and I was able to walk right up to the railings and across Leppings Lane; no one stopped me. I pushed a couple of the barriers and some were bent double, I was just drawn to see what had happened. Some of the railings and stanchions were bent into strange shapes and they had scarves tied to them. There were a few people still milling around looking dazed, but no great police presence or anyone to stop me walking where I wanted to. I couldn't imagine how bad it could have been on there ninety minutes earlier. I wandered about for a few minutes and then walked slowly back to our bus. As we were readying to pull out of the car park an irate Liverpool fan came up the steps and on to our bus. "It's all your fault," he shouted. He got three or four steps along the aisle before he was stopped and taken off. "It's your fucking fault! I blame your fucking lot!" He was just so grief-stricken he needed someone to blame. The Liverpool bus pulled out and we followed it. I wondered what their players could be thinking; people they knew might have died.

That night it was the PFA awards ceremony in London. On the train down to London word quickly spread that there were some Forest players on the train and lots of football fans came to see us and ask what had happened and what had we seen? All we could say was that we'd seen very little. Myself, Webby, Des Walker and Pearcey were due to attend and we did, but in hindsight I think we made the wrong decision. The enormity of what had just happened hadn't had time to sink in. That night the cameras were all on us Forest players. When the death toll approached 100 the next day I was stunned that it could have happened at a football game. The following week was spent waiting to hear what the authorities were going to do. All the players were interviewed individually by the police back at the City Ground. What had we seen before the game? During the game? Was anything untoward? They were just routine questions. We attended a service for the victims at the Lace Market church in Nottingham and we took a minibus to a Sheffield hospital. The replay had been announced when we went to the hospital. We were caught up in the middle. Everton were in the final and we just couldn't win – the swell of opinion was that it should be a Merseyside final. We posed for photos and signed stuff for people who were relatively OK, then we'd go into another ward where a kid was on life support and was brain dead through suffocation. I just didn't know what to say. A few of the victims and their families said thanks for coming but we felt helpless and just tried to give some moral support. It's not something you can prepare yourself for, and the bus back was utterly silent. I hadn't really seen any injuries on the day, but this made it real. It was an awful day.

We were due to play Middlesbrough on the Saturday after Hillsborough. The players had a meeting and the manager said he'd go along with whatever we decided. We decided that we would go ahead with our games. The FA Cup semi-final replay took place at Old Trafford. The manager said, "I've got a game to win, let's go out and win it." All the right things were said but Liverpool had all the emotion and passion to win it, plus they were the best team in the country at the time. We didn't fold, we went 1–0 down early but came back to equalise and it was 1–1 for about an hour, before they went on to win 3–1. After the game Kenny Dalglish knocked on the door. He came in and said, "Thanks for that, lads, all the best." To which Cloughie responded, "Young man, thanks very much. Good luck in the final." I think he knew we were in a no-win situation but was gracious in victory.

Twenty years later I got a phone call asking if I could play in the Hillsborough memorial game at Anfield. Myself, Nigel Clough and Des Walker represented the original Forest side. Kenny Dalglish said it was right that some of those Forest players were there because we were a part of it and hadn't really been mentioned over the years. When the crowd sang "You'll Never Walk Alone" with the families of the victims, and the kop had all their scarves up, it was spine-tingling moment. I was honoured to be part of that.

○ ○ ○

Just a week later we were back at Wembley for the Simod Cup final against Everton. It was an exciting, attack-minded game that went to extra time in front of almost 50,000 fans. I took a knock and had to go off during extra time when it was 3–3, and Franz Carr came on. There had been some discussion between Cloughie and Ron Fenton on the bench about whether Franz should go on. The conversation ended with Cloughie saying, "OK Ron, send Carr on, but if we lose today, you're sacked on Monday!" Luckily for Ron, Franz set up the winning goal. We won by the odd goal in seven and I hobbled up the stairs to collect my second medal in three weeks. I can remember the Forest end filled with inflatables which were all the rage back then. It was a good time to be a Forest fan. In the dressing room the gaffer saw Franz coming out of the shower and went over to have a word. "For what it's worth," said Cloughie, "I still wouldn't have put you on!"

Whereas we'd each been paid a bonus of £10,000 for winning the League Cup, there was nothing in our contracts regarding the Simod Cup. We'd just beaten a good top tier club at Wembley and Forest had made a good amount of money from the occasion, but on the Monday morning we found our bonuses waiting for us in the dressing room. Each player walked in to find a box of Dairy Milk with a ten pound note sellotaped to the top!

We ended the season at home to West Ham. We were close to being a very good team again and I felt that the addition of a couple of quality players could have won us the league. As it was, the gaffer was more concerned to hanging on to what he had. Neil Webb still hadn't signed a contract and there was talk of him going to Manchester United. After the West Ham game Cloughie was on to him in the dressing room. "All the best son," he said to Webby. "I know you haven't signed for United yet – there's always a new contract in my office if you want it." But Webby was off and the manager's words just hung in the air as Neil disappeared out of the door.

We still had no route into Europe, but we'd achieved a lot: Two trophies, a semi-final and third in the league. It was near enough my perfect return. Spurs had done nothing, but I'd got ten goals and was back in the England first team. Webby's fee was decided by a tribunal and he went to United for £1.5 million. I was sorry to see him go.

Our end of season trip was, as usual, to Cala Millor. One day a bunch of us players were sitting around having a drink at lunchtime, a few laughs and a bit of banter, when the manager walked in with some of his cronies. As soon as he arrived we all went quiet. He bought us all a drink, but we were looking around, uncomfortable that he was there. For the next few minutes we all just sat there drinking quietly while the sound of his conversation with his mates carried across the room. Once he had finished his drink he stood up, called over, "Lads, thanks for your company." And off he went, and we all started talking again!

The Not So Beautiful Game

It wasn't just Vinnie Jones who tried to physically intimidate me on the football pitch. Over the years all shapes and sizes tried to have a go at me, from verbal assaults to sometimes silly physical ones. At Forest we had Stuart Pearce, who would frighten many a right-winger, and sometimes put them in the first row of the stand. Then there was the verbal side to the game. It was sometimes tough even to hold your own among your own teammates when the banter started to flow. At the end of my Forest career I'd end up in verbal sparring games with the manager, but for the most part I avoided it with the players. At Forest we had a young lad called Phil Starbuck who was a born-again Christian. Now, anyone or anything that stood out or deviated from the "norm" could be ripe for abuse in the dressing room. Every time Starbuck would come into the senior players' area to use the drinks machine Pearcey would let him have it. "Hallelujah!" would be shouted out, or "Praise be!" Sometimes it was just a gentle, "Morning, reverend." I used to feel for him. He'd just get his milk then slink back quietly to the youth team's changing room.

Back then, most teams had at least one player who was an old-fashioned hard-man. The toughest I came up against was Billy Whitehurst at Newcastle. Playing at St James's Park with Villa I had to fill in at left-back when we got an injury. Within seconds Whitehurst had come over to me and said in a big gruff voice, "Stay out of my way son or I'll break your fucking legs!" He said it in such a menacing way that I certainly believed him. He had a tough reputation and it was well known that he'd "do" his own teammates in training if they crossed him.

In the late 1980s I was being marked by Pat van den Hauwe and at one point in the game when the ball was over on the opposite side of the pitch he just ran past me and whacked me really hard on the shins, for no reason whatsoever. A few minutes later he shouted over and raised a hand, "Sorry, Hodgey." He'd just lost it needlessly for a split second. These days he'd have had three cameras spotting it and he'd probably have been banned.

A tough ground to visit was The Dell, with its tight atmosphere, especially when they had Neil Ruddock and Jimmy Case running around kicking people. In one game Forest were given a penalty and I was waiting to run in for any rebound, just leaning forward, ready to sprint. Suddenly I got the biggest kick up my backside which knocked me into the area on all fours, I turned round and there was Jimmy Case. Again, no one saw it.

The most shocking abuse I got wasn't from a player though. One time, when I was the most hated man in Villa Park, I went over to collect the ball to take a corner. The ballboy must have been all of nine years old, but as I walked over he just snarled, threw the ball hard at my chest and said "Fuck off, Hodge, you wanker!" When the pre-teens are having a go at you, you know you're in trouble.

Wembley Again

In preseason we went to Bordeaux for what turned out to be an eventful trip. I met World Cup star Alan Giresse and we went to watch Bordeaux v Sochaux before the whole Forest squad went out to the local bars and the top nightclub. Here I saw a young Laurent Blanc, the Bordeaux captain, strut in like he owned the place (maybe he did) and we met Jesper Olsen, who I'd played against at Manchester United. The Forest lads were on a daily allowance of just £10 and that night we complained that we were short of cash. The following day, a Sunday, Olsen managed to get hold of a local bank manager and he opened up his bank especially so we could get some cash. I don't imagine the Premiership stars of today having to go to so much trouble for their money.

We were spending three hours travelling each way to play small teams in poor stadiums and the players were restless. We had never-ending bus trips to little provincial towns. We stayed in little chalets around a chateau, more cost-cutting by the club, no doubt, and I was getting bitten to high heaven by the mosquitoes every night. It was like being on a Fred Karno comedy tour. One day we were walking along a beach for a while before we realised that we'd wandered on to a nudist beach. Some nights we'd have a few beers and were like typical Brits abroad. I recall Stuart Pearce walking down a street shouting "Viva La Revolution!" We were just so bored. Another evening myself, Pearce, Colin Foster and Franz Carr were having a beer on the main street and all these ladies were walking backwards and forwards and it took a while for us to realise that we were sat in the middle of the red-light area, something that we just laughed about but today it would probably have made the papers because of the constant press coverage that the players have to endure.

I was injured and played just one game on the trip and I got a chance to watch John Sheridan, who had come in to replace Neil Webb, or at least so we all thought. Once again we started the league campaign with a couple of draws before playing Derby County at home. Peter Shilton was returning to the City Ground and I managed to score an own goal when I glanced a header at the near post. As I was walking back to the halfway, head down, Stuart Pearce was walking behind me and in his cockney drawl he shouted out, "Hodgey, you facking wanker!" That was Stuart's way of making me respond! In the second half I helped to rectify my mistake by chasing a lost cause with Mark Wright and managing to get the ball across the box to where Gary Crosby had a tap-in before Pearce got the winner near the end.

John Sheridan played only one competitive game for the first team. I played alongside him in the reserves at Coventry but I came off after an hour. At Highfield Road there was a massive pillar in the dressing rooms and I'd had a shower and was getting changed when a livid Brian Clough came in with Ronnie Fenton. I don't know if he knew I was there but if he did, he didn't care. I just kept quiet behind the pillar. He was talking about John Sheridan.

"What have I signed him for? He can't head! He can't tackle! He can't run! What the fuck have I signed him for?"

Like he did with some players, he made his mind up very quickly about them and moved them on. Sheridan was sold soon after that but a few weeks later he came back and scored the winning goal for Sheffield Wednesday at the City Ground.

ABOVE: *England v Argentina. Jorge Valdano leans on me as I flick the ball confidently back to Peter Shilton, but history was about to be made.*

LEFT: *We doubled up to try to stop Maradona whenever possible. Here Kenny Sansom helps me out.*

LEFT: *With my Spurs team mate Ossie Ardiles and Diego Maradona, Wembley 1987.*

OPPOSITE: *Enjoying my debut goal for Spurs, v West Ham, Boxing Day 1986. (Daily Mirror)*

ABOVE: *Back to my old haunt, Villa Park, and a flying start to the 1987 FA Cup semi-final as I put Spurs ahead against Watford. (Popperfoto)*

Joy as Spurs go in front just before half-time during the 1987 FA Cup final. (Popperfoto)

Things go from bad to worse at Spurs. Neil Ruddock looks on as I am sent off on Terry Venables return to England. (The Sun)

Lineker, then a Barcelona player, puts four past Spain in the Bernabeau. A memorable night. (Bob Thomas/Getty Images)

As I run towards the Leppings Lane end the tragedy of the Hillsborough disaster is just unfolding. (Rex Features)

Getting Forest back into the 1989 League Cup final against Luton, as Les Sealey brings me down for a penalty. (David Munden)

ABOVE: *Showing off the Littlewoods Cup to hordes of Forest fans at Wembley after we had beaten Oldham to retain the trophy in 1990. (Forman Newspapers Ltd)*

LEFT: *Sir Bobby and Franz Beckenbauer deep in conversation. I just wanted to get my club captain Stuart Pearce off the pitch as quickly as I could. (Colorsport)*

BELOW & BELOW LEFT: *In the dugout before the 1991 FA Cup semi-final. The gaffer was making me chuckle but I was gutted to be left out. He was right, though: Forest won 4–0. (Forman Newspapers Ltd)*

ABOVE: *Robin Hood and the young pretender. On this occasion the young pretender stole the place in the 1991 FA Cup final. (*The Sun*)*

LEFT: *Meeting the future king of England before the 1991 FA Cup final.*

BELOW: *Agony. Just like in 1987, an own goal in extra-time ruined my FA Cup dreams. (Empics/Getty Images)*

Eric points something out to me. (Getty Images)

Like me, Brian Clough was a big cricket fan. We played out a nervy 3-3 League Cup tie at Huddersfield and only went through on away goals and after the game he brought Geoff Boycott into the dressing room. Clough introduced us and sat the Yorkshire legend next to myself and Des Walker. "I've got to ask you a question," he said. "Why did you let Huddersfield back into the game at 3-1 when you had them dead and buried?" I was thinking, "I've got this legendary England batsman asking us this? It's a bit of an inquest here!" The perfectionism of the man and his getting straight to the point was very much like his mate Cloughie. We just spluttered an answer and he moved on.

By the middle of November we were struggling to be mid-table, having lost more games than we'd won. It was always going to be difficult to improve upon or even repeat the events of the previous twelve months, and with Neil Webb leaving we'd lost one of our best players. For me it was an important year, because the Italia 90 World Cup was just months away and it wasn't going as well as I'd hoped.

We got a mini-revival going when we visited Maine Road to play Manchester City. It was a game that signalled more changes coming our way. We performed really well, but at one point I got through the offside trap and was one on one with their keeper. From out of nowhere I got barged off the ball by a teammate. From the floor I looked up to see Lee Chapman going in on goal, then he missed. It was unreal what had happened and we fell out for a while after the game. In the same game we were 3-0 ahead late on when Chapman went for a shot from a tight angle while Nigel Clough was screaming for a pass. Nigel would have had a tap-in for a hat-trick. Chapman was looking to score himself, in a team that was based on teamwork and at the end of the game Brian Clough took him to task. "Young Chapman, what were you doing? Did you not see

Nigel with an open goal?" Chapman brushed it aside with, "Well, if you're not happy, I'm doing my best."

"I don't accept it," replied the gaffer. "That was not your best."

No matter what the score, we were always primed to do the right thing, and that wasn't it. Cloughie made sure that he'd punish Chapman for it and did it in a very public way. He dropped him, and then in a hotel before the next game he called the players together in the lobby and announced, "Same team today, lads." Lee Chapman was standing slightly behind the manager and Cloughie turned right into his face and said, "That means you're not playing." Chappo was gone soon after that. His replacement was Nigel Jemson, a very confident boy whose confidence sometimes caught the eye of the manager a little too often. "Is your mum here today, son?" he asked him once. "Well, go and get her because you should be bloody ashamed of the way you've embarrassed her today." This was in front of the whole dressing room. Jemson had a good start, scored his first goal at the Baseball Ground, and we went on another great run losing just once in fourteen league and cup games. The only loss came in a Sunday FA Cup game live on TV against Alex Ferguson's Manchester United. United were struggling – they eventually missed relegation by just five points – and the papers were filled with speculation about Ferguson's job being on the line. Especially if United got knocked out of the FA Cup at the first hurdle. We didn't care about other clubs' problems, we just wanted to start another Wembley run. Mark Robins gave United the lead and we scored a perfectly good goal to equalise but I was ruled to be offside. TV replays proved that I wasn't and the rest is history. If the goal had stood, who knows what would have happened in the replay at Old Trafford, where we had an excellent record at the time.

Early the next morning we flew to France to play Auxerre in a nothing game. Guy Roux was their manager and Basil Boli their strapping centre-half and we had to immediately pick ourselves up from the FA Cup in front of only 2,000. For some unfathomable reason the game was live on French TV. We just didn't want to be there, but the highlight of the trip came when Des Walker scored his first goal for Forest after playing over 300 games for the club. I'm not sure who benefited from the trip, but someone did.

We beat Millwall in the league and were then back in cup action against Spurs in the quarter-finals of the League Cup. We came out flying at the City Ground and went 2–0 up. They pulled one back and, at 2–1, they were never out of it and they equalised. The replay at White Hart Lane started badly for us when Nayim scored in the first five minutes and we got battered for about the next twenty. We managed to hold out and then, like many of Brian Clough's teams, we were able to break away and score away from home. Gary Crosby set me up and I got in ahead of my old landlord Mitchell Thomas to level things. Nigel Jemson scored a great solo goal for us before Paul Walsh popped up to make it 2–2. Late on I broke into the box and struck a left-foot shot into the corner and we won 3–2; it was another of my favourite goals and again I'd scored twice against a former team.

In the dressing room Brian Clough was in buoyant mood. He called over to Nigel Jemson, "Son, when you scored that goal you should have come and said 'thanks' to me for keeping you in the team. Don't go running to the people who were slagging you off a few weeks ago." The TV crew was asking for someone to do an interview. Brian Laws and I both declined and Nigel Jemson was just about to go out for it when the gaffer stepped in. "I'll do your job for you," he declared before striding out into the corridor. We found out later that he'd used the interview to have a go at Terry Venables which ignited a feud between the two that was battled out through the pages of various national newspapers. Clough loved it if you turned down an interview request; if he heard you say "no" to a journalist you'd be sure to get a big, "Well done, son!" He loved to be the sole mouthpiece of the club.

With no game scheduled for the next ten days I went and booked into a health farm for a mini-break. When I reported back for training at Forest the gaffer asked if I wanted to play for the 'A' team at Chesterfield or in the reserves. "Neither," I replied. "I think the ten days' break has done me good." His response was harsher than I expected. "What a cunt you are," he snapped, then walked away. Clough wasn't particularly happy with me around this time, even though I was in a good run of form and scoring goals. I'd made the mistake of saying to a reporter that we weren't seeing so much of Brian Clough these days. After a game he said, "Harry, would you like to come and help me out at Derby on Tuesday night?" as he was going to watch a reserve game. Nigel Jemson was in the side that night and Cloughie decided he needed to knock the youngster down a peg or two. "Have you ever been punched, son?" asked the manager. "No," came the reply. "Well you have now," responded Clough as he landed one into the player's rib-cage.

We faced Coventry City in the League Cup semi-final, with the first leg played out in a driving rainstorm at the City Ground. Nigel Clough, with a penalty, and Steve Livingstone for City had left the game delicately poised well into the second half. After the Coventry goal our recently signed Icelandic international Toddy Orlygsson, who had lost the ball in the build-up to the goal, was unceremoniously yanked off. My old sparring partner Brian Kilcline was in the Coventry side and he gave away a dangerous free-kick on the edge of his own box.

The Forest side of that era had two dead-ball specialists. Nigel Clough could add a bit of finesse to a free-kick while Stuart Pearce could provide wicked power with deadly accuracy. This particular free-kick was perfect for Stuart Pearce's left foot. As Coventry lined up their defensive wall, I attached myself to the end of it and as Pearce ran up to shoot I leant back into my marker and moved the end of their wall in a little bit. Pearce's shot flew by my head in the space where I'd been standing and whistled into the very top corner, just brushing the underside of the bar. That goal gained me a selection of letters from Coventry fans calling me a cheat but it was something I'd done against Crystal Palace earlier that season after I'd seen Pele do something similar on TV during the 1970 World Cup. It was a case of lean in or get out of the way. Later in the season when we sent Sheffield Wednesday down I jumped up and the shot went under me along the floor and in. I'd just try and get in the line of sight of the goalie. The goal proved decisive because in the away leg it was a backs-to-the-wall job with two solid banks of four and we drew 0–0 in a great defensive display.

Not many teams get to consecutive Wembley finals and Brian Clough wanted photos after the game; he was elated to be back at Wembley again. We had the photos and got changed. As Stuart Pearce headed for the players' lounge the boss called over to him and said that he wanted everybody in for training at ten the following morning. We couldn't believe it – we'd just qualified for Wembley and were going for a party at Steve Sutton's house. The party went ahead as planned and the next morning Stuart Pearce arrived at training, clearly the worse for wear. Clough took great pleasure in having a go at his captain and ordered us to run six sides of the pitch. Then he called us over and said training was over. He sent us home early and gave us all two days off. He was nothing if not unpredictable. Later that week, at a team meeting, he pulled out a letter from the Coventry manager John Sillett which read in part, "Ask Hodgey who picks the team?" He clearly still had my interview about not seeing him so often planted in his mind and he didn't miss the chance to remind me who the boss was.

Never a Dull Moment –
Cloughie on the Road

One year we played at Newcastle and had a stay in a hotel overnight. Cloughie loved going back to the north-east and he was in his element in the hotel restaurant that night. Clough literally took over the dining room and had the pianist play all his favourite old Frank Sinatra songs while he sang along. Clough did all this while the hotel's general public guests were sitting down and having their dinner! The manager didn't care that everyone was having to listen to his singing whether they wanted to or not. I had a pint of lager in front of me which I didn't want to finish as I'd already had a couple and this was the night before a game and Cloughie actually sent someone to fetch me back from my room to finish drinking it. I did, and we had a great night. The following day we drew 1–1. Just being around Clough was an education in football, manners and life in general. After a game at Huddersfield he knew I was a big cricket fan and he introduced me to Geoff Boycott. "Harry, come and say hello to Mr Boycott."

Some of Cloughie's quotes have passed into the stuff of legend and I was there when many of the classics were rolled out. Some of his quips were used over and over until it had sunk into the players. Playing football the "correct" way was at the centre of his teachings. The game should be played simply and on the floor, no long-ball tactics at Forest. Each player had different attributes and they should stick to doing what they were able to. He'd make a big show of walking into the middle of the dressing room, putting a towel on the floor and then placing a ball on the towel.

"Get the ball. They can't score without it."

"Treat the ball like your girlfriend. Look after it, caress it."

To centre-halves, he'd say, "Son, do what you're good at. Head it and kick it." To midfielders it was, "Tackle and pass it to someone who can play." He was also quick to turn on someone if they weren't doing what he expected of them. One day he lost patience with centre-half Paul Hart and snapped, "You took Leeds down, but you're not taking me down! You jump like a seagull with lead balloons on!"

If we had a long trip we'd travel on the Friday afternoon. We'd have to report by 3 p.m. before setting off at six. Clough would tell us to have a five-a-side and he'd watch us closely. Often if someone did something good he'd immediately call a halt to the game. "That's it! We'll end it on that note!" he'd call out before telling us to go and get changed again. I can remember several occasions when he stopped the game like that when we'd been playing for less than a minute!

Usually he'd pin up the team sheet on a Friday. "There you go lads, see you tomorrow at two o'clock," and he'd be gone. Everyone would let him get out of view then sprint over to see what the team was. Sometimes he'd put the Saturday team sheet up on the preceding Monday morning to show that he had confidence in the players. It was all mind games and this applied to referees. We would never harass a referee over a decision. If we fouled anyone he told us to pick the player up and say sorry. "We're nothing if we're not honest and genuine. We don't give referees any trouble," he'd say. He wouldn't criticise them after games or in the press and I'm sure it was to keep the men-in-black on our side. "If you're going to get booked make sure it's for kicking someone on the halfway line, not for dissent!"

I think he badly missed playing. When a linesman came into the dressing room before the game to inspect the boots and studs, he'd say, "If you can get me a game today I'll give you a £100." He was clearly frustrated to have had his career finished early by injury.

At Everton we stayed in Haydock and he took us all on a Saturday morning stroll. He led us to a house and up the front garden where he knocked on the door to get Duncan McKenzie out of bed to say hello. As the whole bus load of us walked up the driveway, Clough said, "If I've got the wrong house we're all in the shit!"

Clough rarely let anyone in the dressing room, but at Watford Elton John put his head round the door. "Come on in yer big fat puff," bellowed Clough. "Now then, when are you playing near me." He talked to Elton, and by the end of the conversation the singer thought Clough was doing him a favour by organising free tickets for all of the Forest team and staff! Another time he called Watford manager Graham Taylor at 1 a.m. and got him out of bed to ask about him getting some tickets to a gig.

He was keen that players took care of their families and if we were on a trip he'd always tell me to, "Get a photo, it's there for ever." He could use other sports to get his point across: "Keep your head still when striking the ball. Look at golfers and cricketers."

When it came to contract talks you just had to hope he was in a good mood. You had to knock on his door before entering, even if it was open and he was sitting right in front of you. Then you had to wait to be asked to sit down. I made the mistake once and he snapped, "Son, did I say you could sit down?" When the club's money was at stake he'd use all the mind games and tricks that he could to beat you down. Talks were purely conducted on his terms. He asked me how much I thought I was worth, so I told him. His reply was straight to the point: "You think you're worth that? Go on, fuck off out of my office!" Another time he called out to the club secretary, Ken Smales. "Ken, can you come in here. Harry thinks he's worth this much a week, plus a signing-on bonus! Now I know he's a good midfield player but blow me, even me captain doesn't get that!" Ken just smiled but kept quiet. Whatever you ended up getting Clough turned the tables to make sure you felt lucky to get it. On the pitch he made sure you were grateful to him too, whether it was for signing you in the first place or picking you for his team, and it was his team, it was his club. "Fuck them out there. When you score a goal go and thank the colleague who made it. Then come and thank me 'cos I pick the team!" And we did. A lot of players had a lot to thank Brian Clough for.

Fun and Games

Forest's league form had improved with our cup run and we went ten games undefeated. A new face in the squad was David Currie, a striker who had come in from Barnsley. The fee had been £800,000, which was a lot of money for a player in 1990. Like John Sheridan and Gary Megson before him, I did wonder why we'd signed Currie, because from the very start the manager was on to him. Before a game at Derby, Cloughie said to him, in front of the whole dressing room, "I must have been daft to sign you. How much did I pay for you?" The poor lad just looked embarrassed – he didn't know what to say. Later Clough asked him, "Have you bought a house in the area yet?"

"I'm still looking."

"Son, I wouldn't fucking bother."

It was funny, but David was just a shy lad who couldn't answer back. He looked like a man who just wanted to disappear from the dressing room. He only started four games before being shipped out again.

One of Brian Clough's favourite players was right-winger Gary Crosby. The slight-framed player was nicknamed "Meat Fly" by the fans and "Bing" by the players. We hosted Manchester City in March and won with one of the most unusual goals I've ever been involved in. Before the game Cloughie welcomed Howard Kendall to the ground. Kendall had recently been appointed as City's manager and Clough called out in the corridor, "Howard, how are you? Welcome back to the madhouse!" An hour later it *was* a madhouse. We were attacking the Bridgford End on a cold spring day and City's keeper, Andy Dibble, had collected the ball in his area. As normal, I'd run in looking for a rebound and then turned and started running back towards the halfway line. I hadn't seen Gary Crosby also run in, he'd stayed back to lurk just behind Dibble. I heard a roar and I just saw the ball in the net and Peter Reid, Gary Megson and Andy Dibble going berserk at the referee. No one on our side really seemed to know what had happened. Howard Kendall was out and confusion reigned. Only on TV later on did we realise what had occurred. Dibble thought everyone had left the area and was standing with the ball balanced on his outstretched hand. Crosby popped out from behind his back, nodded the ball off the bewildered goalkeeper's hand and rolled it into the empty net. It was unprecedented and I don't think the referee really knew what to do. In the end he just gave the goal and we won 1–0. At the end Cloughie asked, "Did you head the ball out of his hands, son?"

"Yes, boss," Crosby replied.

"Well done, son!" Clough cackled. He absolutely loved it; he thought it was hilarious.

One of just many, many memorable Brian Clough episodes came at Arsenal. Forest, despite struggling against Arsenal's set-pieces at the City Ground, seemed to have a great record against Arsenal at Highbury during the 1980s, crowned with an FA Cup quarter-final win in London in 1988. Highbury was a ground that smelt of football, and the changing rooms had a wonderful marble, heated floor. Arsenal manager George Graham was a relatively well-spoken, proud man and didn't like getting his nose put out of joint by the decidedly working-class Brian Clough. Arsenal had been off the pace a little bit for a few years but Graham had them winning trophies again.

Forest arrived at Highbury and the Arsenal manager, as usual, was looking immaculate before the game. Sharp suit, hair slicked down, strolling around like he owned the place, which he almost did. "Look at him, not a hair out of place," spat Clough to the Forest subs as the game started. "He thinks he's fucking Robert Redford!" We started the game well and were passing it around as usual. Arsenal's two centre-halves at the time were Tony Adams and Steve Bould. They would take it in turns to kick you and Nigel Clough, as our centre-forward, took most of the abuse. During the game that evening, Nigel Clough caught Tony Adams with a late tackle. It wasn't much revenge considering that Adams had been kicking Clough for years. As the big centre-half hit the deck, the Arsenal bench was up in arms. Graham had his arms out wide, appealing to the referee, tie flapping in the breeze. The two caged dugouts at Highbury were very close together and Graham approached the Forest bench, finger-wagging. "Hey Brian, that was fucking out of order!" he yelled. Clough was also out of his seat and seemed to agree. In a slow voice he retorted, "George, George, you are right. Our Nige was out of order. I'm sorry. Leave it to me, George." Clough sat down, but thirty seconds later he jumped up and approached the touchline, cupped a hand to the side of his mouth and shouted, "Hey Nige, do him again!" As Clough turned back to the bench the Arsenal subs, especially Paul Merson, were trying not to wet themselves with laughter as their manager's face grew redder. Clough had the final word as he took his seat. "I'm only trying to sell him to you!" he added to Graham.

As Wembley loomed ever closer our league form took a dip. We lost 3–1 at home to Spurs and the manager had an emergency meeting with his coaches about why things were going wrong. We were thumped 4–0 at Everton, and he snapped, "Lads, you'll get me the bloody sack!" He wasn't joking: we lost seven and drew two of nine games. At Anfield, Clough, a Labour supporter all his life, wouldn't let Neil Kinnock in the dressing room on the anniversary of Hillsborough. We found ourselves 2–0 down inside fifteen minutes but battled back for a 2–2 draw.

Second Division Oldham Athletic, managed by Joe Royle, had reached the League Cup final and, despite our poor run of form, and despite their decent side, we were huge favourites. Paul Warhurst, Earl Barrett, Andy Ritchie and Denis Irwin were all too good for the Second Division. They had two rats, Nicky Henry and Mike Milligan in the middle. Both were renowned for putting a foot in and working hard, so I knew it wouldn't be an easy game.

At breakfast on the day of the final I heard Brian Clough telling Liam O'Kane to make sure all the players were drinking plenty of water, or lager if they wanted it. We went for a walk around the ground of the hotel and he called us together for a little pep-talk. "I'm sick of hearing about Oldham," he said. "We're going to piss on them." That was about the extent of the tactical analysis. At the ground the team talk consisted of "Good luck." It was a red-hot day and we were really made to work hard for our 1–0 win. It wasn't a great game to watch, but during the lap of honour the crowd noise was superb and I made the most of it. Joe Royle came over and said, "Well done, Hodgey, you played well." Back in the dressing room the referee came in to present the match ball to the winning captain, as is tradition. The gaffer stepped in and claimed it for himself, though: "I'm having that. He's already got one!"

I was one of the last players in the Wembley bath and Cloughie came in. "Hard game, football," he said.

"It's even harder in that heat," I replied.

"They don't know how hard it is to win a trophy." And with that he slumped into the bath, looking totally drained.

There was an air of anti-climax on the bus home. Whereas the first year we'd had beer on the bus and lots of photos being taken, this time was deadpan with no real joy. The fans were happy; after all, we'd just retained a trophy at Wembley, but for the players it was more a case of "job done" and we headed back to Nottingham just like after a league game.

We had two league games left to play, at home to Manchester United and away to Sheffield Wednesday. The United game was midweek after the cup final and the City Ground was in jubilant party mode. We came out and hammered them – it was 4–0 before the half-hour. Before kick-off the gaffer had taken Gary Crosby and Nigel Jemson to one side and when we came in at half-time he said that they hadn't done what he'd asked them to and that they would have to sort it out in the second half. I thought to myself that it was obvious: he wanted them to kick Neil Webb. He also really wanted us to go for them in the second half because we wanted to win 6–0 or 7–0. In the second half, Bing caught Webby and Garry Parker just turned to me and smiled. It was just what he'd asked me to do when Viv Anderson came back.

Our final game was more important for Wednesday, Derby and Luton – all of whom were battling to avoid the final relegation place. We went to Hillsborough with the attitude of "We do it right, we don't care what's happening elsewhere." We played the game in a thoroughly professional manner and won 3–0 while they went down on a goal difference of two.

Personally I'd had the best season of my career and grabbed fourteen goals, the club's top scorer that year, while making it to the top six finalists for the PFA Player of the Year award. It was the perfect build-up for the Italia 90 World Cup and I couldn't wait.

The Many Sides of
Brian Clough

Brian Clough was a walking contradiction and we all knew
that if he said something one day he might do the exact
opposite the next. Day to day, his moods could swing from
good to bad without warning and each morning I could tell
within the first five seconds whether he was in a good or bad
one. A good one would see him happily strolling in, singing
a favourite song and swinging his walking stick about; a bad
one would see him call into the treatment room to berate the
"lame and lazy" for being injured, something that he could
never accept – that's when we knew to run for cover! Sometimes he'd burst into the treatment room and bellow, "Right,
physio, get this lot out of here and lock the door. I'm sick of
seeing their ugly faces in here when their colleagues are
breaking their necks trying to get me three points at the
weekend! Go on! Fuck off out of here!" Then, on his good days
he was loyal and would give you great praise, which instilled
a real belief that anything was possible.

Despite the public bluster, I think he was sensitive and
sentimental. He'd mention his wife Barbara and say, "Blow
me, did I get lucky when I met Barbara." He often sang the
songs from his youth and asked if we knew this one or that
one, which we rarely did. Usually it was something by the Ink
Spots or Frank Sinatra. If he was in an especially good mood
he'd be clicking his fingers and singing "Nice and Easy" or
"New York, New York". Criticism in the press did hurt him,

and his elephant-like memory made sure that pressmen would get their come-uppance when he got the chance later on.

I was lucky because Clough had come to Forest at the right time in my fledgling career and it seemed obvious to let this man take control of my future. He really did have the Midas touch – just look at the number of international players he created. He knew my character inside-out and used that knowledge to continually bring out my best performances. I could never be sure if he really liked me or not, as he often called me "the little shit", but I was enlightened by Geoff Boycot who told me that that was one of Cloughie's terms of endearment and he knew for a fact that I was one of his favourites. He was certainly *my* favourite manager, no contest really, and I'm glad I was one of his favourites. But that still didn't excuse me from plenty of rollickings along the way!

I think if you were honest and genuine with Brian Clough he would have time for you and would give you his backing. He must have felt that I was a good player and character and knew that my heart was with the club. I'm sure that he was secretly delighted when I made an impact in the first team because it was like he'd found a new player for nothing. I was lucky that my natural playing style fitted in with the way he wanted to play the game. The game had to be played on the floor because it looked better on the eye and required more skill to do well. He wanted to entertain but knew that winning came first. "I'd shoot my own granny for three points!" he'd tell us. His sides played with width and could be exposed by leaving space, but risks were taken and, because of this, he always wanted a strong goalkeeper and back four. Over the years I watched and played in numerous Clough teams which were kept in a game by some last ditch defending and they broke away on the counter-attack and won 1–0.

In my second spell at Forest I definitely noticed that he'd

calmed down and would reminisce about his playing days in the north-east and the people who'd been part of his incredible journey. He would sit at a hotel bar, or on the team bus, and regale us with stories of his childhood, football and cricket, politics, you name it he could talk about it. His own goal-scoring exploits were sometimes mentioned, or, being a Labour supporter, the likes of Roy Hattersley might be around, and sometimes he'd disappear over to Trent Bridge to watch an hour of the cricket. But it was his stories that held you and before you knew it you were hooked and listening intently to the great man's views; he could be spell-binding when in full flow. That's how I like to remember him.

World in Motion

After the disaster of Euro 88, the England squad was going through a period of change as we played the qualifiers for Italia 90. Going back to Forest turned out to be vital in my securing an England place. On some trips we'd have five Forest players in the squad – Stuart Pearce, Neil Webb, Des Walker, Nigel Clough and myself – and all five deserved it. Few teams can provide England with five players in today's game.

I'd been in and out. I came on when David Platt made his debut against Italy, who had an excellent defence. I was marked by Bergomi and had a couple of runs at Franco Baresi. I backed him into the box and tried a couple of shimmies and step-overs but he was still there looking at me as if to say, "What have you got next?" There wasn't even a hint of panic, it was superb defending and we drew 0–0. I was a sub against Yugoslavia and then, in March, I was left out against Brazil. That was my first inkling that I wasn't in Bobby Robson's first XI for the World Cup, but I was back in on the left side against Czechoslovakia. My job was to work up and down, and if Gazza went walkabout, then I had to tuck in and cover for him. He scored that night and sealed his World Cup place. He had more flair than anyone else, was really strong, a damage merchant, and oozed confidence. We beat Denmark at Wembley and I set up a goal for Gary Lineker six yards out. Bobby praised me as one of the best players on the pitch. The only downer was a shock loss to Uruguay just before we flew out for the World Cup. It was England's first Wembley defeat for a long time and I think some of the players had an air of "don't get injured" because we flew out for the World Cup soon afterwards. At half-time Bobby Robson had said to me, "You don't look so perky tonight, little fella," which didn't exactly fill me with confidence for the second half, and at the end there was a row between Peter Shilton and the manager. Bobby thought he should have done better with one of the goals and a loud argument ensued. It showed the passion of the two over a friendly, a nothing game, really. Robson took the responsibility of being the national team manager very seriously, something that even some of the Fleet Street hacks couldn't seem to comprehend. I remember Steve Curry from *The Sun* on board a flight home after a disappointing away friendly as he said to Bobby, "Smile, it's only a game, you know!" The press had been giving the manager lots of flak and Bobby just looked at him and then went to sit down. The press just couldn't feel what he was feeling.

Out of the Uruguay squad, the four players who were not picked for Italy were told separately and they had gone before he announced the squad to the rest of us. The Arsenal boys David Rocastle, Alan Smith and Tony Adams were some of those who missed out along with Dave Beasant. The rest of us flew to Sardinia.

Paul John Gascoigne – A Legend

Gazza was a law unto himself when I met him on England duty. He would do things that no one else would dare, both on and off the pitch. When we played a game in Sweden I was walking up some stairs with Gazza and we passed the Swedish manager, Olle Nordin. I knew that Gazza had a joke-shop electric buzzer concealed in his hand, but the last person I thought he'd try it on with was the Swedish manager – but he did. He gave the Swede a real shock – he wasn't ready for it at all – and Gazza was in stitches. Nordin took it well but I thought, "You can't do that to a national team's manager!"

Before an important game for Gazza against Czechoslovakia, one which might have decided whether or not he went to the World Cup, he was so relaxed. He walked out on to the pitch behind me and when a TV camera was put in his face, he leaned into it and said, "Hello, Mam, put the kettle on!" He told me he was tired of travelling back and forth to Newcastle while he played for Spurs. In training he'd be flicking a ball around while we were being given instructions and Bobby Robson would snap every now and then.

Our final warm-up game was against Tunisia in Sardinia. I was hit in the face with the ball and felt dizzy at half-time. I told Bobby that I felt woozy, and he said, "Don't worry about your place. You'll lose it if you're not right in the second half." So I came off, thinking it was better to be safe and keep my place. Of course he then dropped me and I went from the starting XI to not being in the squad of sixteen at all. In the same match Gazza had a go at their bench. Bobby told him, "You can't do that when you're playing for England." I'm sure Gazza could grasp the gravity of playing international football but at times he just lost his head and he found it hard not to show his emotions.

When I faced Gazza in club football I had to be in his face, constantly annoying him, because if he felt confident and good about the game he would destroy you. He would often say to me early in the game, "Hodgey, be my friend today. Let's enjoy it." I wouldn't react; I just ignored his plea and kept my focus on what I had to do.

At the World Cup he called me "Chicken" because I ran around so much, and one day he decided to let everyone know. He somehow got into the hotel kitchen and found a dead chicken and got to work. When I and the rest of the players were walking across to the evening meal we were greeted by the dead bird, with my number 18 written on the back, perched above the dining table!

I ended up playing tennis with him in Sardinia for three-and-a-half hours until we were both shattered, but then he wanted to go out for another three or four sets. At eight-thirty in the morning he was out there again wanting to play, he just couldn't calm down. Before one game he managed to put twenty-six Wrigleys in his mouth. One night, before we played our first competitive game in Italy, we had a meal. It was Gazza's birthday and also Peter Beardsley's baby boy Drew's birthday. A cake was made and "Happy Birthday" sung, after which Gazza decided to give us a speech about his life story, off the cuff. He began, "Well, it started when I was about seven when me dad bought me a ball." He went on about trials at Middlesbrough and Ipswich, "I signed an apprenticeship at Newcastle on £1,000 a week. At eighteen I made my debut, I scored a hat-trick, was put on £2,000 a week, signed as a pro, offered £3,000 a week, but wouldn't take a pay cut for anyone. At twenty I was wanted by every club in the country, I bought my own television company, and now here I am, a legend." He then sat down to great applause.

I made Steve part of our squad for Mexico in 1986 and he really did an excellent job for me. Four years later he was a natural choice for my midfield in Italy and it was a huge blow when he was injured. We were left one short in the squad and Steve was forced to watch the tournament from the sidelines, which was very hard on him. He thoroughly deserved his call-up in 1990 and was an excellent team member. He always gave 100 per cent for his country and was a popular member of the squad.

Sir Bobby Robson
May 2009

No More Sleeps

Unfortunately I never got to kick a ball during the Italia 90 World Cup but I did keep a daily diary and at times I felt like an embedded journalist. Early on, Bobby Robson told us he'd be leaving the England job after the World Cup. In the press, just before the tournament, he was getting some flak and the timing was terrible. The news of his coming departure wasn't a problem for the players. He called us in and said, "Ignore the press. I want to go out as a World Cup winner." He told us that anyone causing trouble would be sent home, but one night some of the lads went out in taxis to a local bar and they were noisy when they came back. Bryan Robson hurt his toe that night and had to miss the tournament. Still, a few players would pop down to the local Forte Village, which was a party area where the fans and journalists went for a drink as well. Some of the lads needed to chill out and relax that way, but were generally careful that it didn't go too far. Bobby Robson was paranoid about the "news press" that would follow us around and would often threaten to send anyone home who brought any negative focus onto the squad.

It was a great summer for English football, though it ended in heartbreak. I remember going to the games on the bus and everyone was singing "World in Motion". Looking back, the team spirit was incredible. I saw the manager struggling to get his boots on at training – he was going around muttering to himself before finding out that Gazza had stuffed the toes with paper. In the end I was happy just to be around the players and at the centre of the tournament, and right from the moment he confirmed I was in the squad it was a big relief. I started my England diary the next day.

Thursday 24th May 1990
Meet at Luton, Chilton Hotel. Gaffer has a quarter-of-an-hour chat about the morning newspapers which have reported that he had handed in his resignation. He told the players exactly what had happened and the timing of it all. He'd obviously been through a horrendous day and he knew it. Gaffer said, "Shilton had a bad day yesterday. I've had a bad day today, and tomorrow it'll be Gascoigne's turn," referring to an alleged punch-up in a bar in Newcastle.

Friday 25th May 1990
Flew from Luton; the aircraft was named after Sir Stanley Matthews, who was there to christen the plane. Press everywhere. On the flight Gazza has a chat with me about his loneliness in London. He still wants to leave. He also made the front pages of nearly every newspaper for his pub brawl, which he feels was a set up. He also knocks two glasses of champagne over, one of which drenches his suit trousers. Then he put on stewardess's hat and coat and went down the plane asking the players and their wives if they were all right for food and drinks. The papers had a right go at the gaffer, saying that what he had done was a disgrace but I couldn't see what he had done wrong. Arrived at the hotel – it's right on the beach – very secluded, just the job. Gazza started ordering "pina coladas" but as they were arriving for myself, Trevor Steven and Gazza, we realised that the gaffer was sat at a table right behind us. The pina coladas were a yellow colour, and quick as a flash Gazza shouted to the waiter "Three banana milkshakes over here!" As he did, he winked

at the waiter. Straight away the waiter winked back, knowing the score, and everything was fine. Played some tennis and at night went for a meal.

Saturday 26th May 1990
Did an interview for *Today* with Rob Sheppard. More sunshine. The gaffer has a press conference for the Sunday papers.

Sunday 27th May 1990
Trained in the morning, the training ground is lush in grass. Don Howe did a half-hour warm-up, very important but also very boring. Had a nine-a-side across the pitch. Mark Wright has a knock on his thigh. It's not 100 per cent but he says he's OK. This afternoon we went to see Cagliari play at home, a 40,000 capacity gate. There was great colour – red flags everywhere, superb atmosphere. Sat next to Trevor Brooking but Gazza got bored with the game and ended up trying to slap big round stickers on people's backs. Before the game Bobby Robson, Bryan Robson, Peter Beardsley, Paul Gascoigne, Trevor Steven and myself are introduced to the crowd on the pitch and we have a picture with the team. The crowd are fanatical but the game is a dull 1–1 draw, with goals coming in the opening seven minutes. After dinner we played floodlit tennis until eleven o'clock. An enjoyable day.

Monday 28th May 1990
Training – the gaffer says he's resting me from the team to play Cagliari tomorrow. The team only consists of two players who started against Uruguay – Paul Parker and Des Walker. The gaffer feels I looked a bit jaded in training on Sunday. I wasn't jaded, but in the nine-a-side game I was trying to conserve some energy. It was also the first time we had trained for six days and it was pretty hot, so there was good reason

not to go galloping up and down the pitch. Enjoyed training – crossing and shooting at the end with Mike Kelly. Gaffer had a chat with us before training about being careful not to do too much so that we'd be in peak condition for the games. Terry Butcher wasn't feeling too good. After dinner watched *Bloodsports*, a film about martial arts.

Tuesday 29th May 1990
Up at six o'clock because of mosquitoes. On the beach at 8.15 and had four hours of solid rays. A freelance photographer was spotted in some nearby rocks by Mike Kelly's wife. Five officials went and got him. He had a big zoom lens camera. Police came and took him away. The team beat Cagliari 6–0. Peter Beardsley really put himself about. McMahon got involved. Good result though. At night played a cracking game of tennis with Gazza. Chris Waddle arrives tomorrow.

Wednesday 30th May 1990
Went in a car at nine o'clock to do some weights. It's a long way to go for twenty minutes of weights but I feel that I need to do some. At night everybody went into town. All had an hour and a half walking round the city centre shops. Then went for a meal at a beach fish restaurant.

Thursday 31st May 1990
Trained in the morning – some of Don Howe's methods confuse me. Worked on a 3–5–2 formation, but this is new to the players, even though we all agree that we need to try something different and be more flexible. Training is quite relaxed still. I had a word with the gaffer about Pearcey flying past me. Spoke with Chris Waddle about football and playing abroad then watched two videos. At night had a meal and we were joined by Simply Red singer Mick Hucknall. He stayed

all night and we arranged to have a sing song at our new hotel on Saturday.

Friday 1st June 1990

On the way to the airport before flying to Tunisia a policeman fell off his bike. Got to our hotel, ate, gaffer named the teams – I'm playing. Had two hours kip. Got to ground; the pitch was very bobbly and it's very, very warm. Then went on to an FA reception. We're doing too much travelling around. Webby says he doesn't think the gaffer thinks he's fit. On the TV back at the hotel Eurosport showed highlights of England in Mexico '86.

Saturday 2nd June 1990

Up early for breakfast. Meeting at 12. There are a few England supporters in the hotel reception. Lots of people here seem to love walking as a hobby. The locals all just walk around aimlessly or sit all day watching the world go by. On the way to the ground we approached the stadium, only to be turned around by a motorbike policeman, who in turn is stopped by a security man. They end up having a big argument on the street while we curl up, sitting on a really hot coach like lemons. It's laughable. Eventually we turn round again and go to the stadium. Before the game the team had to change in adjacent rooms, the teams in one, the subs in another. This caused a bit of friction, the subs saying "Do we have to knock on the door to come in the room?"

I was pleased the way the first half went against Tunisia. I felt I'd done well. Just before half-time I got a bang on the head from a clearance. Began to feel a bit dizzy. Told the doc and gaffer at half-time. At the time I couldn't remember being hit on the temple. I thought the heat was the problem. So the gaffer said to me to give him a shout if I was still struggling.

As he passed me going to the dugout he said "Don't worry about your place. You'll lose your place if you're not right and you let us down." Anyway, I began to come round but after an hour without me signalling to bench he took me and Terry Butcher off. Terry took his shirt off; he looked angry. After the game the gaffer told him he was playing for England and shouldn't have done it. Steve Bull came on and scored an equaliser near the end to save the blushes. In all honesty we ought to have won 4–1, but we had been close to losing. Gaffer said, "We haven't played badly, have we?" We certainly hadn't but we hadn't played particularly well. On the final whistle the gaffer came to me and asked how I was. In the dressing room he had a go at Paul Gascoigne, because when we had equalised he had gone to their bench and given them some stick. He seemed to want to get involved and make a fool of himself. I think he was relieved because he had cost the goal in the first half. Paul said sorry. I'm the lightest in the squad. On the way back Webby said to me, "Why am I here?"

Sunday 3rd June 1990

In the morning the team that played had a half-hour chat about the way things were going and any grievances. Waddle, Shilton, Bryan Robson, Barnes and Lineker all had their say. The gaffer could see that the players weren't totally happy. He said, "We've got some work to do then". Spent the afternoon by the pool, then on to the golf range with Chris Waddle.

Monday 4th June 1990

Trained in the morning, a lot of shooting and ball work – my shooting was pretty poor. Overheard the gaffer – he's annoyed about the *Sunday Mirror*. Paul Gascoigne to Bob Harris – who he dislikes – "Bob, you're nothing but a first class wanker. I'd love to knock your head off." Saw the *Sunday Mirror* – there's a piece after the Tunisia game and we hear there is a bit of trouble back home to do with Terry Butcher's head-butt. Gaffer says at a meeting, "Would the Dutch reprimand Koeman for pulling someone back against Yugoslavia? I don't think so."

Tuesday 5th June 1990
This morning I did some tests with John Barnes along with Pearcey and Des. Bobby Robson watched us do them. I came on at half-time against a local Italian team – the score was 5–0, the final score 11–1. I missed a great chance with a header at the far post. I was annoyed. It was a poor game – no contest. Peter Beardsley scored three, Webb three and Bull two. I've seen most of the morning papers. They want Butcher and myself out for the Ireland game. I've been blamed along with Butcher even though I thought I'd done quite well in the first half against Tunisia and was certainly no worse than anyone else. The press, I think, will push for Peter Beardsley's introduction up front, John Barnes, on the wing and me out. We'll have to wait and see what the gaffer decides. On the way to dinner, met Nigel Kennedy and his girlfriend. He was very friendly, even though I had left Villa under a cloud. He's here until England are knocked out. Bob Harris asked if I'd taken my stick "personally". I said no but I didn't think I had played any better or worse than anyone else.

Wednesday 6th June 1990
At training the lads took the piss out of me – imitating a chicken – very funny. We had a downpour of rain. Papers saying I will be out. Did a recording for *Top of the Pops*, as the record is number one. Gazza replied, "That question hasn't anything to do with the record," when asked about the training. At night watched a tape of Northern Ireland against Eire, our first opponents. At one point the gaffer said, "Look

at the goalie. He's not interested in giving the ball to the full-backs and they're not interested in having it." But he was talking about Northern Ireland.

Thursday 7th June 1990
Trained in the morning, gaffer put bits on the TV for the game. I'm the only one not playing from Tunisia. Disappointed but I'm not surprised. The press have been dying to get Peter Beardsley in and I've been made the scapegoat because the gaffer can hardly leave out John Barnes. The gaffer just talks about basic things. We haven't really got a system of play, we're just relying on people's individual flair and ability. Once again he's picked the best players, maybe not the best team. He's picked eight of the eleven who got beat by the Republic last time. Saw Koo Stark at the hotel; she came to do a piece for a TV programme.

Friday 8th June 1990
We had an emergency meeting at ten o'clock. Some of the lads had gone outside the hotel site last night and had quite a few drinks. This was against what had been said by the gaffer. The lads had got in at about one-thirty, and they had come into the hotel pretty loudly. All I heard, from my bed, was Bryan Robson attempting to overturn a bed. The bottom end of the bed had come through and landed on his big toe. He thought he had broken it. Not so. But there was a lot of blood around and his nail had to be taken off. He's now got a fight on to be fit for the first game. At the meeting the gaffer said that anyone causing any more trouble would be sent home. He emphasised about dedication to the cause and was clearly angry. His main concern is because he is scared of the press finding out, which I'm sure they will. He asked the players concerned to go and see him, because he didn't know

who was involved, only Bryan Robson because of his injury. He also threatened fines. Sunbathed all day, it's been very hot. Watched Cameroon beat Argentina 1–0, two sent off, proves that the African nations are fast improving. Gazza cut his foot on the diving board.

Saturday 9th June 1990
There have been fourteen arrests overnight in Cagliari. Watched a preview of the World Cup from BBC1 in the video room. Jack Charlton said he wouldn't put Paul Gascoigne in his Irish midfield. Went to meet the mayor. He gave a speech along with Millichip. On the way down the stairs we had a photo at the bottom of the stairs. Bobby Robson was asked to get to the front of the photo. He was going to, until he saw one of the hostesses stood at the front. Straight away he realised what the photo might lead to and he declined to go to the front. Sad. Went on to the ground. First we had to wait an hour and a half until all the players had been given their accreditations. We had to have a photo. In between waiting we watched the USSR v Romania and Colombia v UAE on video. We then trained for the allotted hour on the pitch. The grass is far too long, but it is being cut, hopefully. It's not too bad, the weather. I asked Bryan Robson at dinner how his foot was. He said that it was red raw, but he was going to tell the doctor to put jabs into it to numb the pain. I think he'll play. If not, McMahon will. Italy won their opening game 1–0.

Sunday 10th June 1990
Gaffer announced the team – it is as I thought – Peter Beardsley is back in, for me, the only change from Tunisia. Disappointed, but not unexpected. The team spent the morning doing set-pieces and decided to attempt to catch the Irish offside on free-kicks from deep by pushing up together on the call of "Penalty

Box". Had dinner, then had an hour-and-a-half team meeting, told us all about the Irish, told us too much about them. Also told us about the FIFA fines for bookings and sendings off. They are ridiculous and even in the first five games there have been three sent off and loads of bookings. The fines won't change players' attitudes and commitment – winning is the most important thing. I'm sure the FA will have to pay the fines eventually because people are getting booked for absolutely nothing. Gaffer not announcing subs until tomorrow.

Monday 11th June 1990

Bryan Robson declared himself fit at morning training although he's bound to have a lot of pain whenever he strikes the ball with his right foot. I'm not even sub, can't understand why I've been totally ignored, I'm a little angry more than disappointed. We were hanging on at 1–0 but Bobby took Peter Beardsley off, which I thought was a mistake. Gary Lineker hardly got a kick and we had nothing up front, especially as Gary was struggling with his stomach. Afterwards the lads were down, but at least we have a point. The gaffer said that they only had one shot on goal, but at this level it's all some teams need. Peter Shilton pointed out that Pat Bonner didn't have to make a save and in the second half it was constant Irish pressure. We still have no system, we're relying on individual flair to create something for us. Waddle and Barnes were isolated and we don't look like a team. Most of the players I've spoken to agree that it was an error to take Peter Beardsley off.

Tuesday 12th June 1990

Trained in the morning but I trained badly, still annoyed about being left out completely. Gaffer hasn't said a word to me, but I remember what he said in Tunisia, "Don't worry about your place." Had four hours kip in the afternoon, very tired. Watched Holland v Egypt, Egypt could have won. Chatted with Chris Waddle in Pearcey's room, he wants to play a sweeper system and a diamond formation, we are too predictable and the wingers don't get a kick. Peter Beardsley is also unhappy about how we are playing and something will have to be said because so many players are unhappy. The older boys know this is their last chance.

Wednesday 13th June 1990
Today was an open training session with loads of supporters in. They were quite loud. Some booed Steve McMahon for his mistake against Ireland. The training was designed to entertain the crowd – it shouldn't be like that. Nigel Kennedy entertained us while we ate dinner tonight.

Thursday 14th June 1990
The gaffer came to our breakfast table and said the *Sun* and *Mirror* had us on the front pages with headlines about players and hostesses at a disco. It's absolute garbage. Typical English press. Bryan Robson's wife has been quizzed at her home by pressmen, it's disgraceful, but probably something to do with the fact that the press think the players haven't cooperated with them. We had a meeting after dinner about the Irish game. Peter Beardsley owned up to playing poorly and was honest enough to say that he felt that against Ireland it might have been better to play Steve Bull instead of himself.

Friday 15th June 1990
Terry Butcher is the only concern for the gaffer. He asked Paul Parker about playing right-back. Dave Beasant arrived to replace David Seaman, who has broken his thumb.

Saturday 16th June 1990

I hadn't seen Hans van Breukelen for years and he had a big smile for me before the game on the pitch, he asked about Cloughie. The new system worked well and we looked like a different team. We played well and were happy enough with a point. I wasn't even a sub and with the team responding well to the system I think my chances of playing in this tournament are gone. We linked up better and created some good chances. The gaffer said, "Don't get carried away, we haven't qualified yet." Hans van B told me after the game that he was keen to return to England, maybe back to Forest.

Sunday 17th June 1990

There's a new optimism about the place, but it has to be confirmed when we play Egypt, they drew 0–0 with Ireland tonight.

Monday 18th June 1990

Trained again but tweaked my hamstring. It's OK. Bryan Robson is out of the game so I might get a chance, but doubt it. Platty is in, according to *The Mirror*.

Tuesday 19th June 1990

Hamstring didn't feel right in training. I'm going to rest it for three or four days to get it right – I need to be totally fit. Platty seems certain to start – the gaffer was really encouraging him in training today. Rumours spreading about abandoning the sweeper system. I cant believe it, after such a good performance. I think that if he does change it and we don't play well, he'll get slaughtered. His point is that he's picking a team to win a particular football match, but I'm sure the XI that drew against Holland would get at least a point against Egypt.

Wednesday 20th June 1990

When gaffer got on the bus for training he was two minutes late and all the players clapped. He didn't smile at all, in fact he looked quite annoyed. He's gone back to the flat back four but I can't agree with that. There's a definite difference of opinion between the gaffer and Don Howe. The gaffer wants 4–4–2 but Howe likes the sweeper system. The gaffer said that his formation had played well against Italy and Yugoslavia. Don said, "You can't live in the past, Bob." Don wants more flexibility, at least he wants us to be less predictable and to ask them some questions. At dinner Terry Butcher, Chris Waddle and Gary Stevens dressed up in FA blazers, jock straps and dark glasses and they were sitting at a table surrounded by wine bottles filled with water when the gaffer came in. His face was a picture. He looked so angry for about three seconds then realised it was a bit of fun. At the end of the meal the lads took off their blazers, casually revealing their jock straps and bare legs, then they shook hands with the waiters and walked out. Superb.

Thursday 21st June 1990

At the pre-match meal Bobby asked me about my hamstring and said that if we proceed he still has plans for me. I don't know whether to take his words with a pinch of salt after the Tunisia quote. The pre-match team talk was, as usual, quite long. The gaffer has picked his side on the basis that they play one up front like Holland, but on both occasions they've played two up front. Before the kick-off Bobby tried to fire the team up: "It's just like the Poland game in Mexico. We were there, weren't we, Hodgey, son?" He obviously holds that up as one of his most important games. We didn't do badly in the first half but the same problems surface in that the two wide-men are marked out of it too easily. Mark Wright's header in the second half calms the nerves and we win. In the team meeting after the game Dr Crane fell asleep as Bobby was talking. We've drawn Belgium and if we beat them it is Colombia or Cameroon in the quarter-finals. We couldn't have asked for anything more.

Friday 22nd June 1990

I read in the newspapers that Forest have agreed a fee for me with Real Sociedad. I don't fancy moving abroad at the moment. I got a phone call in my room from Louis Arcanarda, the Real Sociedad manager, who said he was interested in signing me. I politely said, "No thanks." I was tempted, and if they had been a bigger club, one which I knew a bit more about, I might have given it some more consideration. It was still quite flattering and makes me think that a move to Europe might be on one day. Had a Race Night this evening. Peter Shilton and Gary Lineker were the bookies and they got stung because we knew the results of the video races before they started. Fred Street had seen the tapes already and put loads on a horse, a rank outsider. We all kept quiet but Gazza was going mad. The look on their faces was great; they turned to Fred, who just laughed. The chicken is hung over the light in the snooker room.

Saturday 23rd June 1990

My hamstring is OK but I've pulled my groin. Bryan Robson is flying home. He's had two nightmare World Cups.

Sunday 24th June 1990

Left early for Bologna today. The gaffer was already at the airport when we arrived; he'd seen Bryan Robson off. Peter Shilton is captain now – could he emulate Dino Zoff? It was a fifty-minute flight and it's even hotter in Bologna than it was in Cagliari. All I can hope for is to get fit as soon as possible and hope we qualify for the quarter-finals. If we beat Belgium I can see us getting to a semi-final against West Germany.

Monday 25th June 1990
Gaffer asked if I've got a chance for tomorrow night. I told him there was no chance of me being in contention.

Tuesday 26th June 1990
This morning we watched Belgium on video and they looked like a good side. We'll need to play well to beat them. It was a tough game and at first Belgium looked the better team. At halftime Gazza was distraught about his partnership with Steve McMahon. I had a word with him in the physio's room and said he just had to keep his mind on the game. McMahon was playing very deep and Gazza felt he was just chasing shadows on his own. Thirty seconds from time Platty scored the winner and the bench erupted onto the pitch. I've never seen anyone so happy as Gazza in the dressing room that night. He just couldn't stop running around the room singing "Platty, Platty, give us a goal!" It's Cameroon next – the semi-finals beckon.

Wednesday 27th June 1990
Groin is still sore. I want to play in the tournament but it's great to be around as the excitement builds. ITV's Jim Rosenthal was thrown in the pool by the lads. Went on a coach journey to see Mount Vesuvius. It was a bit precarious – few too many close cliff edges. Had a meeting about the press. The gaffer wants to help them a little more and we agreed to give them fifteen to twenty minutes after training.

Thursday 28th June 1990
A boring day. I had more treatment while the lads went training. Pearcey asked the gaffer if we could go and see

Pompeii, but he said no. Disappointing. Can't see why we can't go on a Thursday before a Sunday night kick-off. After dinner gaffer again asked me about my groin. I might try and train tomorrow night. I'll see how it feels in the morning.

Friday 29th June 1990
Groin feels much better so will train tonight. The goalie says he thought we had to create more chances. He is quite happy with the back four and he started off a long debate. Trained at night in the beautiful stadium, on my own. Don't think I'm going to be OK for a game. I've just about had enough: it's so frustrating and I'm the only one injured.

Saturday 30th June 1990
No training for me today, just more treatment and swimming. Platty is taking McMahon's place. I'd have kept McMahon in and used Platty from the bench in case we needed a goal.

Sunday 1st July 1990
I feel as fit as any time during the tournament; I could almost be ready for contention. About Cameroon, the gaffer said that "My scout [Howard Wilkinson] tells me we've been given a bye to the semi-final." It's never been a bye. He shouldn't be saying things like that! He also talked about how the players froze v Argentina four years ago. Terry Butcher was getting everyone revved up in the dressing room; the likes of Beardsley, Pearce and Walker prepared quietly. I went out early to get my usual seat at the end of the bench. The first half belonged to Cameroon: they were flexible, strong, quick and had good team play. Platty scored from a Pearce cross in our first meaningful attack. At half-time the gaffer could sense some danger and stressed that we had to nullify certain players. Shilton said, "A lot of us look lazy and lethargic. We've got to

raise it." The words didn't work though, because Gazza brought
Roger Milla down for a penalty and then they scored again.
Everything was going wrong, our shape and discipline had
gone completely. Shilton made another world-class save to
keep us in the tournament. We didn't look like scoring but
we got a penalty and went into extra time. By then I would
have gladly settled for penalties. I went to the pitch to give
Gary Lineker some water – the players really needed it – but
I got into an argument with the linesman and referee. When
Gary Lineker converted his second penalty I knew it was our
night, even though we'd been second best for most of the
game. The gaffer came in and all he could say was, "What a
game. What a game." Tonight we weren't the best team but
we got through on guts and bravery. Is it destiny? The Germans
will be the hardest test so far.

Monday 2nd July 1990
Left for Turin. At the team meeting Gary Lineker stood up
and offered even money that the gaffer would mention the
war. He did. We all looked round as he said it, it was a serious
speech about the biggest game of our careers. I just had to
look at the floor.

Tuesday 3rd July 1990
It's so disappointing that I'm not likely to get a kick during
this World Cup. I went to Mexico, not expecting to play, and
was involved in every game, and this time I did expect to
figure but didn't even get named as a sub. Fred Street seems
to think I might need an operation and if that's the case and
we lose tomorrow I'd rather fly home the following day instead
of going to Bari for the third/fourth place match. Italy have
gone out which is good as I'd rather play the Argies in the
final than the hosts.

Wednesday 4th July 1990

On the bus to the World Cup semi-final Stuart Pearce said to me, "Any advice champ?" I just said, "You're on your own, son." And later that night he was, literally. The team was the same back five as Cameroon, three in middle, Peter Beardsley and Gary Lineker up front. Terry Butcher stood up and said, "They stand between us and glory." The gaffer didn't say a lot, basically just good luck. We played well first half and at half-time he told everyone that we were playing well and that Germany were there for the taking.

All through the game Franz Beckenbauer remained standing up, leaning on the West German dugout with his eyes glued to the pitch. I remembered him from the 1970 World Cup where he'd played in the semi-final with his arm in a sling. He was a true World Cup legend but I wanted him beaten. We traded goals in the second half and it was extra time for the third game in a row.

I was just praying for Shilton to have a blinder with the penalties. He didn't. Lineker scored for us, Brehme for them. Beardsley netted, so did Matthaus. Platt scored and Riedle replied. The tension went up a notch. I knew Stuart Pearce would go hard and straight with his penalty and turned to say so to Webby. He did and it hit the keeper's legs. I was gutted for him – he hadn't put a foot wrong in six games. Olaf Thom beat Shilton with the next kick and we were on the brink. Chris Waddle came forward and shot over the bar. The noise of the celebrating Germans was tremendous as they ran on to the pitch. Our hearts sank and it was time to go on and console and look after our players. The dream was over.

I went on and had a go at Rudi Voller, who I thought was taking the piss. I had an arm round Pearcey. I didn't like it, and told him, "Fuck off, Voller, you twat!" Litbarski heard me and said calm down. I hadn't even played – imagine if I had.

Perhaps I'd have been shattered but instead I still had all my energy to vent. I got Pearcey out of there as soon as possible. I was devastated and angry, for the players, the manager and the fans. In the dressing room there were plenty of English tears splashing on to the floor. Bobby just kept saying, "Oh, you were unlucky. You're a credit to your country." Then I saw the German defender Thomas Berthold walk in. I thought he might be there to gloat and I just lost it. "Fuck off, you German bastard!" I ranted. Gary Lineker came over and helped me to calm down. I wasn't to know but Stuart Pearce had arranged to swap shirts with the German and that's why he came in. I was using it as an outlet for all of my frustration of not being able to play and for the team losing so cruelly. Overall the Germans acted with dignity that evening. Later on, when we were sitting on the bus under the stands waiting to be driven back to the hotel, the German team came out and started boarding the coach to our left. Their captain, Lothar Matthaus put a bag into the hold and then turned and applauded us all, a classy move that meant a lot and impressed me no end. He knew what it was like to lose having been beaten in the 1986 final. That's probably the nearest any of us will ever get to a World Cup final.

Thursday 5th July 1990
Everyone was naturally subdued. We took a ninety-minute flight to Bari and checked into the sixth different hotel of the trip. We all just want to get home now.

Friday 6th July 1990
Only thirteen days till preseason starts again – nightmare! A quiet day: the subs were announced but I wasn't even asked if I could make the bench.

Saturday 7th July 1990

Lost 2–1 but did a lap of honour with the Italians; it was the best atmosphere so far. I was presented with a bronze medal and swapped shirts with Baggio after the game. On the bus driving away from the stadium, Peter Shilton announced his retirement, saying, "It's been a pleasure working with you all. It's a pity we couldn't win it." At the final team meeting, Bobby went through all the players with a few words for each. "Hodgey's had a good trip, been a bit unfortunate." He himself had missed out in 1958 when he'd been to a World Cup and not played a game so he probably knew how I felt. Then we dunked him in the pool.

Sunday 8th July 1990

We got a wonderful reception at Luton airport. I couldn't believe it. What would have happened if we'd won it? Luton town centre was a sea of people and it was a great experience, a once in a lifetime job. It's good to be home and, while it wasn't a great tournament for me personally, it was great to be included in a second World Cup. It would be nice to make it a hat-trick and go to the USA in 1994. You can but dream.

The Beginning of the End

The 1990–91 preseason would be the start of my final year at Forest. Things had gone so well during the previous two seasons that I thought I'd be offered another contract, but things were about to change. I was fully fit in preseason after the injury nightmare of the World Cup but I found myself in Sweden, in the middle of nowhere, playing one-sided games in boring places. "Do you know Sweden has the highest suicide rate in the world?" Cloughie asked us. "And I can see why, there's nowt to do!" Everywhere was dead and the locals would just sit round drinking beer.

We were stuck on a treadmill of: breakfast, train in morning, lunch, rest in afternoon, play game in evening. Then it would be a day off where we'd have a walk with the gaffer then the next day we'd repeat it all again. We had no English papers to read, nowhere to go, nothing to do but train and then play.

One break in the routine was the night we went for meal on a boat down a river. The gaffer came to me and said, "Can you do a little speech, please, and thank the mayor for his hospitality and for the meal and how well we've been received in this part of the world." So I had to bang on the table. It was embarrassing, but I blurted out a few niceties and sat down again as quickly as possible. Years before, at Portsmouth, he'd come to me and said, "Go and thank Mr Ball for his hospitality and his sandwiches and tell him we have to go back to Nottingham now." These little idiosyncrasies made me want to cringe.

As if five games in Sweden wasn't enough we then flew to Italy, of all places, for more preseason games. I didn't want to go back to Italy again, having already spent most of my summer trailing around the country and not playing in the World Cup. Cloughie didn't appear for this trip and Ron Fenton was in charge. We got stuck in a crappy hotel in the middle of nowhere, with no spending money, and the players were so fed up that we sent the coaches to Coventry. We were pissed off with everything about it and had to endure long trips to games where we faced nasty, kicking teams. It might have been good for a preseason workout but we didn't like it, we just didn't want to be there. We also had to survive on a pitiful daily allowance. We complained about that too. A few days later Stuart Pearce got a call from the manager back in England to say that because of our complaint the money per day was withdrawn completely and that we still had to play that night.

After the World Cup there had been some press speculation about my future because I was entering the final year of my contract. Before the final game of the trip, in Foggia, I walked into the dressing room where Brian Rice had written a message on the whiteboard: "Steve Hodge, available, please call Leeds United Football Club". Ron Fenton saw this and scrubbed it out right away, but Ricey was a devil for stirring things up like that.

On a day off I took a trip to Capri, but it was two and a half hours each way. The boat took an age to get going and on the first stop most of the players got off for a drink, but I was a bit older and wanted to see Capri so I stayed on the boat on my own with lots of Italians. We arrived and I wandered round the market for a little bit but I hadn't realised that I'd been on last day boat out so I only had five minutes when the bell rang to tell passengers that the boat was leaving.

I had to rush back to the quay for the return trip. So I spent five hours on a boat for five minutes in a market.

Back home we had our usual runs around Wollaton Park and one day Cloughie said to me, "Harry, you run like a fifty-five year old! Get yourself to the front!" Our first game of the season at home to Queen's Park Rangers showed me that despite being one of the older, more senior players now, my opinion didn't count. Rangers played three in the centre of midfield while we had our usual 4–4–2 which left myself and Garry Parker in the centre outnumbered three to two. It was a piping hot day and we were having to work extra hard to try and compete in the midfield. We went in at the break trailing 1–0. Cloughie asked if there were any problems. I was usually quiet in those situations but this time I spoke up. "Yes, we're having a problem in midfield. They've got three and me and Garry are overrun." Clough's response was short. "OK, darling, thanks for telling me that." Then he paused before dismissively adding, "Do your best." What he actually meant was, I don't give a fuck what you think; we play 4–4–2, get on with it. We did get a goal and drew 1–1, but I made a mental note not to speak up like that again.

The following Tuesday we travelled to Anfield. I came down with a bug and had to head back home. My place was taken by a young Irish lad who I'd met the previous season as a trialist. He'd come round with Ronnie Fenton and I knew his face but nothing more. That night at Liverpool he was given his debut and played on the right wing: his name was Roy Keane. I'd seen off John Sheridan, Gary Megson, a young lad called David Campbell and others but I was older now and the feedback I heard was that Keane had done all right on his debut and that Cloughie wasn't going to leave him out. I made a note of the competition. We both played at Coventry but I had to come off. My calves kept tightening but there wasn't anything you could see. I was given a course of physio work and watched as Keane scored his first goal against Burnley. I also watched as he played at Old Trafford; he had a good engine on him and was completely unfazed by Paul Ince. That day the Stretford End were giving Stuart Pearce some stick about his World Cup penalty and at that exact moment he stepped up and struck a thirty-yard free-kick into the top corner past Les Sealey. I was starting to have doubts in my mind about my contract coming to an end, my calf problems and realising that Keane was good. We won at Old Trafford but Clough changed the side and put me back in against Everton. I scored twice and felt a tremendous wave of relief, but then my calves acted up again. I was in and out, unable to keep myself fit for a run in the team.

During the season Brian Clough came up with a bizarre new pre-match ritual. From around 2.15 to 2.30 p.m. he'd prowl the dressing room with a tennis ball, bouncing it all the time. Occassionally he'd throw it hard at someone and shout, "Catch it! Catch it!" The players would be getting changed while all the time keeping an eye on the gaffer and the ball in case it came their way next time. It certainly kept us all on our toes and Cloughie certainly knew how to treat his players on a man-by-man basis and could tailor his manner to each player's character. Some players would be dripping with praise, others would get a hard time, but he managed to keep everyone relaxed. Geoff Boycott told me that Clough studied people and it showed.

In the League Cup we were aiming for a third successive trophy. I hadn't lost a game in this competition since returning to Forest. We beat Burnley and Plymouth before facing Coventry again. It was one of the wildest games I ever played in. We were ridiculously bad and 4–0 down after thirty minutes at Highfield Road. It was one of those games where every error we made was punished with a goal. We got one back for 4–1, then I made one for Nigel, 4–2, and a minute later it was 4–3! At the break Clough said, "You back four are going to get me the sack!" Garry Parker completed an amazing comeback when he equalised in the second half but we eventually lost 5–4. It was a bad way to end our run.

We didn't often see Brian Clough at training by then; it was usually taken by the likes of Ron Fenton and Liam O'Kane. When the manager was around the players knew it. I remember after one session the players had just got back to the changing room and were sat around slowly starting to get undressed when the door burst open. The hinges literally shook in their brackets and everyone instantly turned to see the manager standing there, fire burning in his eyes. He started at one end of the room and went around player-by-player, with a white-hot off-the-cuff put-down for everyone.

To Stuart Pearce – "You've been crap since you got that
    new contract!"
Nigel Jemson – "Stop rabbiting to the refs!"
Steve Sutton – "Sign a new contract!"
Steve Hodge – "If possible try and get through ninety
    minutes!"
Brian Laws – "Spend less time at your business!"
Terry Wilson – "Get fit!"
Garry Parker – "Get a kick!"
Mark Crossley – "Get a house in Nottingham or go and play
    for Barnsley!"

And so it went around the room. Everyone got a tongue-lashing for no apparent reason. At the end of the row was Roy Keane and everyone was waiting to see what he'd be bollocked for. As usual Clough surprised everyone. "I love you, Irishman!" he gushed, and with that he was gone. Keane was here to stay and my number 6 shirt was being threatened.

Clough always kept you on your toes. He could be nice

when you expected a bollocking and nasty when you thought you'd done something well. People say he ruled by fear and the threat of being dropped was always there, but because of the way his teams played and the success that he had, many players, me included, went back and signed for him again and again. He knew how to get the best out of people, even if the techniques he used could be called unusual. Not long after the dressing room story above, he slaughtered Roy Keane just because he'd passed the ball backwards one time.

Keane took it all in his stride. When we played Spurs he got stuck into Paul Gascoigne, who was in his full post-Italia 90 pomp. "You fat bastard!" he called in his Irish accent. "The only thing fat about me is me fucking wad!" replied Gazza. It was real, harsh banter; they weren't smiling. I was spending more time watching Keane from the Main Stand than playing alongside him but I got to know him fairly well. We enjoyed some nights out in Nottingham – he'd come from Ireland and liked a night out. I had to deal with rumours about my sexuality, even back to the days when Viv Anderson asked me, "Have you got a bird yet? Well, hurry up or people will start talking." One night I was out with Roy for a drink and when he returned from the bar he just asked me outright, "Hodgey, are you gay?" I told him that I wasn't and he left it at that. But that was the kind of person Roy was. He wouldn't talk behind your back; he'd say it straight to your face and I respected him for that. It was that trait which contributed to the trouble he had with Mick McCarthy at the 2002 World Cup. Brian Clough was just the same. The rumours about me had persisted for no other reason than 'mud sticks'. Being single and a high-profile player without a steady girlfriend I was left open to idle gossip. I've often suspected that the rumours may have been started in the dressing room but I could never prove it.

A New Approach

The autumn of 1990 had been a difficult one for me and obviously my England squad place was now in doubt. Bobby Robson had been replaced by Graham Taylor. I knew about him from Watford; he had a reputation as a tough man and a lover of the long-ball game. He'd always been in the frame to be England manager because he said the right things and was very good with the media. He'd done well at Watford and Villa and made the names of a few people like John Barnes and David Platt.

His first meeting with the England players took place at the West Lodge Park hotel. I was invited and he was there with Lawrie McMenemy. Taylor spoke to us for half an hour and was very professional, confident that he knew what he wanted. He told us that he was "in the business of winning the European Championship, but I won't be shouting it to the papers". He initially put his stamp on things by making some subtle changes behind the scenes. He changed the car arrangements for players on England duty. Now a taxi would collect players from around the country and also take them back home afterwards. The players would assemble on Monday morning not Sunday night so there'd be less hanging around. Any late arrivals would rule themselves out of contention completely. He said he couldn't promise anybody anything. I thought he was a very forthright speaker, and seemed very honest. He told me that he admired Nigel Clough, that he could see his brain ticking, but couldn't give him the extra yard of pace that you need at international level.

For his first England squad he left a message on my answering machine saying I would have been picked if fit, but after I got injured at Coventry Brian Clough phoned Lawrie McMenemy and pulled me out. There were still seven days until the game but I wasn't allowed to train and he wouldn't let me play against Southampton. I probably lost four or five caps after Cloughie stopped me going away with England.

Steve Harrison and Graham Taylor always took training. It was a good laugh and things were kept loose, but it would get serious forty-eight hours before the game. He also had us training at Wembley which we hadn't done previously. For a team-binding exercise he took us to see the musical *Buddy* in the West End. There was a bomb scare and we had to stand outside in the street as passersby wondered what the England football squad was doing hanging around. Afterwards we went for a meal and then to a Karaoke bar. Everyone had to get up and sing a song. I sang "Candle in the Wind"(!), John Barnes did "When Doves Cry", Pearcey murdered Joe Jackson's "Stepping Out" – he was the worst, along with Paul Parker, who spoke his way through "I Will Survive"; Lee Dixon and Tony Adams did "You're the One That I Want". As the wine and spirits flowed I couldn't imagine Bobby Robson doing the same thing. Steve Harrison had come in before dinner dressed like a tramp with a woolly hat, dirty face, long duffle coat and blacked-out teeth. This was the England assistant manager, but he was hilarious. Another time he appeared as Quasimodo on the roof of the team hotel while we were getting on a bus to training. He was a good trainer but was really the entertainments manager.

Gazza and the manager were arm in arm at the end of the night with Gazza throwing water around while singing "Raindrops Keep Falling on My Head", by the end of which he'd drenched Ian Wright. A couple of the lads were sick on the team bus afterwards, and it stank of vomit by the time we got back to the hotel. The gaffer ended the night with a speech about how he wanted us to believe that we could win the Euros. There were a few bad heads the next day.

Taylor wanted a more physical approach and so athletes like Carlton Palmer were brought in. He was not averse to someone launching a long ball and Jack Charlton had had great success with Ireland playing the same way. His favourite motto was "Get it, give it, move it". He didn't put too many restrictions on the players but wanted to get them mentally and physically prepared.

When it came to the day of the match I wasn't in the sixteen. Taylor told me there was no place on the bench or in the stand for me and he'd prefer it if I went home. He left Gazza out of a game against Ireland even though they'd seemed pally and were singing together. I soon learned that he could be ruthless when necessary.

Mind Games

We were at home to Wimbledon on Boxing Day. In the boot room I asked one of the apprentices to put some new studs in on my boots. Cloughie heard me and quipped "I don't know why you're getting them changed, you haven't used them yet this season!" I just walked straight by him without saying a word; I wasn't very amused. Then he got the hump and came gunning for me in the dressing room. I had to come off again in that game and decided I needed to do something about my problem calves. No one at Forest had got to the bottom of the problem so I paid for myself to see a specialist in Holland. In early January I flew to Rotterdam to see this guy who had treated some of the Dutch stars. I was away for three days and in my absence Forest won 6–2 at Norwich and Roy Keane scored twice while I sat alone in my hotel room. My replacement was doing well and I was paying to try and get myself fit. Clough never had much time for injured players and he used my fitness problems to start his manoeuvrings about any possible contract talks we might have had down the line. Looking back through my diaries his methods are pretty plain to see.

January 8th 1991
Cloughie saw me for the first time after Rotterdam. Asked me how it is, said sign a new contract even though he hasn't offered me one. Then he said that Everton and Coventry have enquired about me. Does he want to sell me in an auction?

January 11th 1991

Brian Clough in the *Nottingham Evening Post* says I went in and asked him for a new contract – rubbish! Heard a rumour that he has agreed an £850,000 deal for me with Coventry. Played first game since getting back in reserves at Manchester City. I got through it OK but Cloughie is still on the warpath. After the game he snapped at me, "You're an invalid and you've not kicked a ball all fucking season!"

○ ○ ○

The 1991 FA Cup run became Forest's saviour that season because our league form was decidedly average. Against Crystal Palace in the cup we had a mammoth struggle to get through. In the first replay Roy Keane made a back pass that resulted in Palace scoring a late equaliser. As soon as he walked into the dressing room after the match the manager was at his throat. "Young Keane, what have I told you ever since you came to this club? Turn around and play the ball forward!!" We ended up playing three games, two with extra time and had a couple of postponements thrown in as well. Brian Clough didn't like the rugged way Palace played and in the second replay I set up Garry Parker and we went on to win 3–0 playing some flowing football. The game was won with about ten minutes to go and I saw the substitutes board go up with my number on. As I went off it dawned on me that no one was coming on in my place. I thought, "Has someone not got their pads ready or something?" I went to the baths and it was only a couple of days later that I found out what had happened. Cloughie came to me at a team meeting and said that he wanted to play with ten men to take the piss out of Palace and it was nothing to do with me! He just said it was some fun. He similarly liked to beat Wimbledon and Leeds because of the way they played.

When we went to Barnsley at the end of January things started to get a little bit silly between myself and the gaffer. There had been a little bit in the paper about my contract but at that point I'd had no real contact with anyone else, though there were rumours that Leeds would be interested. During the meal before the game he started taking the piss out of me and the main gist of it was, "Harry, you've shot it now." He was putting doubts in my mind, starting the psychological battle over my contract. Half an hour later he said, "Sorry I was taking the mickey out of you, you know I don't mean it." I wasn't convinced, I felt left in limbo. Did he want me or not? That whole day was a nightmare for me. "I've got you back in the England squad then, Harry," he declared in front of everyone.

"Have you?" I replied.

"Have you said, 'thank you'?"

"What, to Graham Taylor?"

"No, to me, son!"

"Oh, thanks." I was getting a bit shirty, giving him a bit back and then he tossed in, "Oh, by the way, I've just been on the phone to Peter Reid talking about you. He wants to sign you. Get a contract signed here now, son. It's not every day you get offered a contract, get it signed!" I still hadn't actually been offered anything to sign even if I'd wanted to. Then, despite saying he wanted me to sign a new contract, he had a go at me again. He turned to Des Walker and said, "Dessie, Harry told me the other day that he's got seven years left in the game. Well, I'm telling you that he hasn't got seven days never mind seven years!" He went on and on. Then he brought up the Crystal Palace game again where he'd taken me off to play with ten men. With sarcasm dripping he said, "That night I was looking after our star player."

We lost 2–1 at Barnsley and during the game I passed the

ball to Garry Parker but it went out of play. Cloughie was in the dugout directly behind the line of the pass, and he was going mad. "A fucking England player? You're fucking shit! You're shit!" He went on and on. I was on his radar now and everything was being picked on. I knew it was coming because I'd seen other players before get the brunt of it; now it was my turn. Afterwards I knew I'd get an earful. "Harry, for an England player you were a fucking disgrace. If you're ready get out of my fucking dressing room," he ranted. It continued on the bus where all the England players were blamed. "Dessie, you and your England colleagues were a disgrace," he fumed. Des Walker countered by arguing that he'd learned everything in football at Forest. Before the next game Clough was still having a go at me. He shouted across the dressing room to Garry Parker, "Young Parker, I was wrong at Barnsley. I should have pulled Harry off and not you!"

I still hadn't been officially offered a contract or even seen or heard anything about what terms might be on offer. The manager called me to have some contract talks at his house, no agent, just me and him. We were sitting on his couch when he hit me with a bombshell.

"Son, tell me about your problem," he said.

"What problem?"

"Your gambling problem."

Now people who know me would say that I can be a tight arse. "I look after my money. I don't just throw it away," I replied.

"Everyone needs friends, son. If I can help you let me know." I thought what is he on about? But he persisted. "If you had a problem would you tell me about it?"

"I've got family and friends I can talk to before you," I answered. Then he told me a story about someone he knew who had a gambling problem. I eventually told him I thought that either someone was winding him up or he was just talking a load of bull. Either one of his friends was telling him lies about me or he was just deliberately trying to get me going.

Then he said, "Oh, by the way, we're going to offer you a new contract." And that was that. He offered me a drink, which I refused and he called me a bore and saw me off with an "All right, get off then. See your agent and get it signed!" The whole thing left a bitter taste in my mouth. To be accused of something serious just felt out of order. The next day in the *Nottingham Evening Post* it said that Steve Hodge is staying, a story obviously fed to them by the gaffer. I've never ever gambled, apart from a little bet on the Grand National like everyone else. It's absolutely the last thing I would do. To this day I've never figured why he made such a deal out of the non-story.

February 13th 1991

Our second trip up to Newcastle for our FA Cup game; last one was cancelled due to snow. Went to train on a mini junior school pitch; the kids were peering out of frosted windows, we had a snowball fight with them, otherwise it was a wasted two-day trip. The second attempt at the game saw us 2–0 down but we battled back and Nigel scored in the dying seconds to earn a replay. BC: "Well done, number 9. You've kept me in the cup tonight." We are staying in the north-east before playing Sunderland on Saturday.

February 17th 1991

Lost 1–0 at Sunderland. I was dropped, told by Liam O'Kane that I was out, then the gaffer then came in. "Harry, I'm dropping you because you didn't get hold of the ball against Newcastle." Which was just any old reason he needed – I was no better or worse than anyone else. He mentioned that I'd recently played for England and I just said, "It's history; it's gone." Then he went to Nigel, "Number 9, I used to grace this pitch," to which Nigel muttered under his breath, "History." During the game Cloughie asked a steward, "Are you cold? There's a place on the bench if you want to join me, son." Then just before the break he turned to me and said, "Harry, some decision I made leaving you out today!" At half-time he asked if I fancied a run out and usually I'd have said "yes" immediately, but the way things were going I just said, "It's up to you." He snapped back, "I know it's up to me!" Before we left the ground, Cloughie held the team bus up, opened the side door and front door and let kids come on from both angles. Because he was pissed off he made us stay and sign autographs for ages – we'd already been away for three days. I scored in the Newcastle replay as we won 3–0 and then again in the last minute to get a 2–2 draw with Villa, whose fans still gave me loads of abuse.

A little while later he asked me if I'd been tapped up by Liverpool and Manchester City. I said, "Yes."

"If I cancel my holiday will you talk contracts with me."

"Yes."

"OK. Give me a couple of days."

But he never got back to me. In the dressing room he treated me like a youth-team player. "Harry, ask the lads if there's anything they want, get them a drink." If things could get any worse, they did. At Southampton I scored in the FA Cup to salvage a replay but I felt my knee ligaments go. It was a really foggy night at the Dell against a Saints team that included Le Tissier, Shearer and Ruddock. I flicked in a mis-hit cross shot from Roy Keane to score and later, when I chased Rod Wallace, I twisted my knee. I was in the dressing room when the players came off. Stuart Pearce was the first one in.

"Great goal, champ!" he said, using one of my string of nicknames (Harry, Hodgey, Chicken, Champ and probably a few more from Villa fans). The specialist told me to sit out for six weeks but after a week Cloughie was asking if I'd be training tomorrow. Two and a half weeks later I was still injured and walking around the training pitch. "Harry, do you want to join in," he called to me.

"No."

"Mind you don't catch pneumonia, won't you?"

Forest went on a reasonable run while I was out and it was six weeks of sheer frustration. They beat Norwich in the FA Cup quarter-final and I was battling to be fit for the semi-final against West Ham.

April 3rd 1991

Still struggling for the FA Cup semi-final with my knee. Had an injection in it yesterday. Didn't want to but it's my only chance at the moment.

April 10th 1991

Saw Ron Fenton today and told him what I thought about not being offered a contract yet.

April 11th 1991

Trained with the first team today. I wasn't too bad but not perfect. Boss said, "Not bad for someone who's been out for three months." Played at Stockport in the reserves and got through ninety minutes.

April 13th 1991

Cloughie told me today that I hadn't made it for the semi-final, not even to the bench, despite seven weeks of hard graft and injections and even though I've just played ninety minutes.

He put his hand on my shoulder at breakfast and just said, "Sorry, you didn't make it, son." Later he gathered us round and said, "If anybody isn't happy they can fuck off." I know he was aiming that at me; I was simmering under the surface. I could tell that he was nervous – we'd been close to the cup final twice but this might be his last chance.

April 14th 1991

Had to sit with the manager in the dugout and he got a good ovation from the West Ham fans as we walked along the touchline to our seats at Villa Park. Near the bench one of the Londoners kept shouting out, "Oi, Cloughie! You're tha guvna! You're the fackin' guvna. You're the fackin' guvna!" The boss turned to me and said, "Harry, darling, what's he saying?" The chap was now leaning over into the dugout and still shouting, "You're tha fackin' guvna!"

"I think he rates you," I replied. I think he knew what the chap was saying but wanted to hear me confirm it. We won 4–0 but I didn't feel part of it. They only had ten men. He turned to me at the final whistle and said, "Harry, get me out of here." He wasn't that elated. Cloughie finally got to an FA Cup final but we aren't on good terms. I'm selfishly thinking I should have been in the side, but he picked the right team. Nigel Clough said to me, "What an anti-climax." There were photographers in the dressing room after the game but I kept out of the way and felt detached from it all. I've started to think these could be the last weeks of my career at Forest.

April 15th 1991

Played the full ninety minutes at Walsall reserves, no problems with my knee at all. On the way to the game Cloughie called all the young lads over to the side of the bus. "Now, do any of you feel hard done by or that you're working too hard?" he asked. He pointed over the road to where there was a labourer digging at the side, "That's what you call work!" he snapped. Before the match he asked me if I wanted to play that night. What did he expect me to say? I was doing some stretches and he asked me if I was praying. I replied that I fell like doing so sometimes. In the second half one of the youngsters, Tony Loughlin, stupidly kicked an opponent and Clough took him off right away. But he didn't bother to put on a substitute in his place, he left us to play with ten men. Afterwards he told me, "For what it's worth, well done." But it wasn't worth a thing.

April 18th 1991

Played at Rotherham reserves, drew 1–1 but I scored and played well. Think a slight thigh strain will keep me out against Chelsea! At half-time Franz Carr muttered something about the gaffer under his breath. Cloughie heard it and replied, "Franzie, darling, your crossing is crap, you can't run and your attitude is a fucking disgrace!"

April 19th 1991

Today I was named in both England 'B' and full squads!

To say I was shocked at my England call-ups was an understatement. From reserve-team football to the international stage just like that! I'd been involved for the friendly against Cameroon at Wembley but I expected my lack of Forest games to count against me. The Cameroon game had been played in temperatures well below freezing and I don't think Roger Milla fancied it. I came on for Gazza and got about twenty-five minutes but spurned a good goal-scoring opportunity and was frustrated at still not scoring for my country. Gary Pallister was supposed to be coming on too when I did but when he undid his tracksuit he realised that he'd forgot to put his shirt on. I went on alone while someone ran back to the dressing room to get it for him.

My latest double call-up meant a game against Iceland at Vicarage Road with the 'b' team and then a flight out to Turkey. The 'b' team was just a bunch of individuals thrown together and it showed. When I met the full squad we went to a hotel for a meal and a comedian, but the comedian was woeful. No one was laughing and he just got worse and worse and then he collapsed. The pressure of being in front of high profile people and no one laughing got to him. Steve Harrison went on instead and he was great.

Training with Taylor's England was simple: passing, shooting, crossing. Get the ball forward as quickly as possible. It was how teams were playing in lower divisions at that time. Denis Wise and Geoff Thomas were making their debuts. He wanted us to perform at a high tempo and picked me out to say I was a prime example against Iceland of how to snap and harass foreign players. He stressed there was nothing wrong with playing it through the air to a six-foot plus striker and he told Dave Seaman to kick it seventy yards to the striker's head rather than let us play it through midfield. We had an hour long session telling us which areas of the pitch were where the most goals came from. Another motto of his came from his insistence that we all sing the anthem: "Sing and win".

I came on at half-time in Turkey while we were winning 1–0. He took Geoff Thomas off, who I thought was doing OK. I felt some pressure that a draw or loss would now reflect badly on me. In the event we held on and won 1–0. Graham Taylor told me afterwards, "I was helping you get into the cup-final team, Hodgey." It was surreal that I was playing for

England but not a Forest regular. We had a short team meeting at Luton airport on our return and Taylor left us with the message, "Thanks for the result but don't ever underestimate me." That came strangely true for me later in the season and the Turkey game proved to be my last England cap.

Forest played at Spurs three days after the England v Turkey game, but since my return the Forest coaches had been cold to me, it's like I'd committed a crime to play for my country. On the coach to London I was sitting right at the back when Cloughie came and sat next to me. "Harry, I'm leaving you out altogether," he said. I both could and couldn't believe it. I thought, "He's taking the piss out of me because I played for England before playing for Forest. He thinks I should have missed the England trip and played for the reserves in their 4–0 defeat to Blackburn." At White Hart Lane I saw John Motson before the game. He said he'd been told that I was on the bench but I put him right. He was astounded. I watched the match from the stands. In that game Roy Keane injured his ankle and I was watching with great interest. Afterwards Clough came after me. "I thought I told you to sit with me on the bench!"

"I didn't hear you say that."

"Oh didn't you? I'm certain I said it."

"Well I never heard it."

"Well, in future when you're sitting on the back seat, listen very carefully to what I'm saying!"

"OK." Then I just sat looking at him, thinking, "Only two more weeks to go."

Twelve days before the cup final I thought I'd got a break. We were due to play Liverpool at the City Ground and Roy Keane was still injured. Liverpool and Arsenal were neck and neck for the championship but if we beat the Merseysiders the title would be Arsenal's. Before kick-off the gaffer said to

Scoring against Villa, again!

League champions, the hardest one to win. (Colorsport)

Championship celebrations. Eric, far right, had plenty more ahead. (Yorkshire Post)

Mum, Dad and me posing with the trophies I won at Leeds.

Ali and me on our Wedding Day in 1997.

U.E.F.A CUP

WEDNESDAY		SEMI
MERCREDI	1/2	
WOENSDAG		SECOND LEG
25.4.1984		Retour - Terug

RSC ANDERLECHT — **NOTTINGHAM FOREST**

STADE - STADION
C. VANDEN STOCK

LINDEN

A - LANDSKAMP

SVERIGE ENGLAND

RÅSUNDA
FOTBOLLSTADION
10 SEPTEMBER 1986
KL. 19.00

PRIS 5:—

SEIKO SOCCER 1982

SEIKO

TOP SPORTS
FOR TOP ENTERTAINMENT

**AL-QADSIYA CLUB
VS
NOTTINGHAM FOREST**

نخبة لاعبي كرة القدم في أفضل المباريات

نادي القادسية الرياضي
ضد
نادي نوتنهام فورست

Monday, 1st November 1982
at Mohammed Al Hamad Stadium,
Kuwait Kickoff - 5.00 p.m.
Tickets available at the Stadium

على ملعب محمد عبدالله الحمد بالكويت
يوم الاثنين 1 نوفمبر 1982 والساعة الخامسة مساء
التذاكر تباع في الملعب

International Football at Bramall Lane

The Fourth UEFA Under-21
European Championship Final (Second-leg)

ENGLAND v SPAIN

Thursday 24th May 1984. Kick-off 7.30 p.m.   50p

ENGLAND v SCOTLAND

THE ROUS CUP
Wednesday April 23rd
1986 - Kick-Off 7.45pm
Official souvenir programme
£1.00

Wembley
Stadium

ASTON VILLA

NEWS & RECORD OFFICIAL PROGRAMME 50p

ASTON VILLA
v
CHELSEA
CANON LEAGUE
DIVISION ONE
Saturday
26th April 1986

mita

FOOTBALL ASSOCIATION CHALLENGE CUP FINAL

SATURDAY 16TH MAY 1987

KICK-OFF 3 PM

THIS MATCH IS
SPONSORED BY:
...ER COMPUTER
...NALS (UK) LTD

...icial Souvenir Programme £2...

T
O
T
T
E
N
H
A
M

F.A. CUP
FINAL

W WEMBLEY
WHERE ELSE

ФУТБОЛ

ТОВАРИЩЕСКИЙ МАТЧ

СССР

АНГЛИЯ

1986

26.03   20 пр.

FREE! INSIDE
GIANT
JOHN LUKIC

asics

THISTLE
HOTELS

Leeds United

LEEDS UNITED v CREWE ALEXANDRA

SATURDAY 8th JANUARY 1994
Official Matchday Magazine £1.50

FA
CUP 1994

County
Carpets &
Curtains

THISTLE
HOTELS
OFFICIAL CLUB SPONSORS

asics
OFFICIAL KIT SPONSORS

TODAY'S MATCH SPONSOR

SPONSORS
COMPAQ

CARLING
PREMIERSHIP

Queens Park
rangers
Southampton

The FA Carling
Premiership
Wednesday 28th
December 1994
Kick-off 7.45pm
Price £1.50

COMPAQ

QPR

MATCH SPONSORS
'London
parade'

PROGRAMME
MONTHLY
ANNUAL ENGLISH LEAGUE MERIT
AWARDS WINNER 1992/94

...come to Loftus Road

Amber has a soft spot for Gazza. Here they meet at the Help for Heroes game at Reading in 2009.

The kids, Elliot and Amber, meet David Beckham, a brilliant footballer and ambassador for the game.

Elliot and Josh rub shoulders with newly crowned World Cup winner Roberto Carlos.

Meeting football legends: top left: Sir Stanley Matthews at Mexico 86; top right: Gordon Banks and Pele in 2008; and finally, above, from left to right, Ray Wilkins, Ray Wilson, Sir Bobby Robson, Sir Tom Finney, Tony Woodcock and me in 2008. (pauldaviddrabble.co.uk)

Meeting Sir Bobby Robson for the last time in 2009 at St James's Park. He is someone to whom I will be eternally grateful. (Bob Thomas/Getty Images)

Me and Elliot, who is modelling the Hand of God shirt in 1997. (Popperfoto)

me, "Play in *mid*field, not left-back, not striker, but *mid*field."
I played well in a 2–1 win and Cloughie had always said that
he was faithful to the players who'd "got the shirt". Well, I'd
got it now and I intended to keep it. Five days later we ended
our league season at home to Leeds. I knew that this could be
my last game at the City Ground as a Forest player. Before the
game was one of the few times I heard the manager really
want us to get stuck into a team. "Kick them," he said. "Kick
them like they kicked you at Elland Road when they took the
piss," referring to an earlier 3–1 loss. It turned out to be a
great game as we won 4–3 and missed a penalty. I played well
and as I walked off the gaffer said, "Some ninety minutes you
put in today, Harry. Well done, son." Maybe I had booked a
Wembley place after all.

May 13th 1991

England Squad announced today and Taylor has left me out!
I'm picked when I'm injured, now dropped when I play two
excellent games. He did say never underestimate him! Taylor
said I'd done well in Turkey and v Iceland, then he came
out and said he needed to see me playing club football and I
played well in wins over Liverpool and Leeds and I'm bombed
out from Argentina and Australia and don't know what I've
done wrong. Played Notts County in the County Cup today.
Still no Roy Keane in the side.

May 16th

Two days till Wembley and I've got a contract. It's a tiny wage
rise. I feel like an apprentice who should be grateful for any
offer. Now I'm certain to leave. Keane hasn't proved his fitness.
He played in a reserve game but everyone knows he isn't 100
per cent fit. Don't know what Cloughie might do. He left
Martin O'Neill out of a European Cup final. This is the one

trophy he hasn't won so he'll want a fully fit XI out there. He always preaches continuity so that's strengthened my case again.

May 17th

For the first time ever the gaffer has me rooming with Roy Keane. Is he taking the mickey?

○ ○ ○

The day before the final we trained at Burnham Beaches and he "announced" the team on the bus back to the hotel. He came through the partition on the coach and I was sitting at one of two card tables. Nigel Clough was to my side, Stuart Pearce and Steve Sutton opposite me. The gaffer literally threw a crumpled up bit of paper at Pearcey and said, "Skipper, here's the cup-final team." And he was gone. As Pearce unwrapped the ball of paper I looked across at Sutty, who could see what was written. He glanced back at me and gave me a slight shake of his head: I wasn't in the team. I thought Brian Clough bottled it a bit that day – he couldn't face the players he was leaving out. Nigel turned to me and said, "I feel sorry for you. Does this mean you're going to leave the club?" I didn't reply. All I was thinking was "Your dad's a fucking twat." All the "If you have the shirt you keep it" rules weren't applying now. I was a substitute. Nigel Jemson was out completely. In hindsight, deep down, I was happy to be a sub. At least that meant the chance of a winner's medal. I would be part of the occasion, and I might get on. Nigel Jemson didn't have those con-solations. Back at the hotel foyer Jemmo set off to the lifts. I could see his eyes were watering; he was absolutely dis-traught. But Brian Clough called him back. There were some fans in the foyer and Clough said, "Young Jemson, this lady wants a picture." Jemmo had to try and hide the tears and smile for the camera. I don't know how I'd have reacted in that situation. I went back to my room where it was just me and Roy Keane. It wasn't his fault so I was cordial, played the part of the older pro. I didn't think he was fully fit, but I couldn't blame him. He'd come from nowhere to an FA Cup final. I was almost certain that it would be my last game for Forest.

A Travesty at Wembley

On the day of my second FA Cup final I awoke at eight-thirty and sat with young full-back Gary Charles for breakfast. There was an article by Terry Venables in one of the papers: he said that I would be a danger on the day. Little did he know that I wasn't playing. When the cameras arrived at eleven-fifteen I went out for a walk.

At the ground there was no mention of Spurs in the team talk. "Don't freeze on me," Cloughie said. "Don't leave anything in here." I could see that he was uncharacteristically very nervous, fidgeting around and worrying about his tie, "Harry, does it look OK?" As the two teams walked out, Clough was so nervous that he grabbed Terry Venables by the hand. Venables had to pretend to wave to someone he had seen in the crowd in order to get his hand free. In the pre-match introductions I met Charles and Diana, and the Duchess of Kent, who'd been doing her homework. "How are you?" she asked. "I'm told that you've been injured lately." The game kicked off and Gazza was virtually out of control. He ploughed into Garry Parker so high that when a sponge was applied to him as he lay on the floor the stud marks were high on his chest. As usual the Forest players never complained to the referee, Roger Milford. It should have been at least a yellow card. Today it would have been a straight red. Minutes later Gazza scythed down Gary Charles on the edge of the Spurs box. It was so horrendous it wasn't even a tackle. Gazza had just been running around and looked so over-the-top and desperate to win. He was so reckless that he did himself immense damage while Gary Charles sprang up and completed the game. This tackle alone should have been a straight red but Gazza was carried off and Spurs were allowed to continue with eleven men. I think who it was clouded what had actually happened. In the short term, Stuart Pearce scored from the resultant free-kick and we'd had a good start but that soon faded. Ten minutes after half-time Paul Stewart equalised. On the bench the gaffer told Liam O'Kane, "We're playing like fucking schoolboys. Ask Harry if he can run."

Spurs had better, more experienced, players around the pitch. Roy Keane was very young and not fully fit; Lee Glover was a Nigel Clough clone; Gary Charles was young; Ian Woan was not long in league football; Mark Crossley was young. Spurs had the likes of Van den Hauwe, Mabbutt, Lineker, Allen, Walsh, all very experienced, and in a cup final you need more experience. The tide was turning after they scored and I replaced Ian Woan. The manager wanted some energy from me because we looked lethargic. I kicked Paul Stewart and put myself about a bit as the game moved into extra time. As the players took a break before the extra period, Brian Clough famously just sat on the bench. Ron Fenton came and said a few words, but that day Brian Clough, who had never won the FA Cup, was nervous. This was the closest he'd ever been and was ever likely to get, and though his behaviour seemed a bit odd it was exactly what he'd done years before at Sturm Graz in the UEFA Cup. In extra time both teams looked like they'd be happy with a replay until Gary Lineker put me under pressure and I conceded a corner. We never practised set-plays and when the ball came over my head to the back post I saw Gary Mabbutt pressuring Des Walker. I thought, "He deals with that every week."

Des was being leant on and, as I turned, I was in line with his header and I could see exactly where it was going. For a second I thought, "That's going in," and not many other people in the stadium could see what was about to happen. In slow motion the ball drifted into our top corner. It took a second before the roar came and everyone realised it had gone in. Des Walker, who had been one of the best players in the team for years, had scored an own goal in the cup final. We tried to get the ball back and get playing again, but apart from a couple of skirmishes we never created a clear chance. We were nullified. The final whistle went and I'd been there before. The Coventry game had been worse; in 1991 I thought Spurs deserved to beat us. For me it was déjà vu with an extra-time own goal in the same net. I shook hands with Terry Venables and on that occasion he had his day. I knew that was me finished at Forest as I walked off towards the Forest fans and clapped them.

In the dressing room the gaffer asked some medical people to come in and asked how "young Gascoigne" was doing. Clough's own career had ended by injury and he was concerned. He kept saying, "Well played, lads. Well played, lads. Harry, can I have a look at your medal, darling? Harry, show the chairman your medal."

"I don't like showing off runners-up medals."

"Show it him anyway."

The coach back to Nottingham diverted to East Midlands airport where the manager got off and flew straight to Majorca. The city had organised a parade for the following day, win or lose, but I skipped it. A couple of days later I made the long trip to Singapore then on to Sydney with the England squad. I didn't feel very well and, a bit like at QPR three years earlier, the ball was just passing me by in training. The stress about the cup final, waiting to see if Leeds, or anyone else, was going to come in for me, the lack of a contract, troublesome calves. It all came to a head and I just couldn't concentrate. I watched the game in Sydney but felt groggy and run down. We flew to New Zealand, another five-hour flight, but I didn't play there either. And it rained constantly for four days. By now I hadn't trained for a week when we flew to Thailand. Again I watched from the bench while I just wanted to get home and relax and sort my future out. The whole trip was a disaster for me, I don't know how many miles I'd travelled for no caps but it was a lot. When we got back Graham Taylor said, "Go and sort yourself out."

In the middle of June I met Brian Clough to talk about my contract. I was with my agent Kev Mason and Clough was dismissive of him. "Your fat bastard friend might know about facts and figures," Clough said to me, while Kev sat by my side, "but he knows fuck all about football." Then he said to me, "You do realise that you won't be playing for England again, don't you?" I knew he'd spoken to either Graham or Lawrie and then it hit me that he was right. I was stunned as the reality sunk in. Steve Hodge, ex-England international. It was the first sign that my career had hit its peak and now everything would relentlessly be downhill, but I felt I still had a few good years left in the top flight and didn't think the downward slope need be steep. I had no reason to disbelieve Clough's words because I knew that he was friendly with Lawrie McMenemy, who had been number two to Graham Taylor on that trip, so I assumed he'd heard something and I never heard from England again. I told Cloughie my expectations and he went away and came back with a sealed envelope. I didn't open it until I was in the car. It said my demands were excessive and couldn't be met. I didn't know if he was waiting till the last moment again before relenting or if he thought Leeds weren't going to make an offer. I knew his ways so well by now, but the football at Forest was so right for me I'd stay if he'd offered a decent contract. I wanted four years but would have taken two, even though there was no mention of the testimonial that I'd asked for, even though I'd had many years at the club.

I was free to talk to anyone, so I spoke to Leeds. I met Howard Wilkinson at his assistant Mick Hennigan's house. He said they were on the up, had had a good season, big crowds, he was very upbeat. They offered me three years on much better money and I knew that they had a good midfield with David Batty, Gordon Strachan and Gary McAllister, and Gary Speed was emerging. They'd come fourth and I knew I'd have to play well to get in the team. I went to meet Bill Fotherby in the Holiday Inn penthouse with my agent Kev Mason. There was a partition in the middle of the suite. Kev and I knew what we wanted and he went behind the partition and I couldn't hear what was being said and it was a bit farcical. Kev kept going back and forward behind this partition. We were whispering and this went on for about forty-five minutes, toing and froing until finally the deal was done. Ron Fenton called me at the hotel afterwards and said, "Thanks for your efforts. I'll let the gaffer know. You'll always be welcome at the City Ground." Even though my contract was up they got a £1 million transfer fee for me. So they'd doubled their money on me and got a replacement in Roy Keane. Leeds offered me a lot more money and a longer deal; it was the right time to move and I didn't know how good a year I was about to have. Everyone was happy.

I always found Steve Hodge to be a really tricky opponent. In fact, he was one of the toughest I came up against in my career. He was a midfielder who loved to run beyond his own strikers, making him difficult to contain. As I played in the Midlands I saw a lot of Nottingham Forest and always admired Steve and the Forest sides he played in – because of their attacking style they were very exciting to watch.

I first noticed Steve's impact in the Mexico World Cup of 1986 and he proved that he was as good as any in his position. Technically excellent and able to score so many vital goals from midfield, he'd be the equivalent of a Frank Lampard today, who can now command over £100,000 a week. He was certainly up amongst the best midfielders and it's a testament to his ability that he was so central to many of Brian Clough's best sides in the 1980s and 1990s. Brian Clough didn't pick fools.

Some people might have thought that Steve was a little bit quiet but not those who got to know him, which I did. We became friends because we saw the game in the same way and loved the technical side of it, playing football the way it was meant to be played.

Gary McAllister MBE

Sergeant Wilko

Leeds United played a very different brand of football than what I was used to at Nottingham Forest, but the preseason started just the same. Running. Lots and lots of running. We were timed to see how many laps we could do around a cricket pitch in twelve minutes. Gary McAllister won that one by a mile. He was a Rolls-Royce of a player and I knew that back when he'd been at Leicester he'd been keen to move to Forest. He loved the Forest style of play and told me that he'd always wanted to be part of that team. He did get close to signing, but when he met Cloughie for talks he was put off by the unorthodox negotiation tactics. Like me, Gary can talk about football for hours at the drop of a hat.

After the cricket pitch it was lots more running, all around Roundhay Park. I knew Mel Sterland and Chris Whyte from my Under-21 days and Chris Fairclough and Lee Chapman were familiar faces. As seemed to be typical in my career, I soon came up against a former side. In fact, my first game was against Forest. I didn't get to see Cloughie and I spent the entire game on the bench as we won 1–0. I made my debut in a big game when I came on as a substitute for the last ten minutes against Sheffield Wednesday. I was placed out on the left wing, just like my worst days in my first spell at Forest. I scored past Chris Woods, who had been leaving Brian Clough's office when I'd signed all those years before. It was the perfect start at home, which is what I really needed. I was up against John Sheridan, another Forest connection, and my old England and Spurs colleague Chris Waddle, but he wasn't laughing at me this time.

Howard Wilkinson didn't want us to play it out from the back. If John Lukic did give it to the full-backs they usually launched a long ball. Gordon Strachan was one midfielder who would demand the ball, but it would often be straight up to Lee Chapman to flick on for Rod Wallace to chase. The ball wasn't held up for me to pick a run from midfield and I had to gamble when I might get to a flick-on. Consequently I didn't make as many runs. At Old Trafford I hadn't realised how huge a game it was until I got on. We drew 1–1 in one of Ryan Giggs first games – he was just a waif but had quick feet and a turn of pace. I was firmly entrenched as the fifth midfielder but I hoped that when I did get a chance I could do well and he'd have to stick with me. We won at Chelsea and beat Manchester City 3–0 and the crowd went berserk when David Batty scored.

My first start came against Liverpool. It was surprising, but we hadn't beaten Liverpool for eighteen years in the league. I scored the only goal of the game past Bruce Grobbelaar. The roar at the final whistle was massive and we took great belief and confidence from that result. Suddenly I thought that we might have a decent season and we went ten games unbeaten. Our first loss was against Crystal Palace when the referee gave them a last-minute free-kick which led to Ian Wright scoring the winner. I called the referee a cheat because it was never a free-kick in the first place and I was charged by the FA. My hearing took place in Manchester because there were a few cases to be dealt with on that day involving players and managers from that area of the country. I took the lift up to the private room where I had to face a panel of three FA officials. They read out the charge like you would see in a real courtroom and I then had to offer them my defence.

I said I hadn't called him a cheat, but I had, because I really thought that he had cheated. I didn't feel bad about lying because I thought he was in the wrong; if it had been a borderline decision I wouldn't have been so upset about it. The whole thing took about thirty minutes and then I was asked to leave while they debated my case. After just five minutes I was called back in and told I'd been found guilty and would be fined. They offered me the chance to appeal but I knew I wouldn't win that either. I just sat there quietly and listened to what they had to say then walked out. As I waited to get the lift the lift doors opened and Sheffield United manager Dave Bassett stepped out. "How did you get on, Hodgey?"

"Guilty."

"Tough luck," he replied. "I'm in next. Should be fun and games!" I wished him good luck and the lift doors closed to take me back down. I was so angry – if only the ball hadn't fallen to Ian Wright!

Though we had some good skilful players I wasn't finding it particularly easy to play in the Leeds style – although he did admire quality passing, it's fair to say Wilkinson was a firm believer in direct football. That said, I did score twice in another Yorkshire derby against Sheffield United. Both goals came from Lee Chapman flick-ons. Howard Wilkinson would have a team meeting and set out blocks of games in terms of how many points he expected us to get from them. This was good when things were going well and we could assess where we were, but later, when things weren't going so well, it became a nightmare. The number of points we were amassing was just embarrassing and it all became quite demoralising. On a Friday we'd spend ninety minutes practising set-pieces. If I was going to be a substitute that week, which was quite often, then I'd have to fill in as one of the opposition during these drills. Wilkinson was very attentive to things like this, which was the exact opposite of Brian Clough. Wilkinson would have meetings about certain players in the opposition whereas Cloughie wouldn't mention any player on the other side, ever. David Batty was frequently banned from taking part in these practices because he'd get bored easily and would just start kicking a ball around. Wilkinson would send him off to another pitch. He'd disrupt things because of his attention span, just like Paul Gascoigne on England duty. The constant set-piece practising did yield results, though, and we managed to counteract Arsenal, which was something new in my career. No one really did us on set-pieces around our goal.

As well as counteracting Arsenal's aerial threat, the Leeds style meant I saw some success against other sides that I'd usually struggled against. Wimbledon away was, as usual, a game I didn't look forward to, but when I went there with Leeds we were able to play more like they did. The game: to play in it was monotonous; to watch it must have been even worse – we drew 0–0. Even Howard Wilkinson was shouting at us from the bench not to get bored! We then went to Villa and I was again a sub but as we won 4–1 I kept quiet because the team was going well in the league so what could I say? Everton at home was embarrassing for me because I came on after about seventy minutes and soon afterwards someone got sent off so I was immediately withdrawn. I'd sat on my backside for over an hour just wanting to get on and when I did I lasted about six minutes, thinking, "Thanks a lot!" as I trudged back off again. We won that game in the last minute with only ten men and we were top of the table. It was starting to become a two-horse race between us and Manchester United. Leeds hadn't won the title for eighteen years while Manchester United hadn't won it for twenty-three years. The long wait for each of these clubs' fans was becoming more unbearable with each passing year and the fact that the two great rivals were grasping for the same prize made the race even more tension-filled.

I was playing in the reserves to keep fit alongside a lot of young kids which was difficult. I rented a flat in Pudsey which I used for night games or occasionally when I was tired during the week, but otherwise I commuted from Nottingham most of the time. My next opportunity to stake a claim came when Gordon Strachan was injured at Forest and I returned in the centre of midfield at Southampton on Boxing Day. I really thought I'd taken my chance when I scored twice to help us into a 3–1 lead but Alan Shearer and Iain Dowie got them back to 3–3. I was dropped again and Strachan returned for the next game. He was injured again before we went to Hillsborough so I got another chance. Live on TV we pulverised Sheffield Wednesday 6–1, and Wednesday were a decent team. I was nutmegged by a young kid called Chris Bart-Williams, who shouted "megs" as he did it. I thought, "Do you really think I'm bothered?" We were 5–1 up at the time. Wilkinson was cock-a-hoop, not only because we'd hammered his former team but because we were increasing our championship credentials and pressurising Manchester United. I was getting a little run in the first team now and I played really well against Notts County. During the match I ran past the County dugout and was shocked to hear their manager, Neil Warnock, telling his full-back to break my legs. I'd been party to Brian Clough's motivational techniques in the past, but this was something different entirely. To be fair to Warnock, I'm sure he was just trying to fire up his full-back. Warnock is someone who I respect as a manager but I'm not sure about that instruction. This was the game where a relatively unknown Frenchman called Eric Cantona had arrived at the club and was watching from the stands. I think he was impressed with me because he later asked the physio, "Why does Hodgey not play every week?" I'd read in the papers that he'd had a trial at Sheffield Wednesday and we weren't really sure what had happened there or why he was suddenly with us. Overseas players were still a rarity in the English game and we knew nothing about him or his history. He changed next to me, was very quiet and seemed introverted. This was probably because he knew very little English. "Morning, Hodgey" and "See you, Hodgey" was about as far as it went. Right away in training I could see that he had a great touch with both feet and there was an aura around him that smacked of confidence. His debut was the next week at Oldham when he came on for me. I'd played poorly and we were 2–0 down. The press had built up this nomadic bad boy from France and there were lots of cameras waiting for him around the dugout. The cameras would never leave him during his career in England.

No one really got close to Eric – he just wasn't that type of man – but he did socialise with the team and would inevitably be the one buying champagne for everyone. He lived in a very modest suburban house, certainly not the type of house you'd expect to be inhabited by a top-flight footballer. He wasn't bothered about the off-field glamour associated with his profession, only the on-field adulation that he was afforded by the fans.

I probably played more with Eric in the reserves than I did in the first team. In midfield we usually spent large parts of the game watching the ball sail over our heads. From my earliest days at Forest I'd always been taught that the game should be played on the ground. Crisp passing and quick movement. Play the game as it was meant to be played. "Isn't it terrible when you beat these passing teams?" crowed Wilkinson after a 1–0 win at West Ham.

The most demoralising game came at Liverpool reserves on a wet Tuesday night. We'd spent the night chasing young

Jamie Redknapp's shadows in midfield and been well beaten 7–1. Liverpool had a young lad called Lee Jones, who was touted as the next Ian Rush, and he scored four that night, but he never made it in the game. Eric put his arm around my shoulder as we walked off the pitch saying, "Why are we here? Hodgey, this is not football. I cannot play this way." I could only agree with him.

○ ○ ○

I had to have an operation for my calves which were forever cramping up a little. They made a little cut on a sheath around the calf to release the pressure but that didn't solve it. I was struggling in reserve games as they tightened up to the point where I couldn't run. Howard Wilkinson was falling out with me because he'd paid £1 million and I wasn't available. I couldn't prove to him that I was injured because there was nothing physically there to show him. I sat on the bench with the manager during a game against Arsenal, it was all I could do. I gleaned some interesting insights into his knowledge of the game that day. I saw that he could quickly picture certain situations in a game. They got a free-kick about thirty yards out and he saw that no one had spotted Paul Merson, who had too much space wide on the right. Sure enough he got the ball, whipped it in and they scored. Wilkinson had noticed it straight away, none of our players on the pitch had seen it. He'd shouted for someone to get over but it was too late.

Manchester United were just ahead of us and favourites to win their first title since 1968. A draw at home to West Ham put us further behind. I didn't do myself any favours when I said I was fit to play at Manchester City, but really I wasn't. My calves were still sore and in the first half I took a real bang on the shoulder. I was hobbling around thinking, "I'm not going to come off." There was tackle at the edge of our box and I went in half-hearted and got a bollocking from Gordon Strachan. He was right, but I didn't want to get another injury on top of the two I already had. We lost 4–0 and I think we thought it was all over in the championship race, but the following Monday saw Wilko in one of his Churchillian moments. He gave us a speech asking how we would we feel if our fathers, our mothers, our daughters and our brothers entered a race and after four-fifths of the race thought they'd jack it in. We needed to keep going right until the end and, unbelievably, he kept faith with me for the next game at home to Chelsea. I had to laugh at my old Aston Villa teammate, Paul Elliott, who was playing for the Londoners. Every time he went up for a header he'd scream out "Jamaica!" I wasn't laughing when I got chinned by Vinnie Jones, though. We'd had some verbals and when I was waiting in midfield as we were defending a corner he came up behind me and with his right arm he pushed me back and then a left hook to the chin put me on the floor. No one in the ground saw a thing. "Do that again and you'll be on the deck again!" he snarled. Then he shouted over to Andy Myers, "Chin that cunt." Bang on half-time Jones walked over, "You all right, Hodge? You want some more? Come near me and you'll facking get some!" It was a real intimidation job. I don't know if he was always like that or maybe he just didn't like me. I shook it off and we won 3–0. Later we both played in a benefit game for Peter Haddock and he made a jokey remark about it.

We were keeping pace with Manchester United. At Liverpool we got a good 0–0 then hosted Coventry on Easter Monday with three games to go. A Chris Fairclough goal put us ahead in the title race for the first time. Nottingham Forest went to Old Trafford that day and I didn't dare think Forest would win, but they did, when Scot Gemmill scored in the second half. With two games to go we were in front but they had a game in hand. At Sheffield United I was out injured, and we knew that they'd lost at West Ham, which was their game in hand. Bramall Lane was a crazy place to be that day. Wilkinson gave another emotive speech before kick-off asking us to, "Do it for your mums, your dads, your wives, your girlfriends, your kids, and yourselves. You've given the fans all they could ask for in the first forty games – now go and do it for yourselves." It was really windy, with litter blowing all over the place, and we won with an own goal from Brian Gayle. We all ran on the pitch at the end, but Wilko played it down, saying he was going home to do his garden, and warning us not to say anything stupid to the press. We were waiting on Manchester United's result at Anfield. They needed to win to have a chance of pipping us. I watched it on Ceefax for an hour, at which point, with Liverpool winning 1–0, I switched off. It finished 2–0. I'd played in twenty-five games that season and was almost disbelieving at the outcome. At the tail-end of my career I'd won League Cups and now I was a league champion.

Most of the Leeds players had watched it on their own but later I met up with Chris Fairclough and we went for a few quiet drinks to celebrate. Alex Ferguson came on TV looking ashen-faced, saying well done to Leeds United. He felt hard done by having three games in seven days but they bounced back and you know what's happened since. We had a week of parties out around Leeds every night. We had an open-top bus parade and all the usual receptions and things. We met some other players at the *Flying Pizza* and Eric Cantona was buying the champagne. He'd catalysed the team's confidence. He'd partake in minimal banter but his actions on the pitch led us on. And even then I think he felt that Leeds were a stepping stone on to bigger things. He wasn't always a starter, more of an impact player coming off the bench; he could go past people on his own and offered a different dimension to the Chapman–Wallace partnership.

Looking back, I can see that winning the league masked the failing relationship between me and Howard Wilkinson, but despite our differences I'd finished as the club's third-top scorer in the league. After being a professional footballer for over thirteen years I finally had the challenge of the Champions League.

Marching on to Europe

Because English clubs were banned from Europe, I hadn't played a competitive European club game for five seasons, even though Forest and Spurs would all have qualified at various stages. The English clubs were allowed back into the European competitions in the early 1990s but the long absence left them with a lot of catching up to do. The Champions League has gone through many changes since its inception and in 1992 you had to be the champions of your country in order to enter, no runners-up or third- and fourth-place teams, and it was less of a 'league' than the multiple group sections of later years. What mattered to me was that it was basically the same cup that I'd watched Forest win twice while learning my trade and it was the greatest club tournament in the world.

Howard Wilkinson was obviously of the same mind because he started preparations for the Champions League very early in the preseason, experimenting with formations and team play. He tried using Gary Speed in a sweeper role which was specifically designed for Europe, not something we'd ever done domestically. This highlighted another variation from what I knew as the Forest Way. Brian Clough would never change his system because of the opposition: it was always a case of we're good, let them worry about how we are going to play. Wilkinson, while preferring the long-ball game, did have some flexibility and in some ways was ahead of his time using video and specialist fitness coaches. He also used a lot of motivational terminology. In the dressing room there'd be slogans up on the board like, "The difference between ordinary and extraordinary is that little bit extra," and he'd underlined the word "extra". The next week it might say, "If you've failed to prepare, prepare to fail."

We didn't go far during preseason, just stayed in Leeds and a short trip to Ireland, where I got injured in Shelbourne. I was already slipping down Wilkinson's pecking order in midfield as it was. Last season I'd been fifth in line for four places and over the summer he'd signed another footballing midfielder in Scott Sellars. Then, in Shelbourne, at the pre-match meal, I found David Rocastle sitting at a table. "Rocky" was the last person I expected to see there; I'd not heard even a hint about Leeds being interested in him but there he was. All I could say was. "Rocky, what the heck are you doing here?" I was suddenly seventh in line. That night I was carried off and Wilkinson, ever the comic where my fitness was concerned, quipped sarcastically, "Well done, Hodgey, you nearly made it through a preseason there!"

Luckily, I was fit enough to be in contention for the Charity Shield against Liverpool in August. Alongside me on the bench that day was Gordon Strachan and I turned to him and said I just wanted to get on the pitch. He replied, "What about me? I've been here for three years." He had a very good point, because at times he'd carried the team while winning the league. Strachan's fitness was exceptional and he inspired by deeds and words. He also used to run games because he was so good with referees. In the end we both got on in a thrilling 4–3 win.

Having collected my second medal with Leeds inside a year, and with the Champions League coming up, I couldn't really complain but I just wanted a few more starts. It was a nice feeling to open the league season at Middlesbrough as champions. Technically, we were actually league champions and now in the FA Premier League but it didn't matter. Eric Cantona played at Boro and scored but got flak from the manager about his work rate as we got pasted 4–1. This game signalled the beginning of his getting a reputation for not playing well away from home. This was reinforced the next week at home to Spurs when he scored a hat-trick. I was sub for the first seven games and, live on TV, I came on against Aston Villa. Eric flicked it on and I scored a goal, just like I always did against Villa. We were having an indifferent start to the season and my relationship with the manager was slowly ebbing away.

I was involved in an early season supporters' club evening with Howard Wilkinson and special guest Dickie Bird. I was sitting with Dickie and talking about cricket when the manager took the mic to say a few words. There were about 500 Leeds fans at the event and Wilkinson said, "As I came in to training this morning I saw an illusion. I actually saw Steve Hodge training." It got a laugh but in front of so many people it was pretty embarrassing for me and illustrated how things were going to go. At one team meeting Wilkinson even told a joke about me. "Lads, I've got a joke for you. What have Clark Gable, Marilyn Monroe and Steve Hodge all got in common? They're all misfits." I tried to see the funny side but it was hard when my career was ticking away in the reserves or on the bench. Another time he told me, "If you were made of glass you'd shatter."

In the Champions League we had a tough first leg away to the German champions Stuttgart. Even my goal against Villa hadn't been enough to get me into the side. Like me, David Rocastle had been sitting out for most of the games so far but in Germany he was brought in from nowhere. He hadn't played a game but now he was in the starting line-up, having leap-frogged me in the queue. Needless to say, I was substitute again. The manager gave a really good speech before kick-off and reiterated how well-prepared we were. He warned us not to get agitated if the Germans started diving and play-acting. Rocky had a good chance during the opening exchanges, but missed. I thought it was an even game, so I was surprised when Wilkinson called me over after about thirty-five minutes and told me to get ready because I was going on at half-time. I was amazed, because at 0–0 in a first leg, especially away from home, I saw no reason to change it. I wasn't about to argue about getting a game in Europe though and I took Rocastle's place. Our second forty-five minutes were awful and we were pasted 3–0. After the game Wilkinson came in after we'd all got changed and said, "I'm not sure if I should have changed it, but one thing's for sure. When we get back to our place we lose to this lot over our dead bodies!" I got home at 4 a.m. the following morning but was told I had to report back at 10 a.m. for training with just five of the other lads, which I thought was crazy.

Back in Yorkshire for the second leg, I returned to the bench for one of Leeds' great European nights. In front of a big, noisy crowd we poured forward with some good, high-tempo football to win 4–1. They had no answer to us. The problem was they'd squeaked an away goal and with the tie level at 4–4 we were out on the away goals. It was a massive let-down after such an emotional night. The next morning brought an unexpected reprieve. A local journalist had noticed that when the Germans had made their final substitution they had been left with four foreign players, whereas a maximum of three was allowed under UEFA rules at the time. After a quick investigation the game was awarded to us by the standard forfeit score of 3–0, meaning that it was 3–3 on aggregate and away goals were level. A one-game play-off was ordered at a neutral venue. Barcelona was picked as the venue but I didn't even travel to the Camp Nou as my old calf trouble kept me out for a few games. We won the play-off 2–1 in front of an eerily sparse crowd in the massive stadium which set up a tie with Glasgow Rangers.

I returned to action as a sub when we hosted Nottingham Forest. Forest were bottom of the table having had their worst start ever under Brian Clough. They were struggling to score goals having sold Teddy Sheringham and all the press were bringing out the old "too good to go down" clichés. Clough had just brought Neil Webb back to the City Ground from Manchester United and that day he propelled the visitors to an emphatic 4–1 victory. Our fans were bemused and angry. By the end they were all singing, "You don't know what you're doing!" I came on when it was about 4–0 and Roy Keane flew past me. I thought, "I'm not having that!" so I took him down from behind. While I was picking myself up, my old mate Stuart Pearce ran by laughing, trying to wind me up.

The season was going badly, a really poor defence of the championship. Wilkinson had warned us back in the preseason that we'd have to improve just to stand still and that all the other teams would be after us. His words were that we had to 'box-clever' and so far we weren't. One thing that was affecting us more than most clubs was the newly changed back-pass rule which had been modified over the summer. Now for the first time you couldn't pass the ball back to your own goal-keeper and let him pick it up. This changed our options dramatically. Previously John Lukic would hold the ball and he'd launch it to us high up the pitch. Now, if Mel Sterland, say, knocked it back to him Lukic would have to launch it from the floor and the ball wasn't going far enough down the pitch. We were much less of a threat to anyone because the ball wasn't landing or being flicked to the edge of our opponents' area, it was bobbling around in the midfield. Also, teams would now really push up and make him kick it quickly.

In a rare appearance against Sheffield Wednesday at home we were 3–1 up when I made a mistake at the end of the game. Jon Newsome had a right go at me and it was all histrionics. When we got off the pitch I told him, "Don't you ever fucking embarrass me like that again on a football pitch!" I generally got on well with him but being shouted down by a young kid on the pitch wasn't good. Back at Forest Clough would always say, "Keep it in house. Work it out in here, don't let them all know about it out there!" He would always close ranks when things weren't going well, and at Leeds things weren't going well. I was fit but couldn't even get into an eighteen-man squad. And the team was getting past its peak. Individually, several players had had their career peaks the previous season and now were on their way down. Myself, David Rocastle, Scott Sellars and Eric Cantona were all on the wrong side of the manager. Coincidence or not, we were the last four big signings Wilkinson had made. Wilkinson had a heart-to-heart with me before the Wednesday game. He told me that he thought I felt that no matter how well I played I wouldn't get in the side. I replied that he was totally correct. He asked if I felt I'd be better off elsewhere and I said yes. His response was that he couldn't sell me because of my wages, though I was sure that someone else could have paid me the same. He added that I hadn't done enough to cause him a problem, but I disagreed and said whenever I'd played or come on as sub I felt I'd done consistently well. The chat ended there and I knew that nothing was going to change.

In Glasgow for the Champions League game I heard the loudest noise I'd ever heard on a football pitch. I'd played in a Battle of Britain when Forest beat Celtic but this was even more intense. This noise was almost literally deafening when the game kicked-off. It was a lot quieter five minutes later though, because Gary McAllister gave us the lead. Despite the great start we slipped back to our old ways and lost the match 2–1. Eric Cantona was taken off again, just as he had been in Stuttgart and again in the replay in Barcelona. We needed Eric to be our best player and we needed our best player to last for ninety minutes on the pitch. He and Wilkinson weren't speaking much by then and I could see that things were coming to a head. The manager wanted all his players to give 100 per cent effort all of the time and Eric was a luxury player that a struggling team couldn't always afford. It hadn't been highlighted before because as we went for the championship he'd been mainly coming on as a sub.

My troubles were even spreading to the training ground. One day I kicked Gary Speed in training. I wasn't a dirty player, but this went back to the Clough days of go and kick John Robertson. In my mind everyone was fair game. But this time Gordon Strachan ran over and said, "What do you think you're doing, kicking Speedy like that?" I had no answer. I was frustrated because the young kid was playing well and I couldn't get in the side. I felt like a second-class citizen; it was clear that Speed was in and he was being looked after and it made me feel that there was no place for me. In the past I'd always kicked and been kicked back and I just accepted it.

In October we went to London to face Queen's Park Rangers. At a team meeting in our hotel, Eric's Leeds career effectively came to an end. The manager said he'd been calling over to Eric in the lobby but that he'd been ignored four times. Eric, as was his wont, strolled in late. He was wearing a big coat and usually ignored any team dress-code instructions. I could see that Wilkinson had had enough. He said that Eric was completely dropped from the squad for the game. "I gather you want this," said the manager and from somewhere he produced Eric's passport and hurled it across the room. "I suggest you get a taxi because you can fuck off back to France," he yelled. Eric didn't seem to mind, but he seemed to take about five seconds to comprehend that he had to leave. He picked up the passport and left. We were all warned to keep the incident quiet and we did. Wilkinson had also said that Eric thought he was bigger than the club. I was surprised that ten days later Wilkinson picked Cantona for the return leg with Glasgow Rangers. He must have realised that, especially at home, the Frenchman could be a game winner. In his team talk Wilkinson told us that, "This is a chance to succeed not a chance to fail. It's like Frank Sinatra, saving his best song till last, this has to be about Leeds United giving it their best from the first whistle." I was always sceptical about going at teams in a helter-skelter way. I agreed with what Brian Clough had said years before when he explained that he'd wait until the last minute of the second leg to win a European tie. We only needed a 1–0 win to go through on the away goals rule so patience should have been part of the game plan. That didn't mean that we shouldn't have played a high-tempo game but we should have held some caution. We lost 2–1 again and our European adventure was over before the group stages even began. Our route one approach was smothered out by Richard Gough, Brown and Andy Goram. Lee Chapman never got a look-in for us and Rangers had more attacking options. Simply put, over the two legs they deserved to win.

To his credit, Howard Wilkinson realised that things needed to be changed and tried to do so. Unfortunately I was one of a few senior players that felt the brunt of his anger. I was back in the reserves for a game at Bolton alongside Chris Whyte, Jon Newsome, Rod Wallace, Dave Rocastle and Scott Sellars. Wilkinson had a right go at me in front of the players that night. "You're a museum piece," he blasted. "Living in the past with your medals and your England caps. Why don't you just put in a transfer request now and we can get it out in public!" He was taking his first-team frustrations out on me and clearly wanted me to make things easy for him by walking away, but I'd signed a contract and wanted to play to the best of my ability and honour it. I'd be lying, though, if I said I wasn't losing heart in the club because of the way I was being treated. No matter what I did, I'd get dropped.

The Times Were a Changin'

I was at Leeds United when the Premiership was introduced and around this time I started to see evidence of changes in the way managers approached the game and the way that players kept themselves fit. The Premiership didn't really mean much of a difference to us at first: sure there were a few more TV games and dancing girls and fireworks on the pitch when we ran out for kick-off, but the money hadn't really changed and it was nothing like it is today. On Monday mornings at Leeds we'd have video sessions, which was new to me. The fitness side of the game was taken very seriously and Creatine was used to build up muscles. I didn't bother but some players swore by it, and we did lots of physical work. The trainer of the runner Peter Elliott came in and gave us routines on the weights. We were a fit and strong team and Howard Wilkinson was probably ahead of his time getting a dedicated fitness coach in. You can see why the players called him Sergeant Wilko. But not to his face.

Gordon Strachan used to have a spasm in his hamstring and he'd pull up quickly. As I was on the bench more often than not, I'd think there was a chance I might be able to get on but he could give it a minute or two and it would calm down again. There were several times when I'd jump up to get ready but then sit down again. He was a fitness fanatic – I'd see him walking around the dressing room with his fingers on his torso, pressing points on the skin which he believed gave you energy. He even got his own fitness expert in from

Scandinavia. He'd be eating bananas everywhere and he could run all day, so something was working for him.

The scientific side of the game was improving and I have a lot to thank Mick Hennigan for because he prolonged my playing career by several years. No one had ever been able to solve my recurring calf problems until Mick mentioned that I should try some Orthotics, hard plastic inner-soles that you slip into your shoes or boots. As you age, your gait changes and the way I ran, my biomechanics were causing my problems. I had plaster casts made of my feet and they made perfectly fitting plastic inner-soles which would line my body up. It was very odd when I started playing with them, and different muscles ached compared to what I was used to, but the calf problem just went away. It showed me that, in England in the 1990s, the professionals still had only a very average knowledge of sports science. This was something that they'd known about for a while in the United States but I'd suffered for years. The inner-soles, which I wear in my shoes to this day, meant I soon had full fitness. Around this time we all had to do a Health Hydro-test. Out of the eighteen players I came in as the sixth fittest, Despite this I was put back in the reserves again. In fact, even for the reserves I was sometimes a sub. I got a game against Wolves reserves and played well, scoring and setting up two more in a 5–1 win. My calves were OK; I played ninety minutes – but it was never enough.

Shocked

We lost 4–0 at Manchester City in what proved to be Eric Cantona's last game for us. I was at home when it came on the news that he'd gone for £1 million, to Manchester United! I fell off my seat when I heard that he'd been sold to our main rivals, and so cheaply. It was the worst possible thing we could do. After pipping them to the title, Alex Ferguson was living up to his claim of being back again the next year. They were already flying when he signed Cantona but a lot of careers were enhanced by him going to Old Trafford. When we'd won the league and were celebrating on the town hall balcony he'd said, "I don't know why I love you, but I do." Understandably the fans had gone mad, but that was long forgotten when he came back a few weeks later with Manchester United. He got the dog's abuse. There was real hatred in the air but he rose to the occasion, became even more the matador. With his head held high and collar turned up he seemed to thrive on the atmosphere. Eric felt he had arrived when he signed at Old Trafford: he loved the adulation and had players around him to do the work. He was simply fantastic for them and they were the right club for him. That night at Elland Road my abiding memory of him is that as he ran past me down the tunnel he was getting spat on by so many people. Howard Wilkinson once called Eric a fart-around merchant. I couldn't believe he'd said that and had to write it down. The player that became a Manchester United legend was what Wilkinson considered a fart-around merchant!

David Kerslake came to the club for a few games and at his first session the manager said to him, "Dave, you'll find that I'm loyal to the people I can trust and who give 110 per cent for me. Rocky and Steve Hodge might disagree with that and say I'm too loyal to some players, but that's life."

The new year for me didn't bring any change of fortunes. On the New Year's day team sheet I could see that me and Scott Sellars had been written right at the bottom but then we'd been tipp-ex'd out. The lads fell about laughing. I was involved in a friendly at Rotherham, on the subs bench at least. During half-time the manager came in and he went berserk. I was standing behind him and during his tirade he turned to face me and shouted, "I'm talking to you as well! You're a part of it! Yawning in the background!" He turned back to continue his rant then paused, turned back to me and said, "You probably didn't deserve that, but you got it anyway." I don't know why he turned on me and because he half-apologised it must have been bad. I can laugh about it now, but at the time I just wanted to play and enjoy my football. When I wasn't even on the bench I used to watch the home games from one of the boxes that we were allocated behind the goal. After one match I waited in there to get the scores from the teams around us because we were in a relegation battle. When I went downstairs I walked into a team meeting. "Here he is," chimed Wilkinson, "late as ever. This is what today's result means to him: fuck all!" He didn't know that I'd hung around just to let them know what the scores were and I ended up getting another rollicking.

My first-team career at Leeds seemed to be over and I had a year and four months to get through. All the players were called into the first-team dressing room. I went in but Mick Hennigan said, "Excuse me, Hodgey, the gaffer doesn't want you in the meeting." It was another embarrassing episode and I had to walk out while sixteen other players looked on.

The first team was heading for relegation trouble when I got back in to play Forest away. I was so low that I even had trouble getting up for the Forest game; I had nothing to prove there and it was a place that Leeds never seemed to win. There had been some rumours flying around the Trent End about me and some of the songs were getting a bit nasty. I was subjected to some graphic taunts about my sexuality and it hit me hard during that game. I felt really saddened deep down because of the venom it was shouted with and the fact that the same fans had been cheering me on and singing my name just two years before. I went through that game feeling deflated and gave a deflated performance. Around this time I also got a few comments shouted my way during nights out in Nottingham. They were isolated incidents when I was out with my mates but it wasn't nice. I just thought there was no point in reacting.

Wilkinson was putting his faith in the younger players now. Mark Tinkler, Jamie Forrester, Noel Whelan and David Weatherall were all used to try and stop the rot. After we lost 2–0 at Liverpool, when I'd travelled but wasn't even on the bench, I was dropped to a new low. We got back to Elland Road at about six-thirty in the evening and the players got into their cars and headed off. I was about to do the same when Mick Hennigan's Yorkshire accent rang out across the car park, ""Ah reet lads, see yer all on Monday. But you four lads that didn't play can come with me now to do some running." This was a Saturday night and we'd been away all day since about eight in the morning. I hadn't played, we'd got beat, and I just wanted to go down the M1 and get home. He made me train for about forty minutes. I was approaching thirty-one and this was just getting out of hand.

We weren't safe yet but he amazingly put me in against Queen's Park Rangers and I scored in a 1–1 draw. When we drew late on at Coventry the Leeds fans invaded the pitch and the game was cancelled after eighty-nine minutes. That weekend Gordon Strachan took a few players to see Simple Minds in concert and I got to meet Jim Kerr, who I'd been a fan of for a while.

We escaped relegation by two points but were nearly the first team in history to win the league and then get relegated the following season. I was almost part of a trivia question, "Who were the last team to win the old First Division and who were the first teams to be relegated from the new Premier Division?" My second season at Leeds had been a disaster for me and the club; I'd fallen out with the manager but at least I'd got over my injuries. I had one year left on my contract.

I started my last season at Leeds like I had as an apprentice at Forest fifteen years earlier. The first team, of which I no longer felt a part, went to Japan on tour while I went with the kids to play at a tournament with the apprentices. During that last season at Elland Road I had to get changed with the kids in the other changing room – I really was an outcast. Over the summer David Rocastle and Scott Sellars had been shipped out and David White had come in from Manchester City. David O'Leary also joined. He was in his mid-thirties and was unbelievably given a three-year contract, but after only four or five games he did his Achilles and was finished. I spent a lot of time in the treatment room with the genial Irishman and I don't think even he could believe the deal he'd been given. He was around long enough to see the end of the Wilkinson era at Leeds and, of course, his old boss, George Graham came in and made him his number two which eventually led to David getting the Leeds manager's job.

For the first game of the season, can you guess? I was sub.

I didn't get my first start of the season until we went to Norwich in December. I just had five months of monotonous drudgery in the reserves. I was fit but only got the odd substitute appearance. After Norwich, injuries to other players gave me a little run of games and we got some good results. Versus Queen's Park Rangers I was man-marked all over the pitch by Ian Holloway but I scored. I was kept in on New Year's Day at Old Trafford. In the pre-match team meeting we were told to go man-for-man and I was given Roy Keane to deal with. I knew he'd just run and run, so I just ran and ran. We had battles everywhere and while it wasn't great to watch, Howard Wilkinson got it tactically spot on, and it was good to play in. They got a free-kick when I was trying to hold Keane up and slow him down. He'd grown physically and was a real athlete. This was also the game which produced the famous picture of me and Eric Cantona. I'd scythed Eric down, which you could get away with in those days, so I just did it. As I got up he walked to me shaking his finger saying, "Hodgey, non, non, non, non, non." As he got near he just stuck his finger right up my nose, and someone took the picture of me being taken by surprise. My return to the team had helped us go unbeaten against Arsenal, Newcastle and Manchester United. Next we were having a Saturday warm-up for a Sunday game against Blackburn live on TV. Howard Wilkinson walked past and he tapped me on the shoulder, "If Speed is fit tomorrow he plays." And off he strolled. I'd been in for several games, we'd been unbeaten and I scored goals, but I was out again. We lost, live on TV.

That was pretty much me done for the season. I was out of the whole squad by the time we played at Swindon in our last game. We won 5–0 but I was off visiting friends in London. I ended my Leeds career with over fifty appearances as a substitute. My fiftieth appearance as a sub came in the

FA Cup at Oxford. I'd told Jon Newsome, who was also a cricket fan, that when I got my fifty I'd impersonate playing a forward defensive shot as I walked on to the pitch, which I did. I wasn't bothered by then. My Leeds career just wound down until the manager called me in for a meeting at the end of the season. "We won't be offering you a new contract and you're free to leave," he told me. Nothing more, nothing less. As I drove down the M1 back to Nottingham I heard on the radio that Leeds United had released eight players. This was the team that had recently been champions. The radio presenter said that the most high-profile player to be released was former England international Steve Hodge. It hurt to hear that. I knew I was on my way down, but this seemed to make it more official. It was even more galling to find out later that Stoke and Southampton had made offers for me in that final season but that Howard had said I wasn't available.

Free Agent

I spent the summer of 1994 in Nottingham, not knowing where my career was going and wondering if it was going anywhere. The football landscape as I knew it was changing. England had failed to qualify for the USA 94 World Cup, the first failure to qualify for a tournament in a decade. Nottingham Forest had been relegated in the Premiership's inaugural season and Brian Clough had left the club in sad circumstances. I hadn't seen too much of the gaffer since joining Leeds. Our paths had crossed just after I'd scored against Liverpool in my first season at Elland Road. He pulled his car over and wound his window down. "Harry, how are you? Well done at the weekend, son, I was pleased for you, honest." And I think he really did mean it. After all we'd been through in my last year at Forest it was nice to feel the warmth that he was really happy for me. Like most outsiders I'd been shocked when Forest were relegated. When I'd been there for the FA Cup final just two years earlier they were mid-table and doing OK. Certainly there were no real warning signs of such a dramatic decay. When I'd seen photos of his last game in the paper, the blotchy-faced manager in the pictures was not the Brian Clough I remembered and knew. When our paths crossed in the later years of his life he was always pleased to see me and would stop and chat, with him often mentioning my penalty win in 1989.

My agent was trying to get me a club, but there weren't any takers in the Premiership. Even First Division sides were reluctant, probably because of my recent injury troubles even though I'd put my calf troubles behind me. Back then, if you had no club you were still paid monthly until you got a new club. My agent, Kev Mason, was trying everything to get me a decent deal and his search took me overseas. Along with my old Forest teammate, Franz Carr, who was also out of contract, Mason arranged for us to have a trial at Sporting Lisbon. I flew out and checked into the Hilton which allowed us to walk to the training ground each day.

It was a totally new experience for me being abroad. The Sporting manager, though well known now, was practically unheard of outside of Portugal – his name was Carlos Queiroz. I was impressed by his training regime, it was very structured, very friendly. Each morning we'd arrive, and because I didn't know a word of Portuguese I'd nod to this mysterious fellow in the corner who I thought was an assistant coach but couldn't really communicate with because he spoke little or no English. Later I found out his name was Jose Mourinho. We went to watch the local Lisbon derby. Sporting were at home to Benfica but lost 6–3. Joao Pinto scored a hat-trick – the quality of the game was a different class. Figo scored two that night but I didn't know him then. I couldn't get near him in training and soon realised that these were technically excellent players. Paulo Sousa was also there. He looked arrogant on the pitch and could really play. It was a relaxed atmosphere, while in England it was more intense. When they played "get a touch" in the circle it was carefree and they'd try things, they weren't afraid to fail. This was my first indication that Portugal would become the force in European football that they became in the late 1990s. Other names I came across there were Jorge Cadete, who later went to Celtic, and Nelson, who went to Villa. I wondered what they made of me and why I was there, they really had no need for us especially at the back end of my career. They were all young and eager, with their careers spread out before them. I was the experienced old pro with my best days behind me, trying to fit in in a foreign land.

One day I kicked Figo in training. I held up my hand to apologise and in a deep man's voice he said, "It's OK." He was only about eighteen! We did hard training twice a day and I was questioning my own reason for being there. I wasn't sure that I wanted to move to Portugal anyway but Kev Mason kept saying "something will happen". I was wondering what I had to prove at my age and with my experience: either they wanted me or they didn't. I got sick of training for no reason and I flew back after a week. Franz Carr stayed out and Kev rang me to ask why I'd gone back. I said that after a week they should know enough about us to make a decision. Kev said, "You've got to go back," so on the Sunday I flew back again. On the Tuesday we trained. I'd been warned that because we were foreigners we would have had to marry a Portuguese girl to be able to sign a contract and stay in the country. Once you were nationalised as Portuguese you could then divorce a year later. I don't know if I'd have done it had the situation arose, but morally I didn't feel it was right. There was a meeting with Sporting's millionaire chairman Sintra. Kev came back and said, "The deal is off. The owner doesn't trust Englishmen. End of story." I wasn't too upset to be leaving Portugal, but the reality of the matter was that as soon as I was back on the plane I was flying home to an uncertain future. From winning the league title to basically being out of work had come around very quickly and was difficult to come to terms with.

Despite not getting a contract offer in Portugal I wasn't too upset about it. For one thing the marriage to a Portuguese girl would have proved difficult because I'd just met my future wife, Ali, in the summer of 1994 in Nottingham. On the day we met, the friend that she was with at the time told her that my face looked familiar and she thought I was a professional footballer. In fact, her friend said, "I think he's John Robertson!" Ali and I quickly grew close and I was soon commuting back from wherever I was playing to see her.

The new football season started without me and for the first time in my life I didn't have a football club. Roy McFarland was managing Derby County in the First Division and he wanted to sign me. A decade at local rivals Forest could have made it tricky, but Derby had had a bad start to the season and needed help quickly. They only offered me a two-month deal because they were skint. It was Derby or nothing, so I took it. If nothing else it would help my fitness and put me in the shop window. It's easy to be forgotten when you are out of the game, even for a little while. The player whose place I took at Derby refused to even say a single word to me in the six weeks I was at the club. I just thought he was an idiot. It wasn't my fault he was out of the team – he should have asked the manager or questioned his own performances first.

My first-ever game in the second tier was at home against Middlesbrough and my old hero, Bryan Robson. Early in the game I got stuck into a 50–50 tackle and the main stand stood up and there was a real roar of approval at the old Baseball Ground. From that moment on the fans accepted me because they could see my whole-hearted commitment. I really enjoyed my time there, but Roy later told me that the team was filled with too many egos and too many cliques. Just like when I'd gone to Aston Villa, this was another very young team and I was there to add some experience and stability. At least I was old enough to provide it this time. My first football outside the top flight was a bit of a culture shock but I scored four times in eight games and Derby went from sixth off the bottom to eighth from top. Other clubs were noticing me and when Roy said that Derby couldn't afford to keep me, Queen's Park Rangers manager Gerry Francis was in like a shot. They asked me to go and see them play in a League Cup game at home to Manchester City.

Rangers were another club in trouble, stuck in the bottom three of the Premiership, and another very young team. They were lacking a bit of midfield authority so that was my job again. Gerry asked me about my time at Spurs and why I'd left. I explained I was young and homesick back then, but now I was in my thirties, I wanted a contract to the end of the following season; I was keen to play and my maturity wasn't a problem. We quickly agreed terms and I was back in the top flight. It was written in the stars that my first game would be against Aston Villa. I'd played for four clubs since leaving Villa Park but I was booed as usual and the away end could be very loud at Loftus Road. We won 2–0. In the short time I played for him I found Gerry Francis to be an enthusiastic, chirpy, confident coach. Our next game was against Liverpool, live on TV. We won, but trouble was brewing. A consortium was trying to take control of the club and they wanted Gerry Francis out. I didn't know the ins and outs of the situation but Rodney Marsh was involved and the next day Gerry resigned. The manager who signed me was gone just ten days after I'd joined.

My old World Cup England teammate Ray Wilkins took over control of Rangers and my next game was against Leeds United. I was really enjoying being a top-flight regular again and was back to making runs like I had through most of my career. I loved to get down the inside-left channel and John Lukic was berating his defenders for not picking up my runs. A few minutes later I got down there again and crossed for Les Ferdinand to score. I didn't get any trouble from the Leeds fans; in fact, I'd had a few letters thanking me for seeing out my three years. Gary Speed spent most of that game kicking me to high heaven. I told him he'd get himself sent off. He didn't, but we won 3-2. Afterwards I passed Howard Wilkinson and he acknowledged me with a slight nod, but no words or shake of hands. We'd beaten Leeds, Liverpool and Villa, a great start.

On Christmas Day 1994 I woke up alone in the Wembley Hilton Hotel with the prospect of a morning training session ahead of me – the glamour of Premiership football! After training I was invited to the Wilkins family Christmas dinner, a large gathering and a gesture that I really appreciated. We all had a lovely meal before I joined up with the rest of the players that night to prepare for a Boxing Day game against Arsenal. The game proved to be memorable for Arsenal fans because it was the only goal Arsenal's Danish midfielder John Jensen ever scored for the club, and I was supposed to be taking care of him in the midfield! We did manage a 3-1 win, however, but I still got some grief about the goal from the lads. I was enjoying my time at Rangers and just to be playing every week was a relief, even if it was at a supposed "smaller" club. In training, Ian Holloway was a fitness freak, but even he was outdone by coach Billy Bonds, who was in his fifties. Midfielder Ned Zelic briefly appeared from Borussia Dortmund for one day, signed and then vanished. He'd had an idea about what a premier league team was but after he saw the small stadium and poor training ground it was all quashed and he flew home to Germany right away.

We were hammered at the eventual champions, Blackburn. I can recall chasing Alan Shearer when he scored from twenty yards with unbelievable power in his shot. We'd been on a good run before then but that game had been poor and I thought we deserved a rocket from the manager. When Ray

Wilkins came in he just sat on a desk and calmly said, "Right, lads, that just wasn't good enough. See you Monday." That was it. We won the next week, then lost 3-2 against Manchester United when I missed a late chance. We moved clear of the relegation zone and finished eighth in the Premiership. Even with all my medals, caps and World Cup trips, this was one of my most pleasing achievements. I'd really enjoyed it but football was changing. Teams were playing with a back three and I had less holes to run into. I didn't score for Rangers that whole year.

○ ○ ○

Before the 1995–96 season with QPR we went on tour to Italy. We'd lost Les Ferdinand to Newcastle after he'd asked what I thought he should do. I'd told him that Newcastle was too good to turn down. One night outside a nightclub up in the Tuscan hills I was sitting with Trevor Sinclair on a wall. Some kids came by and one said, "Hello, Mr Hodge, how are you?" I thought, "Jeez, I'm up in the Tuscan hills. No one should recognise me here!"

That summer Ali became pregnant with my son Elliot. My life and priorities were changing and I spoke to Ray Wilkins in the preseason and told him, "I've got a bit of a problem." He wasn't too chuffed when I told him that I'd like a move back to the Midlands area. Our opening game at Blackburn came along and I wasn't in the seventeen and then found myself dropped to the reserves without another word. I was left there for several months. We played at Harrow Borough against the southern teams and it wasn't very pleasant for me. Finally, in December, the club phoned to say they were offering me a package to end the contract and I was free to go. It was a sad way to end it and a sad way for myself and Ray to end after we'd been to a World Cup together.

In January 1996 I was effectively out of work and approaching thirty-five. I'd done nothing but play football all my life. I got a call from Glenn Roeder, the Watford manager, offering me a month's contract and the chance to start playing again, which I gladly accepted. Whilst there I had the pleasure of playing alongside a young Kevin Phillips but only managed two appearances because the schedule was decimated by bad weather. Just as my month was coming to an end Glenn was sacked and I was out of a job once again. Graham Taylor took over from Glenn but I didn't hang around waiting for a call. Instead I took a trial with Chris Nicholl at Walsall and he offered me a contract to the end of the season but my Achilles wasn't right. Morally I wasn't happy about taking their money knowing that physically I wasn't right and that my Achilles could go at any time. Instead I phoned up my old mate Gordon Strachan at Coventry and had a three month spell there, keeping myself fit and hoping for a breakthrough in the game somewhere. George Boateng was an unknown youngster at the club, as was Chris Kirkland. Another goalkeeper at the club was Magnus Hedman, who would pull out a little tin and take a shot of snuff before a game or before training, the only player I ever saw do that.

After Coventry I went for a trial at Notts County during the summer of Euro 96. I played some preseason games but Sam Allardyce was having none of it and I read in the paper that they weren't taking me on. He hadn't told me, so I went in the next morning to thank him for offering me the chance and to wish him good luck, but I would have appreciated a face to face chat to find out the bad news!

Out of nowhere I got a call to go and play in Sweden one summer. It was a minor league club and I can't for the life of me even remember the name of it now, but I agreed to go for three months on decent money. I decided to do it while I was still fit, but my heart wasn't in it, I was lured more by the chance to keep playing football – it was all I knew. Also, I just didn't know how to say "no". They were so kind about it and so keen to get me out there that I thought, "When push comes to shove I'll probably say 'yes'." After telling them I'd go I started thinking about the last fifteen years. I'd done so much travelling I came to the conclusion that, with my family commitments, it just wasn't worth it for the time that I'd be away from home. But I'd given them my word and was due to fly out the following day, first to Copenhagen and then somewhere into the middle of Sweden. To be honest, I had no idea where it was or how I was being paid. I was on my own and had no agent. The officials were calling me the night before, leaving me messages, saying that cameras would be at the airport. Late on the night before travelling I finally decided not to go. The phone was ringing but I wouldn't answer and just hoped it would go away, that they'd give up calling and I'd be free of it. Ali said, "You can't do that; you have to talk to them." I checked the answer machine which said, "We're looking forward to meeting you at the airport tomorrow." Eventually I called them and said, "I've got a young family and I can't come. I've had to think deep about it but I can't come. I hope you understand." They were disappointed, but were pretty good about it and let it go. I was so relieved not to be on the 6 a.m. flight. I was later told by Roland Nilsson that the place I'd have been going to really was in the middle of nowhere and I'd have been bored out of my box. I learned a valuable lesson to say no sometimes.

Even when my career was on the way down, it was hard to get away from the pinnacles I'd reached. One Sunday afternoon I was just relaxing at home when the doorbell rang. As I opened the front door I was greeted by a couple of Asian chaps who introduced themselves and said, "Nice to meet you. So-and-so said you lived here, Steve Hodge, ex-England international. Is it OK if our family and friends just said hello to you?" I was a little taken aback but said, "Yes, no problem." Only then did I notice a coach parked a little way down the road. The friends and family must have numbered about twenty-five to thirty people and they politely filed off the coach and formed an orderly queue up my front garden to take it in turns to say hello and shake my hand. Then they boarded the coach, gave me a wave, and were gone.

My final stop as a player came when Orient manager Tommy Taylor gave me a day's notice to play a league game at Scunthorpe in the fourth tier of the league. I hadn't done a preseason but had had both Achilles cleaned out. I only met the other players for the first time on Friday night; they needed a left sided midfielder and I played with Martin Ling in midfield. Brian Laws was managing Scunthorpe and when he saw me on pitch before the game he said, "What the heck are you doing here?" It was a scorching hot day and I played for an hour. In that time I'd touched the ball about five times. It was constantly being launched over the midfield and I was no influence on the game at all. All the other players were really fit and the game passed me by. Quite rightly, after an hour, Tommy Taylor took me off and, as I sat there taking my own boots off, I knew I was done. On my debut I'd had the great Brian Clough taking my boots off. I was glad I'd played that game because it had made my mind up: that brand of football just didn't suit me. I'd had fourteen seasons in the top tier and this was different football. I phoned Tommy on the Monday and thanked him and wished him all the best. That was it, my career was over.

A New Life

When my son Elliot was born I had two years away from the game. For the first time in over twenty years I wasn't playing football on a Saturday afternoon. By the millennium I was thinking about what I was going to do for the rest of my working life. I still wanted to be involved in the game, possibly by getting in somewhere before doing my coaching badges but I found that as soon as you are out of the game you find it is hard to get back in. I phoned Brian Bates at the Notts County academy and he let me go down and do some coaching. I completed enough hours for my 'B' badge, which consisted of eight two-hour sessions for an assessment with a Football Association rep who watches you do a session, then you pass or fail. It's very scary to have your football knowledge judged by a "qualified" person.

With the first hurdle completed I helped out at Leicester City's Academy, but more as a parent. One summer I was at a loose end and decided to do my 'A' badge. I got some funding to do that at Lilleshall and did my hours with Trevor Peake at Leicester City. My first two weeks at Lilleshall were tough, out on the pitch all day apart from an hour for lunch. On the very first day I stupidly pulled my hamstring in the first five minutes. I had to do the rest of it sitting down watching everyone else for two weeks. Tony Adams and Steve Bould were there but not many other high-profile players. If you don't do things the FA way you fail and throughout my career the various coaches and managers had hardly toed the FA line in every aspect of their training sessions. The FA dictated that you had to blow your whistle to indicate this or that at very strict junctures in the sessions and that everything had to be explained in their laid-down formats. Any variations from their script meant you would fail. There were lots of students and schoolteachers there with me and it was a bit strange to converse with people who hadn't been in my sphere and having to have dinner with them and talk to them about their careers. Now there's a fast track for ex-pros to go through. Thankfully I passed my assessment and gained my UEFA A licence, a qualification which will hopefully help me into the game as a coach.

After that I worked on *Talk Sport* for two years with Adrian Durham, a great front man, and we'd bash out the news of the day. Before an England v Germany game one of the German media people came on air with us. It was Thomas Berthold who I'd told to "fuck off" at Italia 90. I took the opportunity to say sorry after all those years, so I apologised live on air and he laughed about it and took it really well. It was an enjoyable, and fairly easy, two years – I can talk about football all day long.

As an ex-England international I've also been invited on trips and to tournaments that have taken me around the world in my retirement. I played beach football and met up with Eric Cantona, now with his big, long beard. It was the usual, "Hodgey, how are you?" and not much more.

I also had trips with the FA to help gain votes for England's 2006 World Cup bid. In South Africa the group I was with had an eye-opening trip to Soweto, where the kids loved their football and played in bare feet on pitches which were littered with broken glass. I played in a charity game in Durban, but we couldn't visit the beach because it was too dangerous. When walking around in the daytime we even had to go in twos and threes.

Another official trip took me to Moscow for the anniversary of Dynamo Moscow's first trip to the UK. We played in an indoor stadium against legends such as Belanov, Dasaev and Michalichenko. At the hotel where we were staying the lobby was filled with gorgeous women and one or two players were caught on camera with these girls, who were prostitutes, in lifts. Nothing happened, but it was still in the press. I took a cab on my own to Red Square to have a wander around. I looked around the sights and as I approached the eternal flame near Red Square I recognised a very familiar bald head being given his own personal guided tour. It was Pierre Luigi Collini, who was in town for the following day's Spartak Moscow v Arsenal Champions League game. Another coaching and ambassadorial role took me to Egypt where I witnessed the world's craziest drivers, and Iran wasn't a place high on my list of places to visit but I was asked to go there with Gary Mabbutt. We did some work with the Iranian coaches and some PR work. The menu at the hotel wasn't the best and I ended up eating chicken for nine consecutive nights, just to play it safe. All the women wore veils and the men seemed to dominate life. We visited the opulent former home of the Shah and took a taxi to go and experience the shrine of the Ayatollah Khomeini. I saw huge murals of Khomeini on the sides of buildings and more sinister ones like a statue of liberty made to look like the devil and with the slogan "Death to America" written next to it. One night we were invited to meet the chairman of the Iranian FA and when I mentioned that I'd played for Nottingham Forest his reaction was, "Ahh, Brian Clough!" It seems that everyone the world over remembered meeting Cloughie. He told me that years before Cloughie had been over to Iran for talks about becoming the Iranian national team manager!

I also had the privilege of playing in the first-ever game at the new Wembley Stadium. Mind you, I didn't quite have Shilton, Pearce and Lineker in my team; this time I had Phil Tuffnell in goal, Chris Evans at left-back and Brian McFadden up front!

O O O

In 2005 Roy McFarland gave me another chance when he allowed me to help out at Chesterfield. I was there for two years, working with the reserve team and watching a lot of League One football. I learned from him how to deal with chairmen and we beat Manchester City and West Ham in the League Cup. At Chesterfield a young lad called Jamie O'Hara came from Tottenham on loan and he looked petrified before his debut at Doncaster. I went over and told him, "Enjoy it, it might be a bit fast at the start but stick in there and you'll be fine." He *was* fine and when he went back to Spurs as a better and more experienced player he got into their first team and the England Under-21s. I could see everything Roy did on a day-to-day basis which was good of him, but in 2007 he was sacked and I left. Now I work part-time at the Nottingham Forest academy so my footballing life has come full circle.

I make a point of keeping in contact with as many people in the game as possible. I like to go and watch people train; it's interesting to see what methods various coaches and managers use. When Carlos Queiroz was at Manchester United he invited me to watch them train and I chatted to Sir Alex Ferguson. I mentioned that I'd been to see Mansfield versus Oxford and he knew the score and scorers. I said I was impressed that he knew such details and he said, "I know football." When I saw Brazil training it was really relaxed, just like it had been when I was in Lisbon. At an England training session with Tord Grip and Sven-Goran Eriksson the manager told me he remembered seeing me when I'd been in Sweden with Forest at small countryside grounds.

The person I probably bumped into the most over the last few years was Sir Bobby Robson. One of the times we met up was in 2007 when he got his BBC award live on TV. He hobbled up to the stage that night and I was the first one he met as he walked up the ramp. We shook hands and I was a bit shocked at his physical deterioration. He got such a heart-felt round of applause that it was a spine-tingling moment. He gave a great, typically down-to-earth speech. In the hospitality suite afterwards he came over and spoke to me and introduced me to his mate Charlie Woods, "This is Stevie Hodge. He's the one that gave that back pass for Maradona." That's the way he was. I mentioned that I was trying to get into the game as a coach and he said there's no respect in the game anymore. Apparently he'd been trying to get one of his ex-players into the game and it really hurt him that he couldn't help the people who had helped him as players. I next saw him at the National Football Awards evening in Blackpool. He did a speech and picked me out in the crowd. I think he had a soft spot for me. I saw him again at a dinner for his foundation in Sheffield but at the following one he cancelled and I knew he was getting worse.

The last time I saw him was when I went to Newcastle to play in the Bobby Robson Trophy game for charity. The first person I saw as I arrived at the hotel was none other than Howard Wilkinson. I assumed he was there because it was a big occasion; I didn't know he was going to be the manager the following day! He was as professional as ever before the game, doing team shape; the warm-ups were professional – and I was on the bench as per normal. It was just like the old days. Before the game I met lots of players I hadn't seen for a while. Gazza was his usual self, calling me "Chicken". Then the manager came in before the game and said we needed to get out there. "Bobby isn't in great shape and we need to get out there now because he's on the way." We were under the impression that he was so ill he wouldn't be able to be there. The line-ups on the pitch for this England v Germany game were a who's who of football on both sides. It was a fantastic crowd and very emotional to see him come out in a wheelchair. He'd aged a lot and you could see he was very very ill and it was all a bit of a tearjerker. I don't think there was a dry eye in the ground as he came along and 'Nessun Dorma' was playing. I could see the esteem he was held in with the size of the crowd. It had been arranged months before and all the players were just grateful to be there for what turned out to be a final farewell. He passed away just a few days later, but it wasn't a big shock after seeing how frail he was. Alan Shearer got the winning penalty that night and we beat Germany. Lothar Matthaus was arguing with the referee and I thought, "Come on, it's a friendly." Angus Deayton had flown in from Italy. He and Jim Rosenthal were on the bench and, with all due respect, the German side was far too good for them. Howard's predicament was that we were leading 3–2 in the final minutes in front of Bobby and a big crowd and could he really put a comedian and a presenter on against the likes of Lothar Matthaus? He did get Paddy McGuinness on for about the last minute and Angus got about thirty seconds, but we couldn't not win that match for Bobby. He had a smile on his face as he stayed to the end then got away quickly.

I recently met Sven-Goran Eriksson and we got talking about Sir Bobby Robson. Sven told me how he'd come over to England when he was an unknown to watch Ipswich Town train during the Swedish off-season. Bobby Robson was generous to let this Swedish nobody into his training and then asked Sven if he was watching the game tomorrow. Robson invited his guest to watch with him from the director's box and talk about football. It summed up his generosity perfectly. As usual the talk turned to Maradona and while Sven was at Lazio he played Maradona's Napoli and won quite easily. Maradona walked by the Swede after the game and said, "Mister, I will play a different tune on Wednesday night," which was the date of another game between the two sides. He was true to his word and in the second game he orchestrated Napoli to a 3–0 lead by half-time. Eriksson's defenders were asking their manager what they could do to stop him and he couldn't offer them any advice. We'd both had to try and deal with one of the world's all-time greatest players in the flesh, and he was just too good.

Moving on to today, it's great that England are bidding to host the World Cup and all fingers are crossed for the final decision. I was fortunate to have been part of the bid to include Nottingham as a host city and when I went to Wembley as part of the delegation it took me full circle from playing in a World Cup to trying to get my city directly involved. There is no doubt that England can hold the World Cup and I think that we have waited long enough for a second shot at it, I just hope that the bid team have ticked all the right boxes for FIFA.

This year's World Cup gives England a definite chance of glory. Looking at World football at the moment the likes of Argentina, France, Italy and Germany wouldn't scare England, only Spain and Brazil are currently better teams but good teams have been known to go out on penalties and Italy proved in 2006 that you don't have to be a brilliant team to win it. We have a top-notch manager with a great track record and we have plenty of top players who have played in World Cups before and Champions League finals. They are vastly experienced players – but there is one player who I believe must be fully fit if we are to succeed: Wayne Rooney.

I'm working at the Nottingham Forest academy and also with the club on match days, and as I write this I firmly believe that Forest will be back in the Premier League next season. It's also great to see Leeds on the way back and Villa and Spurs also having fine seasons. I would love the chance to coach at a good club, so we'll have to wait and see if that little bit of luck comes my way. One thing that does concern me is the lack of opportunities for kids in England. Youngsters from Europe and Africa are being brought into our system and this is bound to have a detrimental effect on the chances for our own kids to make the grade. I can't blame the kids for doing this but I feel that something needs to be done to protect our own.

Have One on Me! A Quiet Drink with Brian Clough

The drinking culture within football during the 1980s and early 1990s had been established years before. Everyone knew that Brian Clough liked a drink and he liked the sun on his back. Our week-long jaunts to Cala Millor in Majorca, after being knocked out of the cup or at the end of the season, were drinking sessions of mammoth proportions. We usually arrived late at night and we'd go straight out on the town. Every day would then follow the same routine: wake up at lunchtime, head down to one of the many bars for a drink, relax by the pool during the afternoon, sleep from 5–7 p.m., eat and then head out drinking until the early hours. Five days of this routine would be a killer, but we all had a great laugh and developed a real team camaraderie. The manager always preached the benefits from this break that we'd see by the end of the season.

One time the Forest squad was at a hotel in Scotland at the same time as a wedding reception. The bride and groom seemed thrilled to have the gaffer at the reception and Cloughie called out, "A bottle of champagne and three glasses please!" Later in the proceedings it was traditional for the newly married couple to walk from either side of the reception hall and meet in the centre of the dance floor. Just as they were about to embrace Cloughie appeared from nowhere, grabbed the groom's kilt and did an impromptu checking of the poor man's wedding tackle, just as he had to

Maradona years before. A couple of ushers arrived quickly on the scene and gently eased the manager away before it went any further!

Drinking was ingrained into the social side of the game and Cloughie would take offence if you refused to join him in a drink. I never saw it affect his managerial decisions or his day-to-day actions but on a match day he'd have a whisky put out in a plastic cup with a drop of orange next to the players' cups of orange that were set out on a table. Sometimes he'd ask one of the young apprentices before a game, "Can you get me some orange with my vodka?" Then he'd add, "Get one for Ronnie too." Ronnie Fenton, ever the faithful assistant, would never openly refuse, but if he got the chance he'd whisper to the apprentice, "Don't make mine a strong one!"

I'm sure that Brian Clough needed a drink as a release from the pressure of just being Brian Clough. His outrageous statements and opinions needed backing up with results and he generated even more pressure on himself through his words to the media. There were people out there just waiting for him to fail and so the pressure on himself grew even higher. By the end of Cloughie's career his appearance started to show the effects of years of drinking. The way that he eventually left Forest was a shambles and not the way he deserved to go out from the game.

I wouldn't say I was close to Brian Clough, but I knew him for many years and played for him for almost a decade in my two spells at Forest. Back in 2001 I called in to see Brian at his Derby home. I didn't ring in advance, I just turned up with my son Elliot, who I wanted him to meet. I pulled up the drive and was sitting in my car with the window down and I could hear Cloughie quite clearly. "Barbara, there's a car on my driveway!" He didn't seem too happy. Then, louder, "Barbara! There's a fucking car on my driveway! Who is it?"

I thought, "Oh no, I've caught him in a bad mood." I got out and approached the house. When I knocked on the door Barbara opened it and said, "Oh, hello, Steve. How are you? Brian, it's Stevie Hodge!"

"Oh, bloody hell, tell him to come in then."

While I was there I took the opportunity to finally ask him face to face why I'd been left out of the 1991 FA Cup final team. I knew there had been a combination of factors: Roy Keane coming through, my injuries, my contract, but he'd always said, "If you do the business, you keep the shirt." So I asked him about 1991 and he just said, "He [Keane] was stronger than you so I picked him." That's all I wanted. An answer. That was his opinion and whether I agreed with it or not I left it there. We shared some stories that day, but when I declined to have a drink with him he called me a bore. I'd known that he liked a drink right back to my early days at Forest. On one of my first overseas trips I was called in to see him in his hotel room and when I got there he was reclining on the bed in his underwear and I noticed a bottle of whisky by the bed, which, to a fresh-faced young player, was quite shocking. He was so outspoken that he had to live up to his own words while many people wanted him to fall flat on his face. That Forest side of the late 1980s and early 1990s was fairly successful. If we'd been achieving those league positions today we'd have been regulars in the Champions League. As it was we had to "settle" for winning the League Cup in 1989 and 1990 and a handful of FA Cup near-misses. I was really pleased when Cloughie named me in his squad of twenty best players; of course, he named nineteen players that he'd managed and also added himself!

The last time I saw Brian Clough was when I visited the family's newsagent shop in West Bridgford shortly before he passed away in 2004. He came out from the storeroom at the back and said, "Someone told me you were in the shop. I was

looking for a fat little forty year old but you're looking well!"
We went on to talk about the Anderlecht scandal, which still
hurt him. As we parted he said, "If I can ever help you, just give
me a ring."

Steve Hodge, ex-Professional Footballer

Being left out at the age of fifteen for being too small actually did me a favour in the long run and Bobby Robson made "that little centre forward" a very proud man in the 1980s. I think even Brian Clough would acknowledge that the "player who couldn't play" did a pretty good job! My proudest achievement is that I managed to stay at the top level throughout my career. It was a long journey and I remember that after we beat Sturm Graz to get through to the UEFA Cup semi-final in 1984 I was sitting in a night club with Ian Bowyer. "Harry, is this your first semi-final?" he asked with a wry smile. "Yes," I replied. "Well, wait till you've been through the mixer!" he laughed. I didn't quite know what he meant back then, but by the end I did, and boy, had I gone through the mixer!

The Shirt

After the final whistle at the Azteca, I think a couple of players wanted Maradona's shirt. I didn't really think about swapping shirts, I just wanted to get off the pitch as quickly as possible. The Argentinians were going crazy and I just tried to be dignified and walk away. I'd kept all my England World Cup shirts, but as we were out I decided to try and swap one. I went over to shake Maradona's hand; Chris Waddle was with him and he was being mobbed by people and it was bedlam all around him so I didn't bother. I just wished him all the best and walked away with Chris Waddle. I was asked for an interview by Gary Newbon which delayed me, and a couple of minutes later I walked off in my own world. It was all over and I just wanted to get away. The teams had two separate tunnels that came up on to the pitch but underground they joined up and led back to the dressing rooms together. I just happened to be walking down our tunnel as Maradona came walking along the Argentinian tunnel. We looked at each other and I tugged at my shirt. He nodded and so I did: it was pure chance. He put his hands together in a little bow gesture of thanks and we walked away.

Back in the dressing room a few people were complaining about the hand ball and it was only then I really twigged what had gone on. Sitting in my corner I knew I could have done better but I realised there was nothing I could do about it now. Bobby Robson was moaning but philosophical: "He got away with it. It was clear from where I was standing." Terry Butcher was angry and in an aggressive mood and all the players were talking about it. The feeling of being cheated was overwhelming. I just kept quiet and put his shirt in my bag. I wondered if people were blaming me but not saying so. I still felt the back pass was something that I would have done 99 times out of a 100, but a part of me was saying, "Why did I do that? Was it too risky?" One thing was for sure, we were going home, the adventure was over.

There was talk of Ted Croker putting in an official complaint to FIFA but nothing like the outcry that greeted Thierry Henry's hand ball against Ireland in November 2009 when governments threatened to get involved. Bobby Robson had seen it at the time and knew exactly what had happened. I thought many times back to the game a quarter of a century ago. The manager hadn't wanted to change our system to accommodate a man marker and perhaps we didn't have enough flexibility to do so. After the Argentina game it was very sad. As we readied to go home, Bobby Robson was going to go to Acapulco before watching the semis and final. At the bus back to the airport he was shaking our hands one by one. "Well done, Hodgey, son," he said. "You've done really well; I'm chuffed for you. Another week here would have been great but the experience will do you the world of good. Thanks a lot." Those words meant, and still mean, a lot to me. The whole seven weeks from build-up to the Argentina game is something that I'll never ever forget.

○ ○ ○

Back home, I put the Maradona shirt in my attic and there it stayed until in 2002 I saw the news that Pele's 1970 World Cup shirt had sold for over £150,000 at auction. It was a new world record for a football shirt and I realised that Maradona's 1986 shirt could be comparable. The shirt soon became a talking point and, after retiring, it was the thing I was most remembered for. When I was first invited to be on Sky's *Soccer AM*, Craig Bellamy was on the show and he was keen to get a photo with the shirt which I'd taken along. A year or so later I was invited back and travelled down to London the day before. At eleven o'clock that night I got a call asking if I'd brought the shirt with me. I hadn't and was in a London hotel. I had to convince my mother-in-law to go round to my house and go up into the attic to get the shirt and give it to a motorcycle courier. It was then delivered to my hotel at about 2 a.m. and I must say I was quite nervous about it getting to me in one piece. I also took it on to the Johnny Vaughan show where I appeared with Frankie Dettori and Jimmy Greaves. Part way through the show, and totally unplanned, Frankie decided to try and put the shirt on. Like all shirts from back then, the Maradona shirt was pretty small and tight so when I realised that he was actually going to pull it over his head it was more than the studio lights that were making me sweat! I was worried that he might rip it and I don't think he realised how old it was. Luckily it survived in one piece.

I eventually thought I'd better dust it down and get it insured, but that proved hard to do because no one was willing to put a value on it. I eventually decided to loan it to the National Football Museum at Preston, back where I'd made my reserve-team debut all those years before, and they house and insure it.

I get more questions about the Maradona shirt than anything else and I get asked to appear and talk about it just so people can see that shirt, even though we lost the game. It's never been washed and still has his sweat and DNA embedded in the fabric. The Hand of God really made a mark on people's consciousness; it's usually the first thing people think of when they hear the name Maradona.

Afterword to the Paperback Edition

As I sat down to write the final chapter of my autobiography, it was in the aftermath of a hugely disappointing World Cup for England and a heartbreaking attempt to bring the tournament back home. England's 2018 World Cup bid was disastrous, but was it really a surprise? UEFA and FIFA do not seem to be on our side. The powerful Premier League might be envied, but England lacks influential people on the powerful committees of UEFA and FIFA. While encouraging new footballing frontiers is commendable, the selections of Russia as hosts in 2018 and Qatar in 2022 were inevitable, given the level of resources that was going to be poured into the tournaments by each of them. Irrespective of our excellent bid and spine-tingling presentation, the Three Lions strode into Zurich like lambs to the slaughter.

The lack of form of the creative players at the 2010 World Cup lead to a dull group-stage campaign in which defences were on top. The few quality games came towards the end of the tournament, the Netherlands producing a stunning fightback to beat Brazil in the quarter-finals. Germany's skill and teamwork completely dismantled Argentina's attacking threat in their quarter-final, during which they cruelly and ruthlessly exposed Argentina's porous defence to end the reign of manager Diego Maradona, who had looked on course to emulate Franz Beckenbauer as a World Cup winner both as captain and manager. Maradona did bring emotion, joy, passion and anger to the touchline, his press conferences were magic and his team seemed to love him, but the Germans love to spoil a party. Upon his return to Argentina, even though the people still wanted him, he stood down.

The final itself was a poor spectacle. Holland had decided, as the underdogs, that their best route to victory was to stop Spain's fluid passing and so they continually fouled their opponents and had no interest in making the game a flowing encounter. Even though I would not condone their tactics on the day, their game plan nearly succeeded, and had Iker Casillas not saved from Arjen Robben when he was through on goal midway through the second half, the outcome might well have been different.

Many words have been written and spoken about England's performance and a number of factors have been discussed, including tiredness, boredom, the manager, injuries and the players not being good enough. Tiredness is one excuse, but I'm not convinced. The England players in 1986 and 1990 all had long seasons, were only granted a short break before the finals and yet still performed well. In 2010, players such as Van Bommel, Robben, Iniesta, Xavi, Puyol, Ramos, Casillas, Lahm, Schweinsteiger and Forlan all had long arduous seasons, the bulk of them having reached a semi-final or final in European competition and a few of them a domestic cup final also. But they all performed superbly throughout the whole tournament. The big four English clubs were all out of the Champions League at the quarter-final stage and the top players were rested during the season, so I don't feel that the excuse of tiredness carries much weight.

Boredom during a World Cup can be an issue, but, for me, just to be selected to represent England at a World Cup would be enough to keep me upbeat and remain positive. Players these days have endless channels of communication and entertainment, far more than just the TV and Walkman that I had.

When boredom sets in, it can bring a squad together: humour can be generated and camaraderie forged. The manager is crucial in this respect. To this end, I like to compare Brian Clough with Fabio Capello because of their brilliant track records and their focus on discipline. The vibes coming out of the England camp were that it was too strict, too rigid. When I returned to Forest from Spurs, Clough looked me in the eye and said, "Do you want to play for me, son?" I'm not sure that all the players wanted to play for Capello. Clough would often say to us, "Lads, smile. The alternative is to cry," or, specifically to me, "Harry, say hello to your popular manager," when he knew he'd annoyed me for whatever reason! He was someone who'd ridicule anything or anybody. He kept the life and spirit constantly flowing, and he also liked the players relaxed, hence he invented the mid-winter break in the sun, which the players loved. "Everybody needs something to look forward to," he'd remind us. "Let's go and get some sun on our backs." Capello, on the other hand appears to be a serious man, and in today's era of "player power" the players don't easily accept the strict rules of another period. Communication of instructions and feelings is obviously vital to the relationship between the manager and his players, especially players who are not selected initially.

When I returned to Forest from Spurs, I can recall that before we went out to play Aston Villa, Clough turned to me in the changing room and said, "Harry, you're playing well, son. It's like you've never been away." This boosted me, as I'd had a slow start on my return, and he sensed that he was able to alter my mental state by good man-management.

On tactics, there are similarities between Clough and Capello, especially when it comes to relying on the 4–4–2 system. This stubbornness was one of the things that eventually caused Forest problems. Other managers studied ways to nullify that system, yet Clough wouldn't change. I'm not saying that 4–4–2 is not a good system – it is still very popular – but it can be tinkered with, and there are times in a match or against clever opponents when you and your players need to be more flexible to accommodate different systems. Clough had a disregard for rehearsing set-plays. Everything was done off the cuff and his only instruction when defending corners was to "watch the ball and go and head it".

England's team selection at the World Cup was another area of concern. Ultimately, the first-choice goalkeeper should've been told who he was prior to the tournament. It's such a vital position that the number one needs to feel that he's secure and that he's got the confidence of everybody. To find out only two hours before the kick-off of the first game at the World Cup finals probably made Robert Green feel as though it'd been a close decision and that the manager wasn't sure. This is the way that Capello has previously worked and it has served him well. On the other hand, I'm sure Clough would've made it clear who the number one was going to be before the team set off. Unfortunately, the selection of Green backfired, but Capello was brave enough to replace him with David James, something that I agreed with, even though it was tough on Green.

Losing Rio Ferdinand was catastrophic – he was the captain, a winner and still the top defender. It was, I believe, the pivotal moment in the summer for England. Rio oozes confidence and lesser players feed off that. It meant that England had to chop and change Ledley King, Jamie Carragher and Matthew Upson, and the back four had to continually adjust, which, to their credit, they did until we faced our first tough opponent.

Brian Clough used to say, "Show me a player who can head a ball, and I'll show you a player." What he meant was that he liked and trusted people who were brave and honest, those who weren't scared to get hurt, and, for all his problems before the World Cup, I thought John Terry performed well until the Germany clash, as did Ashley Cole.

One man had to shine if we had any chance of lifting the World Cup, but, unfortunately Wayne Rooney, along with Ronaldo, Messi, Torres and Drogba, had a poor tournament. Whether it was boredom, tactics, injury, tiredness or personal issues, our star player was doing the simplest things – which he does with his eyes closed most weekends – badly. He didn't appear to be happy with himself or his team, and his frustration boiled over at the end of the Algeria game when he let his feelings be known on camera. I have to say that I've never seen England play that badly in a finals match. We lacked the one thing that all fans expect – passion. It was the World Cup, but it didn't appear that way on the pitch.

I think Rooney is a fantastic talent, a complete footballer who understands the game and could play anywhere on a football pitch. He's also mentally strong, and he'll bounce back because of his talent and attitude. Clough used to think that way about Glenn Hoddle. Clough once stated before facing Spurs, "Young Hoddle isn't physically strong, but he's mentally strong. He'll have the ball anywhere because he's talented, and I love watching talented people at work."

Eventually, Jermain Defoe was given his chance to do what he does well – sharp, angled runs which lose the best defenders and brilliant finishing! The most puzzling thing was the lack of opportunity afforded to Peter Crouch (seventeen minutes) and Joe Cole (forty-four minutes) during the whole tournament, even though England often seemed to need something different or someone who was fresh. On reflection, Capello probably picked the strongest squad available, give or take a couple of big decisions. However, taking Ledley King and Gareth Barry didn't work, Rob Green made a bad error in the first game, the captain was injured before the tournament, and our main striker hit poor form and everybody around him suffered.

After a disappointing World Cup, questions were bound to be asked. For example, why did the FA extend Capello's contract before the World Cup? Without the security of the extra two years he would perhaps have walked away after South Africa, as we saw elsewhere, with plenty of managers falling on their swords. It is understandable that the FA wanted to act quickly, because, on the back of a brilliant qualifying campaign and with high hopes for the World Cup finals, they feared he'd be head-hunted, so they were protecting their prize asset. If results had gone well, the FA would've been applauded for securing the services of an in-demand manager. As it was, Capello's stock fell dramatically. It may all end up happily, though. England have bounced back and are on course for Euro 2012, young players like Joe Hart and Adam Johnson have taken their chances, and Capello's stock is slowly rising again. After disaster, sometimes better times can quickly follow, as Sir Bobby Robson proved after his own debacle at Euro 88.

France and Italy did not live up to expectations either, and these two great footballing nations have some thinking to do. Is it down to the coaching, the manager or the players? I feel it's a combination. Coaching, especially technical work, has to be the main priority. At the top level, you have to be skilful. "Be a master of the ball", as Brian Clough would say to us. Tactically, both the manager and his players need to be bright and intelligent, putting strategies in place that enable them to have the best opportunity to win. Coaching must start from a young age, and players must be encouraged to practise their skills regularly. In other countries the young players complete more practise hours than our kids do each week. The young players also need to be hungry for success, to keep coming back after every knock-back, as this shows who has character. Many young players are handed three- or four-year contracts after a few promising first-team games, which, on the face of it, is fantastic but it can also be a crossroads in a young player's development. Some naturally driven young players are thirsty for the next challenge; others can be inclined to sit back, accept their money and prestige, and they consequently lose their drive. At Leeds, if things were not going well, Howard Wilkinson had some down-to-earth Yorkshire guidance for the players: "Forget your fancy mobile phones, your TVs and newspapers. Get back to being ordinary and get your minds back on the important things, like playing football." This is sound advice.

It is also my opinion that there are far too many foreign players playing football in England. No one can blame them or their agents for wanting to come to these shores whilst the money is so good, but, unfortunately, it will continue to have a detrimental effect on the national side if the rules aren't amended to give the young home-grown players a sniff of first-team action. Germany has changed its rules, which means that more home-grown players are allowed to develop, and they're now reaping the rewards. Germany should be our template: four players from their successful European Under-21 Championship team in 2009 – Neuer, Khedira, Boateng and Ozil – were taken to South Africa. They all embraced the chance they'd been afforded and were only knocked out by Carles Puyol's towering header in the semi-final. Germany consistently produces top teams and top footballers. After their elimination by Croatia at France 98, they responded by reaching the 2002 World Cup final, only to be beaten by the dazzling Brazilians. They suffered a poor campaign at Euro 2004 in Portugal and so decided to do something to address the problem. They appointed Jurgen Klinsmann as manager and had an in-depth look at how their football should move forwards. The results since then have been impressive, the team having reached two World Cup semi-finals and a

European Championship final, and they have invested in a new, youthful team for the future. But even these achievements will not be enough for the Germans, who'll strive to become winners again. Germany's elite performers down the years have all been technically good and mentally and physically strong. In midfield, the list is pure quality: Netzer, Bonhof, Overath, Littbarski, Stielike, Schuster, Matthaus, Magath, Hassler, Moller, Hamann, Ballack, Effenberg, Sammer and now Schweinsteiger. I can recall facing Effenberg in a friendly between Leeds and Bayern Munich, and it was a tough experience. He had great poise, and when he had possession it was impossible to get the ball off him, such was his height and strength. I spent the entire evening trying to annoy him just to put him out of his stride, something that I achieved in the second half when he turned on me after I'd clipped his ankle and told me in his German accent what he thought of me!

As a country we cannot accuse foreign managers of disregarding our young players. All managers try to do the best for their own clubs and have worldwide scouting networks so that they're aware of every top prospect emerging. But, as a result, being a young home-grown player at a top club during the last ten years has been tough. On 30 December 2009, Portsmouth played Arsenal in the Premier League and not one Englishman started the match – the alarm bells were ringing that night, and the bells were even louder after the 2010 World Cup. The lack of English players coming through the system has meant that there's been very little challenge to the established stars in the England team.

One area in which England have never struggled is in producing world-class goalkeepers. When I was growing up, we had Shilton, Clemence and Corrigan, and when I was playing we had Shilton, Woods and Seaman. Recently, however, when England played Hungary at Wembley, England had Joe Hart, who looks to be the heir apparent to the position at twenty-three years of age, and two Under-21 goalkeepers on the bench. Most weekends in the Premier League you'll see no more than five English goalkeepers involved: Joe Hart, Scott Carson, Paul Robinson, Robert Green and Ben Foster. This leaves the England manager with a lack of quality and competition for places in the goalkeeping department.

The England manager has a fantastic but ultimately tough job. Clough once said to me, "Harry, management is easy when you're winning. You earn your money when you can't win a game and there will be times in a season when you can't *buy* a win." Capello had a smooth start, then in South Africa he got a win but he couldn't get a good performance. Let's hope that at Euro 2012 he can prove why he was employed in the first place.

The manager nowadays needs to be flexible and to be able to adjust his team formation, meaning the players that he selects must be intelligent enough to perform different roles. The manager's style of management is of paramount importance. Clough had a way that he wanted the game played. "The first person I see get the ball down on the floor will get my applause," he'd calmly tell the players just before they went out – in other words, let's pass the ball on the grass, be brave and play. He had phrases that we knew off by heart: "Always expect the unexpected"; "The run dictates the pass"; "Every player needs to have something that he excels at". These were regularly drummed into us, and it was common-sense coaching. If we were ahead in a match and the time was nearly up, he'd be barking, "Get to the corner flag. Get anything, but keep that ball away from my goal." Or if a winger had the ball near the opposition penalty box, he'd shout, "Don't put that ball into the box for their goalkeeper to catch it and boot it into my penalty box. Learn how to win a football match."

He was constantly challenging you, questioning you and

pushing you. I played a good pass at the City Ground one day and a second later Clough was out of his dugout chastising me, "Harry, don't just stand there admiring your pass. Go and help your mate out." He had many words of knowledge and wisdom. If we were playing poorly but were still level, he'd turn to the subs and say, "If you offered me a draw now, I'd snap your hands off." In his calmer moments, often after a bad result, he'd tell us, "Lads, if you stay in the game long enough, you will get your own back. The trick is to stay in the game." On life itself he would sarcastically say, "Whoever said life begins at forty was talking crap. Take it from me: it stinks." Clough was a positive, upbeat character, though, a glass-half-full man who tried to promote positive thinking before every match. "If I didn't think we could win, lads, I wouldn't bother turning up," he would say. If we were playing in a less important cup competition, he'd say, "We've all turned up and left our homes. We might as well try and win tonight." Before some games he would enthusiastically say, "You're young, you're fit, you're full of yourselves, so let's go and put a show on." If we were losing comfortably and coming to the end of a game without having scored, we'd hear him pleading for someone to get a goal: "Come on, lads, let's get a goal. Let's get something." He wanted something good to take into the next match, something to give him and us a boost.

He had his own beliefs, which he stuck to religiously. As a club, Forest didn't practise playing the offside trap: "We don't play offsides at this club. We defend properly." This probably explains his loathing of Arsenal's highly successful and organised back four who became renowned for always having their arms in the air appealing for offside. He disliked teams who played a more robust style of football, as he didn't picture the game that way. "It's far easier to destroy than create," he'd complain when talking about certain teams. He took great pleasure in beating the likes of Wimbledon and Crystal Palace in the '80s and '90s.

Another thing that would infuriate him was the needless giving away of penalties. If a penalty was conceded and Clough believed it could've been avoided, he'd show his displeasure with a mixture of anger and frustration. "Why did you have to bring him down?" he'd say, gesticulating. "He had a long way to go to goal. My goalkeeper was in his goal, and for all you know the striker might've had a heart attack – that was crap!"

The strikers always had Clough's suppport: he'd been there; he knew what they felt and what they went through and he had empathy for them. But there was a limit to his support and if the striker wasn't doing his job, eventually he'd replace him. "At the end of the day, strikers are judged on the number of goals they score, and I should know because I *could* score a goal. Have you seen my record, lads?" He wasn't happy if the ball was flicked away by his strikers; to him, it wasn't taking care of the ball for the team. If a striker tried a fancy flick and it didn't get to its intended target, he'd smack his arm against the coaches and rant, "Who does he think he is flicking the ball away like that? I'm telling you, Maradona, Pele, Puskas and Di Stefano wouldn't have tried that." He also believed that some players flicked the ball away because they were scared of getting kicked. In today's game, the inventive flick or back heel can open up a tight defence, and I do feel that this aspect of the game is more accepted now by managers and fans.

Clough imparted assurance, arrogance, knowledge and self-belief to his players. They had trust in his methods and he'd take great pride in telling us, "I haven't got any O levels – I was a bit thick at school – but I've got plenty of medals. They're my O levels."

Today's top players have all the power and a manager needs to be careful in his dealings with his players. Players no longer fear being dropped or accept being verbally abused; they all sit on long contracts and are set up for life. The days of Clough shouting at the Forest players with the words, "You'll all leave this football club before me," are long gone.

I'm not sure that today's young players would readily accept the treatment that we received when we were trying to make our names. We had to smile and take the ridicule, which could be hurtful but was designed to keep our feet on the ground. I once went to see Brian Clough in his office after a home game. When I walked in, Bobby Gould was having a chat with him.

"Harry, say hello to Mr Gould."

"Bobby, Harry thinks he's a good player, but I've had to tell him the truth," he calmly stated. I smiled with embarrassment, said hello and then quickly made my exit.

Even as an older professional you had to take the criticism. After playing at Liverpool one Saturday, we were told by Clough that we had to be in at ten-thirty the following morning to prepare for Luton Town on Easter Monday. I groaned under my breath but was heard by Clough, who promptly turned on me and said that I was to be in for 9 a.m., making the tea for the players when they arrived at 10 a.m. In my final season at Forest, when I was substitute on a few occasions, I'd be sat contemplating the game ahead and wondering if I might take some part when the gaffer would interrupt my thoughts with, "Harry, ask our lads if there's owt they want or get them a drink. Do your job." There were no prima donnas! I doubt that today's Premier League stars who find themselves on the bench would be asked to fetch and carry for the other players.

Modern football has its drawbacks, but it is still a game watched by millions of people who are passionate about it. People accuse the game of having fewer characters than it used to have, which is probably the case, but managers such as

Sir Alex Ferguson, Jose Mourinho, Harry Redknapp and Mick McCarthy are all big personalities who speak in their own unique ways about the game and who are clearly immersed in it. They all bring frankness and humour to their jobs, characteristics which I personally appreciated in my manager. One day, at a team meeting, Clough, knowing I was single, made me an offer. "Harry, I could set you up with our Libby [Clough's daughter]," he stated. "Apparently her dad's loaded and got more money than you!" I kept quiet and smiled. "I'm only joking, son," he chuckled. "Can you imagine having me as your father-in-law!" The lads were in stitches. Later on in my Leeds career, when I'd reclaimed my first-team place, we met in the City Ground car park, as I'd gone to watch Forest play. "Harry, good to see you back in the Leeds team at the weekend. It's been too long," and his words were sincere.

Clough, undisputedly, should have managed England at some stage in his career, but it's fair to say that the FA would've found him a handful. He never missed a chance to have a sarcastic dig at them. We were once losing a game at half-time and as we sat down for our drinks Clough's eyes were drawn to Brian Laws, who was at that time taking his FA coaching badges. In a stern, mocking voice he asked the full-back, "Coach, have you got any advice for the second half from your FA coaching manual?" Laws, sensibly, didn't reply!

Football is continually changing, and one thing that was highlighted in South Africa was the need for goal-line technology. Frank Lampard's brilliant non-goal may or may not have altered the outcome of the contest against Germany, but it was clearly a goal and should've stood. It was a bizarre decision, but the officials were unsure precisely what had happened; a quick check by the fourth official on a TV screen would have swiftly confirmed the goal. If TV evidence had been used at Mexico 86 the Hand of God incident would never have happened.

Maradona would've been shown a yellow card and England might have beaten Argentina!

Brian Clough was a good judge of a player. In 1983, at the end of the game between Barcelona and Forest at the Camp Nou, he suddenly appeared next to us. "Hey, lads, get his shirt," he implored as we trudged off, having just been mesmerised by Maradona's brilliance. He knew he'd just witnessed a special player with God-given talent. I'd already swapped my shirt with the Spanish International Victor so was in no position to go and ask for Maradona's, but Kenny Swain took Clough's advice and did exchange shirts with him. Of course, I did get another chance three years later to heed Clough's words.

Diego Maradona's infamous Argentina shirt, with the shiny silver number 10 on the back from Mexico 86, will go down in the annals of World Cup history. It will remind everyone of a footballing god without equal, of one of the most controversial moments in World Cup history, of perhaps the best goal ever scored in the World Cup and of a very painful day for English football. As for me? Well, I will probably always be known as the "Man with Maradona's shirt!"

Appendices

Appendix 1

Interlude: The Players

Looking back I know I've been lucky enough to play with and against some of the best players of the 1980s and 1990s, I've been managed by some of the game's legends and been involved in some of the most controversial games of that era. I never thought my career would go as it did when I was a youngster, I just tried my hardest and hoped it would take me somewhere good. My career took me to some unforgettable places and I wouldn't have missed it for the world.

Best team I ever played against:

Schmeichel

Nilsson   Buchwald   Baresi   Maldini

M. Laudrup   Matthaus   Souness   Cruijff

Maradona

Rush

<u>Subs:</u>
Shearer, Scifo, Dalglish, Stojkovic, Adams, Figo, Schuster, Zola.

MY CHOICES

Peter Schmeichel:
He had everything, great presence, superb handling, large frame and excellent on crosses. I faced him one on one several times but I never managed to beat him.

Roland Nilsson:
Strong and intelligent, he could use his pace going forward to great effect and reached the World Cup semi-final with Sweden in 1994.

Guido Buchwald:
A man-mountain defender with great composure and the obligatory strong German mental attitude, comfortable in defence and midfield.

Franco Baresi:
The Italian organiser of the back four, not tall but had a great spring when jumping and very quick across the ground.

Paolo Maldini:
I played against him for England when he was just a young left-back who bombed forward whenever he could. Even then he defended with intelligence and the calm assurance of a veteran.

Michael Laudrup:
A brilliant attacker who liked to float around so you had to concentrate hard when playing against him. He had two great feet which meant he could beat defenders on both sides and had a devastating change of pace.

Lothar Matthaus:
Energy, technique and aggression were the German captain's strengths. He scored and made goals and defended with great discipline which culminated in his lifting the 1990 World Cup.

Graeme Souness:
A strong-minded, combative central midfielder who controlled games with his passing, goals and drive. He possessed an aura of self-belief and his haul of medals was a just reward for his qualities.

Johan Cruijff:
Playing against him was a daunting challenge. He had complete mastery of the ball and that night in Milan it was just a privilege to be on the same pitch as the great man.

Diego Maradona:
The best player I ever faced by some distance, built like a tank, aggressive, brave, total ball mastery, a fantastic dribbler, supreme confidence, the list goes on. He was arguably the best player ever and although the cheating of his Hand of God goal tainted his image, his pure talent was from another planet.

Ian Rush:
He had the knack of being in the right place at the right time and then his finishing excellence took over. The top-class Liverpool midfields of his era provided the ammunition but Rush was the executioner supreme.

Best team I ever played with:

Van Breukelen

Anderson   Gough   Walker   Pearce

Waddle   Keane   Gascoigne   McAllister

Hoddle

Lineker

Subs:
Bryan Robson, Cantona, Beardsley, Ardiles, Shilton, Strachan, Barnes, Robertson.
Joint managers:
Clough, Bobby Robson.

MY CHOICES

Hans van Breukelen:
Maybe a surprise choice before Peter Shilton but Shilton's last game for Forest was my first and I didn't play that many times with him for England. I also only had one season with Ray Clemence before he retired. Hans came from Utrecht as a virtual unknown but quickly got to grips with the top flight in England. He was hugely popular with fans and players alike and he went on to win the European Cup with PSV and Euro 88 with Holland. It was a big mistake to allow him to leave Forest in 1984 and I don't think they've had such a good keeper ever since.

Viv Anderson:
A brilliant attacking full-back, I was privileged to watch and then play with this all-conquering player who also grew up with the Brian Clough philosophy. A big character who

defended superbly and could also score and create goals. I can't remember him ever being taken to the cleaners by any winger and his character makes him a must for any dressing room.

Stuart Pearce:
Another big character who was plucked from Coventry for a small fee. Inspirational with his actions, he wasn't that loud on the pitch but when he felt you needed it you got it! Mentally very strong he bounced back from his Italia 90 penalty miss to score sixteen goals from full-back and take Forest to the 1991 FA Cup final. He had the reputation of a hard man but he was also fair and his record of only one sending off in a long career shows how clued-in he was. We often used to go to gigs together but I never did get into his love of punk music!

Des Walker:
Mr Consistency. I remember watching him in a trial match at the City Ground and he did well at full-back but you wouldn't have guessed what he'd go on to achieve. Eventually he settled in at centre-half where his pace and intelligence comfortably kept the opposition at bay. It was always reassuring to know that Des Walker was playing behind you and if you made a mistake your opponents would still have Des Walker to beat. Easier said than done!

Richard Gough:
"Stroller", as he was named, made the game look a doddle. Strong and aggressive, quick over the ground, he and Gary Mabbutt were the cornerstones of the brilliant Spurs team of 1986–87. It was a real shame that he returned to Scotland, but he went on to win many trophies with Rangers and caps with Scotland.

Chris Waddle:

Deceptively quick and tricky as they come, he scored and made many memorable goals for Spurs and England. Probably had the ball more than most players in that Spurs team of 1986/87 and he used it brilliantly. He probably benefited from my arrival at Spurs because he swapped to the right wing and his career really took off.

Gary McAllister:

A class act and pass master. He knew when to go long and when to keep it simple and could deliver both kinds of pass with quality. He was also a real athlete who covered the ground as the best midfielders can do and also scored his share of goals. His teammates knew they could rely on him even in the toughest away games. He gave me one of the biggest compliments of my career when he named me alongside Roy Keane and Patrick Viera as his three toughest opponents.

Roy Keane:

Came from nowhere and immediately I knew I had a battle on my hands. Supremely self-confident and talented, he made everything look simple, when it wasn't. Another inspirational box-to-box player, he grew and matured at Manchester United and it was always a tough order playing against him.

Paul Gascoigne:

A unique talent, someone with imagination, dribbling skills, confidence, no fear on the pitch, a player who comes along once in a blue moon. As an older England player I could see that whenever you could, you had to give him the ball because he would cause damage. His ball manipulation and retention in tight areas was sensational and he inspired

England in Italia 90 when English football became sexy again. For a couple of years between 1989 and '91 he was one of the best players in the world.

Glenn Hoddle:
For a midfield runner like me, Glenn Hoddle was a dream. He would deliver the right pass, with the right pace on it, with either foot and he could see your runs when lesser players couldn't. The system that England used probably didn't allow him to show his true potential, but in the Spurs team he was king: when he had a free role he was devastating.

Gary Lineker:
I knew about Gary Lineker early in my career, when he was the pacey striker in Leicester's youth team. Gary's attributes were his obvious pace and his ruthless finishing. He didn't get involved too much in the build-up play but a ball over the top or a cross into the six-yard box would make him come alive. He scored his goals against the best sides in the biggest games and so nearly took England to a World Cup final.

Appendix 2

CAREER STATISTICS

	Appearances	Goals
Nottingham Forest 1982–85 and 1988–91	277	66
Aston Villa 1985–86	70	16
Tottenham Hotspur 1986–88	54	8
Leeds United 1991–94	66	10
Derby County (loan) 1994	11	4
Queen's Park Rangers 1994–96	15	0
Watford 1996	2	0
Leyton Orient 1996	11	0
England (Full Caps)	24	0
England (B Caps)	2	1
England (Under-21)	8	3
Totals	540	108

HONOURS

World Cup	Bronze Medal	1990
Premiership	Champion	1992
League Cup	Winner	1989, 1990
European Under-21	Champion	1984
Charity Shield	Winner	1992
Simod Cup	Winner	1989
FA Cup	Finalist	1987, 1991
PFA Team of the Year		1990
Midlands Player of the Year		1986

Thanks and Acknowledgements

Steve Hodge:

Finally I have to thank my wife Ali and kids, who, after I finished playing football, probably, or should that be definitely, had to put up with days when I was grumpy or pining for the game. I'd like to thank them for their constant love and support. The year or two after you retire is the worst time in a player's career. My son Josh is nineteen. He loves his cricket and we can talk about it for hours and, occasionally, he will tell me about the two centuries he has scored so far. At that point I put him back in his place by asking if he scored either of them at Trent Bridge, which I did in a pro-am game in the mid-1980s. It's all part of the banter!

Elliot plays for the Forest Academy in the Under-14s and is doing fine. He probably gets more criticism from me than any other player in the team, but he listens and takes it all on board. When I took him to see Manchester United train, Sir Alex told him, "Practise, practise, practise. It's the only way." It makes me proud to see him wearing a Forest shirt and he is a bit of a "rat" himself. He knows how hard it is to make it in football but he's keen and determined and I could never accuse him of a lack of effort. He's also played county cricket for Notts and Derbyshire, and as you can probably gather, he's an all-round sportsman.

Amber, age ten, plays cricket for Derbyshire – she's an all-rounder and very good for her age – and football for her local club team where she is a fast little striker who scores plenty of goals. The sight of her at a young age dribbling past the bigger kids makes me chuckle. I've always championed the smaller players' cause after my own experiences! Amber was with me at an England training session once and I had a chat with John Terry. Afterwards she asked me, "Dad, was that you talking to John Terry?"

"Yes," I replied.

"Does he know who you are?"

"Yes," I replied once again as her face showed signs of mounting shock and disbelief.

"Dad, you must be a legend!"

My children's sporting endeavours have thankfully kept me busy and involved in sport since I retired and I'm really grateful for that and they all make me very proud.

I'd like to thank my mum and dad as well, Violet and Brian, for all of their love, support and encouragement. As a parent now I can appreciate the time and sacrifice they put in to allow me to have the chance to try and achieve my dreams.

I'd also like to thank my cousin Paul for being so competitive when we played football and cricket together when we were kids. He would beat me quite often because he was slightly older, but those battles fostered the competitive nature in me. I would also like to thank the rest of my family and friends for their support.

My thanks must also go to my ghost-writer Rob Jovanovic, who has patiently listened to me talking about my recollections over the last twelve months. My diaries and decent memory have meant that he's been constantly changing and adding things to the story but he has steadfastly continued with his work and I thank him for that.

Rob Jovanovic:
Many thanks and love to Carolyn, Milan and Cece. Tim Bates was persistent in getting us the deal and then became a joint critic and cheerleader (not literally!), as did Ian Preece. Thanks also to Gaby Young, Alan Samson, Hannah Whitaker and Vicki Harris.